Maternal Optimism

Maternal Optimism

Forging Positive Paths through Work and Motherhood

JAMIE LADGE

AND

DANNA GREENBERG

Oxford University Press is a department of the University of Oxford. It furthers
the University's objective of excellence in research, scholarship, and education
by publishing worldwide. Oxford is a registered trade mark of Oxford University
Press in the UK and certain other countries.

Published in the United States of America by Oxford University Press
198 Madison Avenue, New York, NY 10016, United States of America.

CIP data is on file at the Library of Congress
ISBN 978–0–19–094409–4

9 8 7 6 5 4 3 2

Printed by Integrated Books International, United States of America

*To Carole Greenberg and Bobbi Shapiro, our working
mothers who have been models of maternal optimism.*

CONTENTS

PREFACE: DEFINING MATERNAL OPTIMISM

Maternal optimism: The desire or willingness to see the positive in events or conditions of combining motherhood with paid work with an expectation of favorable outcomes.

Outdated yet persistent societal norms and expectations imply that good mothers are those who do not work outside the home and devote all of their time and attention to their children. Yet, for many women, this is not an option or a choice, primarily because most women today work. The challenge for many working mothers is feeling they can successfully meet the needs of their family and the responsibilities of their work roles. Maternal optimism assumes that mothers can and do have positive work and family experiences.

What drives maternal optimism? One way to determine this is to ask the following questions about the degree of optimism you have as a future or current mother: Does the uncertainty of becoming/being a working mother make you worried or fearful about the future, or are you optimistic about what the future holds as a working mother? Do you hold more positive or negative thoughts about what the future holds as a working mother? The purpose of this book is to help working mothers alleviate some of their negative thoughts, worries, and fears, and focus on the positive aspects of becoming/being a mother who works.

While there are many books and popular press articles that have addressed the bias, guilt, and anxiety that mothers who work often face

when making work and family choices, the goal of this book is to provide you with stories and research that support the notion of owning and
feeling confident in the choices you make as future or current working
mothers, even if they don't always work out the way you may have hoped.
We address the origins of deep-seated expectations and stereotypes often
attributed to working mothers and explore ways in which women have
forged paths that are unique to them and make sense for them, rather than
ones that are expected or based on what worked for someone else. Every
working mother's path is unique and should be celebrated, not lamented.
Women often instinctually look to what others are doing for comparison
and answers, but what women really need to do is look inside themselves
to decide what works best for them. There is always someone who is going
to be managing work and family differently. You may see their approach as
better or worse than what you are doing. But instead of evaluating them,
working mothers need to ask themselves what they can learn from those
experiences while crafting their own paths. We hope women will pick up
this book at times when they may not be feeling confident, when they may
regret a choice, or when they are stepping into an unknown situation, so
that they can reframe any negative emotions they may be feeling into a
more positive light. We believe that if women approach uncertainty about
their current or future state with hope, rather than fear, they will have a
greater likelihood of living life with maternal optimism.

   This pressure for working mothers to do it all and have it all seems to
have increased in recent years with the rise of bestselling books (noted in
italics) that focus on intense parenting alongside the pressure to *Lean In*[1]
at work. On the home front, working mothers are responding to societal
norms that continue to *Praise Stay-at-Home Moms*[2] and reward *Intensive
Mothering*[3] and *Ambition Decisions*.[4] There is a growing expectation that
parents need to dedicate their entire existence to raising their children if
those children are to successfully navigate the uncertain world they will
enter. Mothers, in particular, are expected to apply the same intellectual
and physical energy to childrearing that they might apply to pursuing an
advanced degree. In their professional lives, working mothers are also
being urged to devote themselves fully to pursuing their careers. Working

mothers are advised to *Lead Gracefully*,[5] *Find a Sponsor*,[6] or *Pushback*[7] as they work their way through the *Leadership Labyrinth*[8] in an effort to break the *Confidence Code*,[9] *Get the Corner Office*,[10] and *Thrive*.[11] Working mothers often feel if they are not leading the charge to break the glass ceiling or at least striving for the next promotion, they are not succeeding professionally.

With these competing demands to be fully devoted at work and at home, it is no surprise that so many working mothers are left feeling *Overwhelmed*,[12] *Maxed Out*,[13] and in a perpetual *Time Bind*.[14] The stress and insecurity that often surrounds working mothers has led to an expansive market for books, websites, and life coaches that provide working mothers with sound—and sometimes not so sound—advice about managing work and family. Working mothers, and working mothers to be, are looking for *The Plan*,[15] *The Secrets to Success*,[16] and *7 Solutions to Be a Guilt-Free Working Mom*[17] to manage the complexity of integrating work and motherhood. Our concern is that the overemphasis on helping working mothers have it all, even with a postmodern twist, has led to a one-size-fits-all assessment of work/family that has little connection to the reality of working mothers' experiences and leaves many women feeling inadequate as professionals, as mothers, and/or in how they are integrating work and family.

This book takes a different approach. To begin, we do not see mothering and work as two distinct spheres of life. Maternal optimism presumes that engaging in paid work is part of being a mother, just as it is for fathers. Even decisions about taking time off from paid work are inherently decisions about being a mother and determining how to integrate work and parenting over the course of a career. Furthermore, maternal optimism does not assume there is a right way to integrate work/family, nor do we seek to provide working mothers with the "seven steps" to successfully manage work and family. What is right for one working mother is not right for the next, and what is right at one point in time is not likely to be right at another point in one's life and career. Thus, the goal of this book is to impart wisdom from research and from stories of women at various life and career stages who craft their work/life paths based on their unique and evolving circumstances. The paths we share are from working women pursuing varied careers in different industries who have a range of life circumstances. These stories highlight the challenges and disappointments along with the joys, opportunities, and successes many women experience as they integrate work and family over time. By connecting these stories to decades of work/life research, we uncover key insights of navigating work and family over the course of one's career and varying life circumstances. By providing readers with new insights, we hope to empower working mothers to feel more confident as they craft their own paths.

FORGING POSITIVE PATHS THROUGH WORK AND MOTHERHOOD

This book begins from the premise that every working mother is crafting her own unique path. Each working mother will need to navigate her particular work and life circumstances as she makes decisions about how to integrate work and family in a way that is best for her. While most women will feel less optimistic many times in their lives, each working mother is an individual with her own values, career aspirations, organizational demands, and family needs. While the challenges, opportunities, and choices that come along with being a working mother will vary, similar questions may arise for all working mothers, such as: Should a woman return to work after her first child is born? Does it make sense to scale back or take time off from work as children age or when responding to the needs of a sick family member? What impact will a promotion or taking on a more challenging work opportunity have on her family? We also recognize that differences in family structure, cultural beliefs, sexual orientation, race, and religion will play a role in how women's work/life stories unfold. In this book, our objective is to help women navigate work and family by addressing the common questions and choices they may confront and offer existing research, data, and personal stories of success and failure that may be used to help them make their own choices based on what works best for them. It is also meant to serve as a guide to help individuals who are in positions where they have the capacity to shift organizational practices to better support women as they integrate work and family.

The second underlying premise of this book is the recognition that integrating work and life is not stagnant, but instead unfolds over time. Frequently, we reduce work/life challenges to a single point in time, such as the decision to return to work after the birth of a child. Work and family decisions are anything but stagnant, rather, they are filled with unpredictable events. For example, childcare arrangements that work well at one point in time may need to change as children get older or when you accept a new promotion at work. Priorities around work and family may shift as your family expands or when dealing with work and/or family interruptions. As Mary Dean Lee and colleagues stated, "Individuals lead complex lives that consist of entangled strands of work, family, personal and community life that shift, flow, unravel, synchronize, get wound up in knots, and untangle as careers unfold."[18] In this book, we assume that just as a working mother begins to feel comfortable in how she is navigating work and family, that equilibrium will shift. Working mothers need to recognize that their own unique paths will unfold over time across anticipated and unanticipated circumstances. By understanding and anticipating these shifts, working mothers can develop the resiliency they need at home and at work.

Finally, the notion of forging your own path does not assume that every woman experiences the journey through work and family in the same fashion. Given the financial pressures on today's families and the instabilities of the economy and the workplace, most mothers will be integrating work and family in various ways throughout their lives. While some women will continuously work full time for their entire careers, many women will experience ebbs and flows in their careers. Working mothers may pursue flexible work schedules, seek short-term project-based work, or start their own businesses to navigate work and family at different points in time. Even women who have the financial resources to leave paid work are more likely than ever to use this time to continue to develop their skills and prepare for a return to paid work. The false dichotomies between stay-at-home and working mothers, between on and off ramping, and between the mommy track and opting out need to be eliminated as they are suggestive of an "either/or" rather than an "and" approach. Thus, we use the term *working mothers* to refer to all women who combine work and family, even for those mothers who may be temporarily out of the paid workforce. Also, by considering work and family integration over time and by broadening the focus to a variety of life circumstances and individual differences, our hope is that working mothers move away from striving to have it all and instead learn to embrace their own stories that will unfold with their own narratives, supporting players, and plot twists. This book is about empowering working mothers to be the writers, the narrators, and the central protagonists of their own paths.

HOW THIS BOOK ORIGINATED

The foundations for this book were set in motion close to a decade and a half ago when we began a study about women's experiences being pregnant at work. At the time, there was little discussion or appreciation in the business community for the unique experiences of pregnant working women as they transitioned to working mothers. However, as researchers on this project, we had each experienced being pregnant at work and had heard enough informal stories from other pregnant women to believe that this was a significant identity shift for women that was critical to their work lives. We were not mistaken. The women we interviewed articulated clear visions of how they imagined their lives would look after their babies were born and were already creating plans for their future lives as working mothers. For some women, these visions were empowering, and for others, these visions were already leading them to question how they would integrate work and family. We also began to see how individual and organizational differences strongly influenced pregnant women's visions of their futures as working mothers.

Over time, as our own lives evolved, our research shifted to a deep intellectual and emotional interest in the lives of working mothers, their partners, and their families. We also recognized that pregnancy was just one aspect in a working mother's life, and if we were to better understand working mothers, we needed to conduct more research. We began additional projects—sometimes together and sometimes with other talented collaborators—on such topics as working mothers' experiences negotiating flexible work arrangements, working mothers' return to work after maternity leave, working fathers, diversity issues with working mothers, and women entrepreneurs. We also began to speak to and coach working mothers, both formally and informally, as they navigated various transitions related to work and family. Out of this research and practice emerged the foundational principles for this book. No two women have the same work/family path, yet too many women struggle as they judge their paths against mythical ideals.

While our research and that of others form the basis of this book, the ideas presented here are also informed by our personal work and family experiences. We both are working mothers, and on the surface, our stories seem quite similar. With regards to work, we are both tenured professors at prestigious universities in the Northeast. In the family domain we each have three children. Yet, these similarities are only surface level. As working mothers we have had to pursue our own unique paths that have included navigating pregnancies that didn't always align with our careers, determining when and when not to pursue challenging career and leadership opportunities, shifting to part-time work and back to full-time work, navigating health crises, and encountering unexpected turns with partners and children. Like the women we study, we have had to learn to value, find, and take pride in our own maternal optimism in the work/family paths we are crafting.

HOW TO USE THIS BOOK

This book is divided into two main sections. The first section follows the life transitions of working mothers as they move from not-yet-expectant mothers to new mothers, then to mothers of school-age children and adolescents, and then to middle-aged mothers with children out of the home. Chapter 1 begins before a woman even becomes pregnant. While it may seem premature (no pun intended), we know women are already making life and career choices based on past experiences and future expectations about becoming a working mother. Chapter 2 explores the foundations of working motherhood as women become pregnant and begin to negotiate professional and mothering roles as they disclose their pregnancies at work and prepare for maternity leave. Chapter 3 continues with the reality of becoming a working mother as women reenter the workplace and move from envisioning to enacting life as working mothers. In Chapter 4, we move on in years as we focus on growing families and the new questions that arise as children move from preschool to adolescence to high school. The final chapter in this section considers working mothers later in life as they age and experience motherhood with adult children.

The second half of the book moves beyond life stages as we explore nontemporal transitions working mothers may experience that are driven by work or family circumstances. This section begins with Chapter 6, which focuses on flexible work arrangements. Workplace flexibility is often romanticized as an answer to all of the challenges working mothers face. In reality, workplace flexibility is more complex and can introduce new difficulties for a working mother. Chapter 7 moves beyond job flexibility to consider career flexibility. As working mothers integrate career and motherhood, they may take different paths such as taking time off or starting their own businesses. These paths come with their own obstacles and opportunities. Chapter 8 moves away from work transitions to focus on life transitions. In this chapter, we explore life disruptions that can arise for working mothers. We look at personal disruptions that may occur due to health crises or chronic illness, as well as interpersonal disruptions such as a sick child, divorce, or caretaking of extended family members. We consider how these life disruptions impact women's careers and how working mothers manage through these experiences. In Chapter 9, we then turn our attention to the men in working mothers' lives. We consider how, as life partners and as allies in the workplace, men are integral to our evolving notions of work/family and are pivotal in supporting working mothers.

In each chapter, we focus on the key questions and decisions that arise, the new opportunities as well as the challenges that surface, and how all of this affects a working mother's evolving sense of self. We highlight the paths some women have followed as they work through these transitions and connect these experiences to work and family research so that working mothers can learn from the experiences of others, compare them to their own, and chart their own course. While the chapters build from one to the next, you can enter the book at any point, turning to the chapter that connects to your particular circumstances. We encourage you to focus your attention on those aspects of the book that are most engaging to you now, put the book down, and then return to it time and again as life progresses. Our hope is that this book becomes an important reference that empowers working mothers and fosters your maternal optimism.

REFERENCES

1. Sandberg, S. (2013). *Lean in: Women, work, and the will to lead*. New York, NY: Alfred A. Knopf.
2. Schlessinger, L. (2009). *In praise of stay-at-home moms*. Grand Rapids, MI: Zondervan.
3. Ennis, L. R. (2014). *Intensive mothering: The cultural contradictions of modern motherhood*. Ontario, Canada: Demeter Press.
4. Schank, H., & Wallace, E. (2018). *Ambition decisions: What women know about work, family, and the path to building a life*. New York, NY: Viking.
5. Tallon, M. S. (2016). *Leading gracefully: A woman's guide to confident, authentic & effective leadership*. San Francisco, CA: Highest Path Publishing.
6. Hewlett, S. A. (2013). *Forget a mentor, find a sponsor: The new way to fast-track your career*. Boston, MA: Harvard Business Review Press.
7. Rezvani, S. (2012). *Pushback: How smart women ask—and stand up—for what they want*. San Francisco, CA: Jossey-Bass.
8. Eagly, A. H., & Carli, L. L. (2007). *Through the labyrinth: The truth about how women become leaders*. Boston, MA: Harvard Business Press.
9. Kay, K., & Shipman, C. (2014). *The confidence code*. New York, NY: HarperCollins.
10. Frankel, L. P. (2014). *Nice girls don't get the corner office: Unconscious mistakes women make that sabotage their careers*. New York, NY: Warner Business Press.

11. Huffington, A. (2014). *Thrive: The third metric to redefining success and creating a life of well-being, wisdom, and wonder.* New York, NY: Harmony.

12. Schulte, B. (2015). *Overwhelmed: How to work, love, and play when no one has the time.* New York, NY: Macmillan.

13. Alcorn, K. (2013). *Maxed out: American moms on the brink.* Berkeley, CA: Seal Press.

14. Hochschild, A. R. (1997). *The time bind: When home becomes work and work becomes home.* New York, NY: Henry Holt.

15. Downey, A. (2016). *Here's the plan: Your practical, tactical guide to advancing your career during pregnancy and parenthood.* Berkeley, CA: Seal Press.

16. Dey, M. (2017). *The secrets to success for the working mother.* CreateSpace.

17. Fair, M. (2013). *Tilt: 7 Solutions to be a guilt-free working mom.* CreateSpace.

18. Lee, M. D., Kossek, E. E., Hall, D. T., & Litrico, J. B. (2011). Entangled strands: A process perspective on the evolution of careers in the context of personal, family, work, and community life. *Human Relations, 64*(12), 1531–1553.

ACKNOWLEDGMENTS

The process of writing this book has been years in the making, and we have many people to thank for their insights, friendship, collaboration, love, and support. Many of the insights from our research and ideas discussed in the book have been shaped by the many working mothers who have shared their stories with us over the years. We are grateful and awed by all the working parents who have participated in our research, joined us for a seminar, or taken our classes. You openly and honestly shared your fears, concerns, and triumphs large and small. This book draws on your collective experiences and personal anecdotes. This book is your story.

Our perspectives on work and motherhood have also been influenced by our many academic colleagues. Our deepest appreciation to Judy Clair, who collaborated with us on our initial research on pregnancy in the workplace. We have also been very lucky to have engaging research collaborations with numerous colleagues, including Kim Eddleston, Caroline Gatrell, Kerry Gibson, Brad Harrington, Beth Humberd, Sharon Kim, Elaine Landry, Laura Little, Courtney Masterson, Wendy Murphy, Gary Powell, Katina Sawyer, Alexis Nicole Smith, Dana Sumpter, Christian Thoroughgood, Liz Volpe, and Marla Baskerville Watkins. Your partnerships have provided us with laughter, friendship, and new insights around work and motherhood—many of which are discussed in this book. We also are deeply appreciative of all our colleagues at Babson College, Northeastern University, the Work Family Research Network, and our other academic friends we have met through our involvement and participation in the Academy of Management who have informed and encouraged this work.

We also offer our sincere gratitude to our Oxford University Press family, who have partnered with us on this project. Abby Gross, our editor, provided us with support and encouragement as she understood personally and conceptually the vision behind this book. Katharine Pratt, along with multiple anonymous reviewers, provided helpful feedback along the way that deepened our thinking and challenged us to explore the complex, varied stories of work and motherhood. While not part of the Oxford family, we also want to thank Jenn Cassie, who helped us edit our work prior to submitting the manuscript. Jenn was essential to our final editing as she helped ensure our writing was engaging and straightforward. We are eternally grateful for her positive reception to the book and our ideas, which gave us the confidence we needed to live up to the book title: maternal optimism!

Lastly, but by no means least, as working mothers we see the deep connections between our own families and this book. Our families have supported us and been patient with us as we devoted many hours to our book. A special thanks to our partners in life: Michael Tobin (Danna's husband of twenty-five years) and Todd Goldberg (Jamie's partner of eight years) for only occasionally (!) complaining about additional home responsibilities as we devoted extra hours and emotional energy to this project. When we talk about men being allies at work and at home, we know how lucky we are to have you in both these corners. As working mothers, we are also forever indebted to the cadre of devoted, loving childcare providers who have entered our homes. Our children and our lives have been enriched by the care you have given our families. Finally, we cannot celebrate our own maternal optimism without sharing our deep love for our children. Charlie, Jackson, and Corey (Jamie's children) and Micaela, Jonah, and Seth (Danna's children), you have patiently, and not so patiently, waited for a much-needed ride or a call back, or entertained yourself while we squirreled away in Jamie's office for just one more minute. You are always there championing our dual role as mothers and professionals—you gave us the reason to write this book.

PART ONE

The Expected Path

Envisioning the Future as a Working Mother

It has been really hard for me to make a decision about when and if I wanted to have a baby. I have struggled with it for years. My husband was ready to have kids two years ago, but I wasn't. I didn't want to give up my life. While I knew that you don't have to give up your life when you have kids, I think you definitely give up part of it. You see, I am someone who has always been very busy with my interests. I have a large circle of friends, I enjoy exercise, sports, and social events, and I need sleep. I love my work, and having time for something fun or relaxing is really important to me. I just started thinking, "What am I going to have to do without so I can add kids into our life?" I really didn't want to take anything out of my life, and I still don't. And that's going to be the hard choice to make when we have children. However, after much debate I finally decided I want to have the experience of having children and being a mother. I don't want to miss out on that. So I have finally decided I better start thinking about getting pregnant before it gets too difficult. You can see, though, I am still wondering how I will fit children into my life. That, I still haven't answered.

—MARA, *hospital administrator*

The decision to have a baby can be one of the most difficult choices a couple can make, particularly when both individuals have a successful career. Many women spend years focusing on building a career, taking the time to acquire essential human capital skills that make them valuable resources in the workforce. However, there comes a time when all women begin to think actively about their future and determine whether or not that includes having children. As Mara describes in the opening quotation, when women have built a career and a personal life that they find satisfying, it becomes hard to imagine how children can be integrated into the mix. Important questions women often have at this important juncture in life include: How does having a baby impact a woman's career? How much does it cost to have a child? How does having a baby affect personal freedom?

Beyond working through your own thoughts and visions of combining motherhood with paid work, you may also find that you are frequently responding to family, friends, community members, and sometimes even coworkers who are weighing in on when you should start a family. You may find their comments both a help and a hindrance as you consider the answers to these questions. In this chapter, we explore how you can more consciously think about what the future may hold as a working mother and what impact the decision to have a baby can have on your career and personal life. Although we assume that most professionally employed women carefully plan the timing of their first child, we also consider unexpected challenges and opportunities that cannot be predicted or managed.

CRAFTING A SUCCESSFUL CAREER

After graduating from college, few women question whether they will enter the workforce. In comparison to the 1960s, many women are encouraged by their families, teachers, and women in the workplace to work hard and build a career and life independent from others. As Annika explained,

> My parents were always very clear with all of us. We needed to work
> hard and create a life for ourselves regardless of what happened with
> marriage or family. So, it was never a question of whether I was going
> to have a career.

The drive to succeed is reflected in some of the recent statistics on women
entering the workforce. For every two men who graduate from college or
pursue a higher degree, there are three women doing the same. This difference is significant in part because higher education is associated with
higher wages. Educational differences partially account for why childless
women in their twenties are out-earning their male counterparts by close
to 8%. While this pay difference can reverse as women age and move into
senior leadership positions, the early career stage is often a highly productive time for women.[1]

Early in their careers, women often find they have the freedom to make
work choices based primarily on their financial and professional needs
rather than on the needs of their family. While young women may be concerned about student loans and daily financial pressures, these burdens
are not the same as concerns about supporting and caring for children.
If a job is not challenging or the career direction one has begun is not
fulfilling, women at this stage may be more inclined to alter their career
path. Indeed, women without children experience greater job mobility
than women with children not because they are more qualified but because they have the freedom to pursue a job or company without taking
into consideration childcare management, job flexibility, or workplace
support for working mothers.[2] For example, when Lindsey was interested
in leaving the nonprofit sector to pursue a career in human resources, she
considered job openings across the country. During the search process,
Lindsey knew this was the time for her to be open to new opportunities
and new geographic locations, as she anticipated feeling more constrained
by family needs in the future. Lindsey ultimately accepted a job in a new
city a thousand miles away, which provided her with both personal and
professional renewal. During this early career stage, women need to take
advantage of increased job mobility not only to achieve economic stability

but to build up skills that make them more marketable in the future.[2] Taking advantage of career mobility can give women the power they need to advocate for themselves later in their careers. Unfortunately, the gains of mobility are not experienced equally by all women. Research suggests that African American and Hispanic women on average experience less job mobility than white women, particularly for those who are not college educated.[3]

While women may be actively building their careers during this period, this does not preclude them from pondering how to combine work and family in the future. These future visions about work and family form early in life as women are influenced by their families and other important role models. As Heather reflected on her views about work/family, she pointed to the important model her parents set for her about combining work and motherhood. Heather explained,

> There were four children in our family, but my mom and my dad always worked. I saw that my mom was able to manage it all. I mean it was crazy, chaotic, frenzied and she had much help from my grandparents and other family members, but it worked. So as a child and in high school, I never imagined not having my own family and a career.

Heather's family history provided her a valuable life preview. She understood that combining work and motherhood can be simultaneously chaotic and fulfilling. Being aware of some of the work/family conflicts that parents, parental figures, or other role models experience can be empowering to women as they begin to recognize that work/family challenges are manageable and do not always prevent them from having a successful life as a working mother.[4]

Parents can also provide important models that affect the extent to which women may expect they will be solely responsible for managing work and family. Women whose mothers work often have less traditional views about combining work and family, particularly when they grow up in homes where both fathers and mothers are active caregivers.[5] Further, women who expect their partners will be active caregivers are likely to have fewer concerns about eventually managing work and family. As Nina shared,

> My parents were always pushing me, making sure that I got the best education, making sure that I worked hard. While it was the typical stuff, they said that I could do anything that I wanted to do and that I should always fulfill my best expectations, that I had many abilities, that I should make sure to follow them. So I did that, and if you're supposed to do that, you cannot just give all that up.

In Nina's case, the expectations that her family set were not just about combining work and parenting but also were about the importance of a woman crafting her own identity and pursuing a meaningful career. Nina in part built her career based on these encouraging messages, so work became more central to her sense of self. When it came time for her to have a family, she was not willing to give up this part of her identity, which she had been taught to value.

These early models about work and family also affect how women make career-related decisions long before they have a family. As early as high school, if young women are concerned about combining work and family, they show less desire to pursue a college education, which may lead to a lower future career commitment.[6] Anticipating future concerns about balancing work and family may lead women to unconsciously make choices that will limit their long-term career opportunities and earning potential. Women who anticipate challenges in combining work and family also start demonstrating less ambition and drive related to their career. This effect is particularly true for women who plan to start a family before they are 30.[7] Some young women's concerns about work and family start to erode their confidence in their ability to be a working mother long before they even launch their careers.

Other women who might not have these early concerns about integrating work and family sometimes find concerns start to arise as they pursue more significant career opportunities. As women engage in activities that help build their careers and themselves as professionals, they may find it particularly difficult to imagine a future life that integrates motherhood into a full professional life. As careers progress, women may find they work longer and more unpredictable hours and spend more time socializing with colleagues, building their professional networks, and participating in professional development activities. Engaging in these extra work-role behaviors creates additional time and role strains in women's lives, which can lead them to start to question how they will combine work and family in the future. For example, while Monique was not thinking about getting pregnant anytime soon, she did occasionally wonder how she might integrate a baby into her work-focused life. As she explained,

> My mom worked as far back as I can remember. I consider her a strong independent role model. Growing up, I didn't feel like I wanted to be a mom. I did not think that was something that I was going to be interested in. So, I have been focused on myself and, you know, reaching goals that are important to me. Now I am starting to think about, how can I be career focused and have a baby?

Women who are in leadership positions are particularly attentive to the potential conflicts that can arise in combining family and work.[7] Unfortunately, there are not enough women in visible senior leadership positions who can serve as role models for combining work and family.

Some women may become so preoccupied with future concerns about combining work and motherhood that they make choices that slow down their career progress with the hope that by setting limits now they can decrease work/family conflicts in the future. A woman may choose not to pursue a promotion or switch to a new job or take a position that involves travel or relocation because she is worried these career shifts may make it more difficult to integrate future work and family demands. As we mentioned earlier, women who anticipate challenges managing work and family are likely to compromise their careers in the present.[7] At the same time, career choices that are made in part to accommodate having a family in the future can prove to be good choices. Both authors pursued careers in academia partially due to family reasons.

Early career advancement can also help women more successfully integrate work and family later in their career. Women who have accumulated extensive work experience before having a child pay less of a motherhood wage penalty relative to their peers who have less work experience.[8] With higher wages, women may be able to afford additional childcare or household help that can ease the stress of home responsibilities. Women who are in more powerful positions also have an easier time adjusting their work roles to better integrate work and family. These adjustments include negotiating an extended maternity leave, a flexible work arrangement, and different role responsibilities so that they can more successfully be a working mother.[9]

RACIAL AND CULTURAL FACTORS THAT SHAPE HOW WOMEN ENVISION MOTHERHOOD

While we use the term *working mothers* to refer to all working mothers, we recognize experiences vary significantly based on other aspects of a woman's identity, including race, ethnicity, and sexual orientation. The word *intersectionality* is used to refer to the idea that multiple identities will intersect to create a whole that is different from simply adding together the individual experiences associated with each identity.[10] Intersectionality is critical to our discussion of working mothers because it reminds us that while there are commonalities to this experience, there are important differences that arise in each phase based on one's multiple social identities. Throughout this book, we note some of the ways that intersectionality leads to variation in working mothers' experiences. Specifically, we focus on differing experiences based on race, ethnicity, and sexual orientation, as well as nontraditional parenting (e.g., single mothers). At the same time, we recognize we cannot account for the full range of differing experiences at each stage of the work/life story. As such, we encourage readers to be cognizant of how their experiences of becoming or being working mothers may differ based on their unique intersecting identities.

Socioeconomic background is one such factor that affects the visions, ideals, and assumptions women hold about combining work and motherhood. While work often is framed as a choice for women, this is very much dependent on class. Women who come from middle-class or working-class backgrounds may never have to question whether they will integrate work and family. Victoria's working-class background strongly influenced how she imagined integrating work and motherhood in the future:

> My mom always worked. My dad always worked. I came home and I was a latchkey kid before I even knew what a latchkey kid was. It has never bothered me. I turned out okay. So, I feel like I have choices. If I didn't have those experiences to draw upon, I am not sure I would be as confident about becoming a working mother.

For some women, familial models of working mothers may go back multiple generations, particularly when women come from a working-class background. Angie shared,

> My father's side was very working class. His father stopped school at eighth grade. His mother finished high school and she always worked even though it was a time that women didn't necessarily work. Most of the families I grew up with were families where a mother had to work for the family to survive. The whole family knew how to work together and were happy supporting each other. I think I have had some nice models. I never really thought about not being a working mother.

Race is another way in which a woman's background may yield differing visions around combining work and motherhood. Black women frequently draw on their familial and racial history when explaining their lack of concern over becoming a working mother. Unlike white middle-class women, black women historically reject notions of domesticity and traditional family roles. Driven by both need and choice, black women ascribe to a different cultural discourse about their career, family, and community.[11] As journalist Ylonda Gault Caviness reflected in a column in the *New York Times*,

> One thing that makes it easier for black women is that, unlike many white women, most black women in America come from a long line of mothers who worked outside the home, and have long been accustomed to navigating work and family. My mama worked, as did her mama and her mama before that.[12]

Caviness goes on to explain that because black women come from a lineage of working mothers, they have grown accustomed to navigating work and family. The cultural norm is about having a family and a good job rather than making a choice between one or the other. One could argue that black women are socialized into a cultural expectation that women will combine work and motherhood. This would partially explain why black working mothers have the highest rate of labor force participation of any racial group, with over 76% of black mothers working compared to 69% of white mothers.[13]

Women who come from more conservative, patriarchal cultures may have more trouble reconciling their cultural ideology around work and motherhood with their desire to combine work and family. In explaining how her cultural background impacted her future visions about work and motherhood, Priya shared,

> I come from a conservative Indian background from the northern part of India. It's one of those places where women were educated, but a lot of times they didn't continue on with their careers. It was definitely the man that led the family. So my father was the head of the family. My mom had her Ph.D. in physics, but she gave that up. She decided that she wanted to raise a family and be 100% focused on that. That was and still is what women are expected to do.

Even though Priya lived in the United States and knew she wanted to keep working after she had children, her background gave her pause for concern. She recognized she was deviating from the dominant norms of her culture. She was concerned about sharing her choices with her family and community and how they might judge her. Women who make choices around work and family that deviate from the norms of their community may feel more conflicted about their choices and ability to succeed as a working mother.

The point of highlighting these racial and cultural differences about expectations of work and family is to raise women's awareness of the messages they have received and how these messages may be affecting them very early in their careers. Some women will find their backgrounds empowering and affirming of how they envision navigating work and family. Women who experience a disconnect between the messages received and their desires regarding work and family may want to consider how to alter these expectations. Connecting with women from one's cultural background who have followed a similarly "deviant" path around work and family can be particularly helpful in providing guidance and support. If such individuals are not available, women may simply want to make sure they are connecting with other positive role models whom they can learn from and envision becoming. Affinity groups may be the place to find such role models. Affinity groups are often established in organizations to help support women and minority workers.

WORKPLACE BIAS AFFECTING WORKING WOMEN'S DECISIONS TO BECOME MOTHERS

Even though a woman may not yet have found her life partner and may be solely focused on her career, in some instances her colleagues may already be imagining and acting as though she is a working mother. In some organizations and industries, simply being a woman signals one's inevitable transition to motherhood. Take for example the case of Jane, who talked about a job interview she had where the hiring manager began describing the many family-friendly policies available to working moms:

> I just remember when I was getting ready to graduate from college I was interviewing with one of the senior managers. I was very excited about the company and the job, and I knew they were supportive of women. But I found it really funny that she shared, "I don't know if you have kids or not but we've got a great maternity leave program. We are big on family, and flexible work arrangements, and part-time Moms, and things like that." I was shocked. I just said, "Okay, I'm not thinking about that right now."

Jane found it odd and unnerving that this woman would focus on her life as a working mother even though she had not begun to build a career, let alone a family. While the interviewer might have been trying to be supportive, Jane found the conversation demeaning and undermining. She worried that everyone in the organization would focus first on her gender and second on her career.

Organizational anticipation of motherhood can also have a negative impact on the career opportunities that are given to women before having children. For example, young women in finance and professional service firms have faced documented gender discrimination based on biases about them having children someday.[14] In *Selling Women Short*, Louise Marie Roth describes the rise in discrimination cases at Wall Street firms based on subtle cultural forms of bias toward women from male colleagues, managers, and clients. As a result, women get fewer, less challenging work assignments, which leads to harsher performance evaluations and limits women's pay and promotional opportunities.[14] These early biases can sour young women's perceptions about eventually navigating work and motherhood. Such biases are perpetuated in the media, particularly social media. For example, a recruiter on LinkedIn suggested women should not wear their wedding rings on job interviews, implying it signals "high maintenance," impending motherhood that requires accommodations, and an eventual lack of work commitment.[15] Even an abundance of organizational policies that are designed to support working parents may fuel implicit biases against women. The assumption becomes that this is something *all* women will eventually make use of and in so doing they will create costs and workload burdens for their department and organization.[16]

Early in their careers, women need to be mindful of these gender role biases. While they are not the norm in most organizations, if women detect this covert or overt behavior, they will need to determine how to address it. If the organization has a women's affinity group, this might be a community to engage with to get support and identify next steps. Reporting this behavior to human resources is one option but should be preceded by talking directly to the perpetrator. If women continue to detect the same biases, it may be time to find a new group in the organization to work with, or a new organization entirely. Sometimes, outdated gender norms and expectations are deeply ingrained in organizations and may be impossible to address. However, by not reporting incidents of bias, even if they are subtle, the behavior will only continue.

For women who are older and do not yet have children, organizational colleagues may respond in slightly different, though equally problematic, ways. The assumption that all women want to become mothers is so entrenched in society that women may find themselves fielding questions around fertility from various organizational meddlers. Sarah Silverman described the pressures she feels from her family and the public about being childless:

> I'm 45 and I don't have kids and, you know, when you're a woman, I'm finding out . . . you get so much pressure . . . I got two emails within the span of a week, two weeks ago, from people in my life, who I don't necessarily know really well, who just out of nowhere said, "You should really have kids" and "I've been thinking about you." It's such an odd thing to put on someone.[17]

It is challenging enough to navigate the pressures of building a successful career, but when the pressure of whether and when to have children is added into the mix, it can create additional psychological burdens.[18,19]

When faced with this line of questioning, it is best to challenge others' assumptions about women, motherhood, and combining work and family. Disregarding the ignorance of others only perpetuates bias rather than calling attention to difference. Just because something diverges from the norm, it does not mean it is wrong; it is just different. For working women, there are multiple pathways to becoming successful that may or may not include children. However, since this book is about working mothers, we now shift our attention to the issue of timing childbirth.

HAVING A BABY: IS THERE EVER A GOOD TIME?

One of the biggest questions working women want an answer to is this: When is the best time to start my family? In general, professional women are waiting longer to start a family. In the United States, the average age at which women had their first child rose to 26.3 in 2014, up from 24.9 in 2000. Women of Asian descent have the highest average age (30), and women who identify as Native American or Latina have the lowest average age (23). This overall increase in age of first-time mothers is affected partially by the steady drop in adolescent births, but also by the increase in women who are waiting to have children until their careers are more established.[20] The proportion of first births to women aged 30 and 34 increased by 28% between 2000 to 2014, and for the first time, in 2016, data from the Centers for Disease Control and Prevention showed that the birth rate among women aged 30 to 34 surpassed that of women aged 25 to 29.[21]

Education level also affects when women choose to become pregnant. For college-educated women, starting a career often takes priority over starting a family. Hence, educated, career-focused women often are older first-time mothers.[22] More than half of women with master's degrees wait to have a child until they are 30, with 20% of these women waiting until they are at least 35.[23]

The main consideration for many working women when planning to start a family is how having children will impact their careers. To begin with, women's earnings (regardless of experience, education, hours worked, and spousal income) decline by 4% for each child they have.[24,25] While these findings are impacted by reductions in hours worked, moving to part-time work only partially accounts for the wage penalty of motherhood. Women with children often contend with fewer promotions, which further accounts for the reduction in wages. Although some may argue that working mothers may be less willing to take advantage of promotions that come with increased responsibility, research shows that mothers are offered fewer new opportunities and are often discriminated against for not acting on them.[26] In fact, mothers are less likely to be considered for jobs and are offered $13,000 less in compensation compared to fathers and $11,000 less compared to childless women.[26] The wage gap for women with children is 10% to 15% higher than women without children.[27] Often referred to as the *motherhood penalty*, this may be a short-term phenomenon that shifts as women move higher up in the organization. Although there are fewer women than men in the top 10% of most organizations, they are compensated more equally to male colleagues, regardless of whether they have children or not.[24] This would suggest the importance of women using the pre-child phase to build their careers so they are closer to these top positions and less impacted by a motherhood penalty.

Given the potential negative career impacts, it is no wonder why so many women decide to delay childbirth until they are more established in their careers. This strategy makes sense from a purely economic perspective, as for every year a woman delays starting a family she is likely to see a 9% increase in earnings.[25] Women can benefit in their career development by not having any interruptions during this period.[8] Conversely, women who bear children early in their careers face a more significant career penalty with regards to income and promotions.[8] Full-time professional women who delayed motherhood until the age of 35 made on average $50,000 more at age 40 than women who had their first child at age 20. Even women who had given birth at age 30 were making $16,000 a year less at age 40 compared to those who delayed motherhood until age 35.[28] Women who wait to become mothers are likely to have accumulated status, bargaining power, and knowledge, which yields this financial differential.[28]

One shortcoming of the research on the effects of timing of child-birth on women's careers is that it focuses solely on objective, financial outcomes such as salary and promotions.[29] While objective outcomes are important to measure, subjective career outcomes such as career satisfaction and learning may be more important in terms of how women craft their careers. A study that one of the authors conducted found that when measuring for subjective career success—that is, how satisfied a woman is with her career—neither number of children nor age at first birth was found to influence subjective career success. Although many women delay having children so that they may build their careers first, the findings of the study suggested those who had children earlier in their careers had higher levels of career satisfaction than those who delayed childbirth. The time that had elapsed since first birth was found to be positively related to subjective career success, suggesting that women's career engagement may increase as their children get older.[29]

The decision of when to have children is also influenced by the financial realities many working women face. Having a child is costly. According to recent statistics compiled by the US Department of Agriculture, the average family will spend nearly a quarter of a million dollars on a child from birth until the age of 17, a figure that doesn't include the costs of college.[30] While pregnancy cannot always be planned, couples who establish a solid financial base before having children can alleviate some of this potential financial stress.

While working women often believe they have full control over their lives, family timing decisions can be the first of many of the unpredictable aspects of integrating work and motherhood. Some women find themselves pregnant before they had expected, others wait years to become pregnant, while still other women have to speed up their pregnancy timing due to health or life complications. Candice, who was in her thirties and single, found herself diagnosed with premature ovarian failure. At the time, she was not engaged to her boyfriend and the two were perfectly happy with their careers and single lives. Her diagnosis changed her plans. As she explained,

> I always wanted children but I figured, I am 33 years old and I have plenty of time. I also was just starting on a whole new career. Then I was faced with "you probably have less than a 1% chance of getting pregnant." So my boyfriend and I made the decision we were going to start trying. That expedited everything—marriage, getting pregnant, having children.

INFERTILITY AND WORK

Once women decide they are ready to conceive, the unfortunate reality is that the process of becoming pregnant is not as easy as many women anticipate. In the United States, approximately 10% of women aged 15 to 44 will struggle with fertility issues. For women in professional and managerial careers who often wait until they are older to have a baby, these percentages are often higher. Research shows that almost one third of women over 35 who are trying to conceive for the first time will encounter issues of infertility.[31] Older women are also more likely to be treated with more expensive, invasive procedures such as surgery, artificial insemination, and in vitro fertilization (IVF).[32] Thus, while there are career advantages to waiting to conceive, there are health and family tradeoffs.

As with all aspects of motherhood, working women find themselves in uncharted territory as they navigate infertility at home and at work. While infertility issues affect men and women in equal percentages, it is more typical for a woman to undergo more invasive, costly medical procedures.[33] These procedures may require daily monitoring over the course of weeks and months, along with countless doctor visits. Navigating infertility can be both mentally and physically draining. Furthermore, the length of infertility treatment, which can be months or years, is not known when women start the process. To cope with the physical and psychological stress of infertility and the time demand of treatments, women may need to make adjustments at work. Women who have a great deal of freedom to control their work schedule may find it easier to conceal the stresses of infertility. But women who have less control over where and when they work may have to explicitly discuss their infertility treatments with their manager to negotiate the accommodations they need. Having conversations at work regarding infertility may be particularly difficult since this opens up discussions with a manager about issues related to sexuality, reproduction, and the body—none of which are comfortable. As these conversations signal motherhood, women may worry about the possible negative repercussions on their careers.

To prepare to speak to their managers, women will want to do some advance planning. They may find it useful to gather information first about company policies as they relate to infertility support, flexible work arrangements, and personal/sick time. It can be helpful to get advice from other women about how they managed work during infertility treatments and handled discussions with their managers and human resources. It is not necessary to discuss extensive, private details about your situation, but it is important to provide factual details such the fertility treatment schedule and the time, stress, and emotional demands you are facing. This typically leads to discussions about the options for adjusting a woman's work situation should the need arise. Women should also be prepared to discuss how they plan to complete their work responsibilities if they need accommodations. While the conversation should center on the short-term accommodations you are requesting, it is important to remind your manager that fertility treatments can be a long, arduous process and additional support may be needed in the future.

When Jayla started the IVF process, she met with her direct supervisor and explained that she would be starting a round of infertility treatments and would have to leave work at set times for the next seven weeks. While her boss was initially supportive, he began asking her to switch her appointments to accommodate a client deadline. Looking back, Jayla wondered if she might have had an easier time if she had first discussed the situation with human resources and worked out a formal arrangement. Jayla's story is a reminder that it is important to be detailed and explicit in these conversations, consider how formal they need to be, and consider making sure you follow up in writing.

In discussing infertility at work, women need to remember that work colleagues, like family and friends, will come into these discussions with their own experiences and perspectives. When Barrie approached her manager about reducing her workload to accommodate her infertility process, he was very supportive:

> When I requested a reduced workload, it was intended as a short-term solution to allow me time to pursue fertility treatments and/or adoption. My direct supervisor was very sympathetic because family is very important to him. He believes that happy people with stable families make happy employees, so his only concern was that we create a plan that would enable me to continue to work but remain focused on my treatments and overall health.

Yet not all managers are understanding of the infertility process. For example, Mia shared,

> This process has been really hard, because with five miscarriages my heart had been broken many times. When I finally got pregnant on IVF, I was very pessimistic because of all the miscarriages I had before. What made it even more difficult was working through the experience with my boss. The last miscarriage was right before Christmas, and my boss's response was, "Maybe you should consider not having children of your own. Consider adopting." It was a very upsetting conversation for me. So when I had to tell him I was pregnant again, I was prepared to get some negative feedback. I thought a lot about what to say. When I told him I was pregnant again, I reminded him that none of this has ever impacted my work. I also explained how he was very fortunate not to have the issues I was having. I told him that getting pregnant was very important to me and I hoped he could be supportive. I reminded him that none of this had any impact on my

job. He acknowledged that none of what I had gone through before had impacted my job and he was very appreciative of that. That was the best response I could hope for in the situation.

While infertility issues are increasingly common, many people still do not understand differences between infertility treatments, some have religious or ethical views on infertility, and some simply lack the empathy to understand why a woman might pursue this arduous process. By preparing for both positive and negative comments, women who face infertility can better shield themselves from these remarks. Such a shield can diminish the potential that these comments will impact a woman's confidence about becoming a working mother. Some women find it helpful to have at least one confidant at work whom they can talk to about the daily challenges of the infertility process and work. Hiding the stress of infertility can be exhausting and lead women to question whether they will have the strength to combine work and motherhood. Having a confidant to share these feelings with can provide emotional release as well as the needed support to help a woman through this phase.

Single women or lesbian women who are trying to conceive face many additional challenges that are akin to those of women who face infertility. Finding a donor and planning time off for treatments or working with adoption agencies can raise logistical issues, particularly when women may feel uncomfortable revealing to their coworkers or managers that they are trying to conceive or adopt. Married and/or partnered lesbians also face uncomfortable and difficult decisions about which partner will carry the baby. Our research shows that in lesbian couples, as the birth mother discloses her pregnancy, she may claim her identity faster and feel more validated as a mother than nonbirth lesbian mothers, who often feel their maternal identity is invisible to others. Supportive workplaces make a difference in these women's experiences and, interestingly for some, taking on a new identity as a mother may lessen any bias related to their identity as a lesbian, as their colleagues start to see them as aligning with a normative gender role.[34]

GAINING ORGANIZATIONAL SUPPORT WHEN
CONSIDERING HAVING CHILDREN

Although many organizations support women in advancing in their careers, approaching the topic of starting a family can be daunting. We spend our time at work focusing primarily on job-related issues and tasks, and engaging in conversations about personal decisions can be a challenge, particularly for women who may be concerned about unconscious bias. As was discussed previously in this chapter, even women who do not have children may face unconscious biases from managers who see them as mothers in the future and assume that they will not be as committed to their careers in the future as their male counterparts. While it can't be solely left up to you to challenge such behaviors and assumptions, recognizing that bias might exist in your organization may be the first step to understanding how it might affect you in the future. In our own experiences and in the stories shared to us by others, there are a variety of strategies that can be used to counteract any potential discrimination. Some women are able to confront any bias upfront by articulating their career goals and family goals to their colleagues and bosses. Others decide to wait and see how others will react and find they are pleasantly surprised by the degree of support their managers and organizations provide to them. Regardless of the strategy you choose, there are signals in organizations that you can be on the lookout for. For example, are managers in your organization evaluated on the extent to which they are supporting women in their career development? Does your organization have any "integrating diversity" metrics that are applied to a formal review process? Such policies send a strong message about an organization's values and the degree of support you may encounter. While more organizations are supporting women's affinity groups, often these groups are focused more on those who are already mothers. Does your organization have any women's affinity groups that support women in the pre-pregnancy phase? Are they inclusive to women at all levels of the organization? Many women find that workplace support groups can help them think through work/family challenges before having children, gain an understanding of the policies and procedures offered by the company, and prepare for the potential complex life of working motherhood.

The range of options provided to prospective mothers varies immensely across organizations. Some firms provide support for women dealing with infertility. This is particularly tricky given the constraints of "body time" on women's work.[35] If fertility is a concern, find out what resources your organization offers. For example, some organizations offer benefits to help cover the cost of infertility treatment for employees, which has a significant impact on employees' morale, particularly for those going through infertility.[36] In Candice's case, the change in her employer turned out to be critical in her ability to have a family because they provided financial support for the infertility treatments. Without this support, these treatments and perhaps her twins might have never happened. Infertility support can also strengthen a woman's commitment to her career. Research shows that state mandates to cover assisted reproductive technology increase the probability that a woman will invest in a professional degree and a professional career.[32] Even if your organization cannot provide this level of support, your manager may be educated on infertility and infertility treatment so he or she may be more receptive and understanding of women who are undergoing these treatments.

Some organizations take the issue a step further. Apple and Facebook have become creative with regards to the issue of infertility by providing egg-freezing benefits for women who are delaying childbirth and want to lessen the risk of infertility. The cost of egg freezing is about $10,000 per round, with a $500 fee per year for storage costs. Facebook COO Sheryl Sandberg decided to offer this benefit after one of her female employees with cancer needed to freeze her eggs but her insurance wouldn't cover the costs. Some argue that these are good business practices for organizations. At the same time, this practice is controversial as it further supports a culture that prioritizes work and signals an underlying message to women that they have to choose work over family if they want to be successful.[37,38] Doing research upfront to know what your organization offers—both formally and informally—in terms of policies and procedures will preempt some of the challenges you are likely to face in the years to come and can create opportunities to guide the timing of starting a family with navigating your career.

CHAPTER TAKEAWAYS

1. Early role models, personal family backgrounds, cultural norms, and racial and socioeconomic differences affect each woman's thoughts and plans on when to have children and how to integrate work and family life.
2. Prepare for and counteract biases from work and home sources pertaining to both childless and pre-pregnant women.
3. Unpredicted and unanticipated occurrences such as health crises, career shifts, and infertility can surprise anyone. Planning is essential, but there is never a "good time" to start a family.
4. Seek support, encouragement, and guidance from organizations, colleagues, affinity groups, and family and friends.

REFERENCES

1. Luscombe, B. (2010, September 1). Workplace salaries: At last, women on top. *Time.* Retrieved from http://content.time.com/time/business/article/0,8599,2015274,00.html.
2. Fuller, S. (2008). Job mobility and wage trajectories for men and women in the United States. *American Sociological Review, 73*(1), 158–183.
3. Alon, S., & Tienda, M. (2005). Job mobility and early career wage growth of white, African-American, and Hispanic women. *Social Science Quarterly, 86*(supp. 1), 1196–1217.
4. Basuil, D. A., & Casper, W. J. (2012). Work-family planning attitudes among emerging adults. *Journal of Vocational Behavior, 80*(3), 629–637.
5. Davis, S. N., & Greenstein, T. N. (2009). Gender ideology: Components, predictors, and consequences. *Annual Review of Sociology, 35*, 87–105.
6. Marks, G., & Houston, D. M. (2002). The determinants of young women's intentions about education, career development and family life. *Journal of Education and Work, 15*(3), 321–336.
7. Savela, A. E., & Brien, K. M. (2016). Predicting college women's career plans: Instrumentality, work, and family. *Journal of Career Development, 43*(4), 335–348.

8. Taniguchi, H. (1999). The timing of childbearing and women's wages. *Journal of Marriage and the Family, 61*(4), 1008–1019.

9. Greenberg, D., & Landry, E. M. (2011). Negotiating a flexible work arrangement: How women navigate the influence of power and organizational context. *Journal of Organizational Behavior, 32*(8), 1163–1188.

10. Collins, P. H. (2015). Intersectionality & definitional dilemmas. *Annual Review of Sociology, 41*, 1–20.

11. Landry, B. (2000). *Black working wives: Pioneers of the American family revolution.* Berkeley, CA: University of California Press.

12. Caviness, Y. G. (2015, May 2). What black moms know. *New York Times*. Retrieved from https://www.nytimes.com/2015/05/03/opinion/sunday/what-black-moms-know.html.

13. U.S. Department of Labor. (2015). *Current population survey, annual social and economic supplement.* Washington, DC: US Bureau of Labor Statistics.

14. Roth, L. M. (2006). *Selling women short: Gender inequality on Wall Street.* Princeton, NJ: Princeton University Press.

15. Hurwitz, B. (2016). When interviewing for a job, lose the ring! *LinkedIn*. Retrieved from https://www.linkedin.com/pulse/when-interviewing-job-lose-ring-bruce-hurwitz

16. Konrad, A. M., & Cannings, K. (1990). Sex segregation in the workplace and the mommy track: Sex differences in work commitment or statistical discrimination? *Academy of Management Proceedings, 1990*(1), 369–373.

17. Stern, C. (2016, January 11). "You can't have it all": Sarah Silverman, 45, says women face too much pressure to have babies, as she admits she "aches for kids" but loves her life more. Retrieved from https://www.dailymail.co.uk/femail/article-3393994/Sarah-Silverman-45-says-women-face-pressure-babies-admits-believes-T-all.html.

18. Park, K. (2002). Stigma management among the voluntarily childless. *Sociological Perspectives, 45*(1), 21–45.

19. Gerson, K. (1985). *Hard choices: How women decide about work, career, and motherhood.* Berkeley, CA: University of California Press.

20. Matthews, T. J., & Hamilton, M. S. (2009). *Delayed childbearing: More women are having their first child later in life.* Washington, DC: National Center for Health Statistics.

21. Stobbe, M. (2017, May 17). Women in 30s now having more babies than younger moms in U.S. *CNBC*. Retrieved from https://www.cnbc.com/2017/05/17/women-in-30s-now-having-more-babies-than-younger-moms-in-us.html.

22. Gustafsson, S. (2001). Optimal age at motherhood. Theoretical and empirical considerations on postponement of maternity in Europe. *Journal of Population Economics, 14*(2), 225–247.

23. Livingston, G. (2015). For most highly educated women, motherhood doesn't start until the 30s. Retrieved from http://www.pewresearch.org/fact-tank/2015/01/15/for-most-highly-educated-women-motherhood-doesnt-start-until-the-30s/.

24. Budig, M. J., & Hodges, M. J. (2010). Differences in disadvantage: Variation in the motherhood penalty across white women's earnings distribution. *American Sociological Review, 75*(5), 705–728.

25. Miller, A. (2011). The effects of motherhood timing on career path. *Journal of the European Society for Population Economics*, *24*(3), 1071–1100.

26. Correll, S., Benard, S., & Paik, I. (2007). Getting a job: Is there a motherhood penalty? *American Journal of Sociology*, *112*(5), 1297–1338.

27. Krapf, M., Ursprung, H., & Zimmerman, C. (2014, January 11). *Parenthood and productivity of highly skilled labor: Evidence from the groves of academe.* Federal Reserve Bank of St. Louis Working Paper No. 2014-001A.

28. Gregory, E. (2007). *Ready: Why women are embracing the new later motherhood.* New York, NY: Basic Books.

29. Valcour, M., & Ladge, J. J. (2008). Family and career path characteristics as predictors of women's objective and subjective career success: Integrating traditional and protean career explanations. *Journal of Vocational Behavior*, *73*(2), 300–309.

30. Vasel, K. (2017, January 9). It costs $233,610 to raise a child. Money.com. Retrieved from https://money.cnn.com/2017/01/09/pf/cost-of-raising-a-child-2015/index.html.

31. Chandra, A., Copen, C. E., & Stephen, E. H. (2014, January 22). *Infertility service use in the United States: Data from the National Survey of Family Growth, 1982–2010.* National Health Statistics Reports No. 73. Retrieved from https://www.cdc.gov/nchs/data/nhsr/nhsr073.pdf.

32. Kroeger, S., & La Mattina, G. (2017). Assisted reproductive technology and women's choice to pursue professional careers. *International Research on the Economics of Population, Household, and Human Resources*, *30*(3), 723–769.

33. Berkson, M. (2017). *Working women and infertility: Addressing the changing needs of women in the workforce today.* Retrieved from https://infertilityanswers.org/working_women_and_infertility.

34. Hennekam, S., & Ladge, J. (2017). When lesbians become mothers: Identity validation and the role of diversity climate. *Journal of Vocational Behavior*, *103*(A), 40–55.

35. Payne, N., & Lewis, S. (2018). *Combining work and fertility treatment: Conflicts and identity dilemmas* Presented at the Annual Work Family Researchers Network Conference, Washington, DC.

36. Isaacs, J. C. (2008). Infertility coverage is good business. *Fertility and Sterility*, *89*(5), 1049–1052.

37. Parsons, S. (2014, October 20). Female tech CEO: Egg-freezing "benefit" sends the wrong message to women. *Business Insider*. Retrieved from https://www.businessinsider.com/apple-facebook-egg-freezing-benefit-is-bad-for-women-2014-10.

38. Alter, C. (2015, April 24). Sheryl Sandberg explains why Facebook covers egg-freezing. *Time*. Retrieved from http://time.com/3835233/sheryl-sandberg-explains-why-facebook-covers-egg-freezing/.

2

Nine Months and Counting

Balancing Pregnancy and Professionalism

I never took a sick day when I was pregnant. I was determined to manage it. I was in a new job, and I said to myself, "these guys do not know me; they do not know me at all." I worked for ten months to prove to them that I was worth hiring, I am serious about what I do, and I am coming back. So, I probably pushed it too far. I did not get sick, though, and I did not jeopardize the babies.

As I was preparing for maternity leave, I was working closer with my boss, and I just tried to keep making him understand that he had to judge my performance and have confidence in me. It took a little while to get my boss on board about my leave and my return. He admits to me now that he had no idea whether I was going to come back or not, and I feel as though he kind of rolled the dice with hiring me, as I did with him. He had been looking for someone who could handle this function for a couple of years. My maternity leave was going to come just as I was building this function and entering the first formal budgeting process, which is a core competency of this job. I was going to walk out on this team during this process and I was not going to be there for the closing of our fiscal year, so I worked up until four days before the twins were born. I had always been a fifty- to sixty-hour worker, but towards the end of my pregnancy I started coming in at 7 a.m. leaving at 3 p.m., which was hard for my boss, but I was comfortable slowing down, and I guess I was cocky in the end because I knew what I brought to the table. My husband had been telling me to stay strong whether they accept it or not. He would say, "It's not against the law to have a child."

When the babies arrived, I think my boss and colleagues really thought I was never coming back. Then, when they heard my daughter was sick with an extremely rare disorder, they *really* didn't think I was going to come back, and I even had to convince myself otherwise. I thought to myself: "In just ten months you switched your job, you got pregnant, you got engaged, you bought a house, and you planned a 250-person wedding. During all that you did not skip a day of work."

—BRENNA, *IT manager*

Brenna's story reflects the complex, paradoxical feelings about work and family that you may be facing as a professionally employed women who is pregnant for the first time. As we discussed in the previous chapter, women are often entrenched in their careers when they begin to think about having a family. Our identity is often tightly connected to our career. Working women often feel quite confident and competent at work because they know what is expected of them and what it takes to achieve certain career goals. However, this confidence may erode as a woman finds herself pregnant for the first time and entering new, unchartered territory. There is little you may have done up until this point that prepares you for the choices, decisions, and opportunities you will navigate as you transition from being a working professional to a pregnant working professional. As you begin this process and face the unknown, you may hold on tight to what you know and are most comfortable with—your work identity. However, the question of "having it all" may begin to enter your mind and wreak havoc as you consider how you will blend work and family and what you life might look like in the future. Proving to yourself and others that you can do it all may become your modus operandi as you try to keep up with your achievements and commitment to work. We have conducted studies that look at the internal struggles that pregnant women wrestle with as they try to envision themselves as working mothers. If we could wave a magic wand, we would encourage women and organizations to disavow this notion of "having it all." Given the stronghold this trope has on working mothers, it is important to explore how it affects women during pregnancy.

While every woman has her own thoughts, feelings, and visions about who she is and who she hopes to be as a working mother, there are some commonalities to this transition process that we highlight in this chapter. Based on our research and conversations with pregnant, professionally employed women, we have found that there are three significant adjustments that most women work through as they begin to integrate pregnancy and work. The first is a psychological adjustment that starts as a pregnant woman begins to envision her future and questions her identity. The second adjustment is a physical one that stems from how a woman copes with her changing body in the workplace. A pregnant woman cannot control the physical changes of pregnancy, nor can she control how others see and respond to her changing body and all that it represents. The last adjustment is an interpersonal one and relates to how a pregnant woman contends with interactions with her boss and her colleagues. We consider each of these adjustments in more detail before exploring how they play out at two pivotal moments during pregnancy—disclosure and negotiating maternity leave.

PSYCHOLOGICAL ADJUSTMENTS: WHO AM I?

Even when there is not yet a baby to care for, many pregnant women often begin to question who they are as professionals and as mothers. Pregnancy, like other life-altering experiences, may lead you to wonder how to answer the following questions about yourself: Who am I? Who do I desire to be? What are my priorities in life? And how will motherhood change who I have always been? Riya, a communications specialist, articulated how these questions arose for her:

> Up until now I have defined myself by my work and being part of this organization. I am now constantly wondering how this will change, if it will change, and when. I assume it will change in some way because I have seen it change with friends and colleagues. However, maybe it will not. Maybe I will not feel any differently about work when I become a mother.

Like many women, Riya is wrestling with questions about her personal and professional life and how they will intersect. She expresses uncertainty and self-questioning as she ponders her future. On one hand this lack of a coherent future self can be challenging, while on the other it provides an opportunity to consider priorities.

This process of examining how your current identity as a working woman may or may not change after having a child is fairly typical of anyone who is experiencing a significant life transition. Pregnancy is a liminal, in-between period when an individual is in the transition from one stage of life to another.[1] During the liminal phase of pregnancy, women no longer solely define themselves as working professionals but have not yet moved into their new lives as working mothers. This period can be difficult, as a working mother may be experiencing feelings of ambiguity, self-questioning, and disorientation and might be starting to feel disconnected from your old life but not fully centered in your new one.[2] One of the most significant challenges associated with beginning to envision your life as a working mother is the influence of societal expectations regarding work and motherhood. Unfortunately, these expectations generate confusion—both for women and for those in their lives—because pregnancy and motherhood signal assumptions about gender roles and a woman's place in society. Although many women work (women represent nearly half of the working U.S. population!), gender role expectations are deeply rooted in societal norms, making them difficult to break down.

One of the more entrenched societal norms around parenting is intensive mothering, the belief that mothers are expected to direct the majority of their psychological, physical, emotional, and financial resources towards childrearing.[3] This norm has arisen in part from the uncertainty and fears parents feel about raising children in today's world given social, economic, and political pressures. Consequently, mothers tend to hold on tighter, do more, and work harder to excel at parenting—more so than they might even do in a high-responsibility profession.[4] While many pregnant women feel the pressures of the intensive-mothering expectations, anxiety around these expectations is particularly strong among women who expect to be working mothers—and how could they not? Just the term "working mother" suggests that a woman will violate this expectation, as it suggests that a woman's time and energy will not be fully dedicated to her child. It is no wonder why nearly every pregnant woman begins to worry about whether or not she can be a good mother, particularly if she will be a working mother. As Leah shared,

> I was feeling guilty that I was not going to be perceived as a "real" mother. I felt like everyone thinks I should want to stay home with the baby all the time . . . and dedicate my whole being to raising this tiny being in the best way possible, even though that is not who I am.

Although 70% of mothers with children under the age of 18 work,[4] the ideology of intensive mothering can make women believe that working motherhood is a nontraditional and unseemly path.

The intensive-mothering rhetoric can also affect how women experience being pregnant. The messages women receive about how to be a good mother while pregnant are plentiful and forceful, whether they are about the impact of maternal nutrition, sleep, exercise, and stress on neonatal development, or about the need to read and talk to your child during pregnancy to begin bonding. The challenge becomes whether to uphold or defy these cultural messages, which only grow in intensity for women who work. Working women can struggle to meet societal expectations of intensive mothering while also meeting the expectations for an "ideal worker"—that is, an employee who is expected to have little to no outside work responsibilities and can therefore commit all her time and cognitive energy to her workplace.[5] Although ideal worker norms may not be explicitly stated, they often exist as unwritten expectations. Like many working women, you may have made a significant investment in your career as you abided by these ideal worker expectations. However, now that you are pregnant, you are likely beginning to see how expectations around motherhood may conflict with ideal worker expectations. These conflicting expectations tend to make pregnant women insecure about their position in their organization: they may wonder if they will be able to continue to fulfill their own, and others', expectations at work following the birth of their child. As Charlene, who was early in her career, explained,

> I do not want the people I work with to think that this is going to affect the way I do my job. I'm young and new in the position. While I don't feel like the organization took a risk hiring me, I don't want anyone thinking that I'm not going to meet those expectations.

Charlene was afraid that her colleagues would see her as less capable and less professional now that she was pregnant. To manage her concerns and protect her work identity, Charlene took on extra work and worked longer hours than she had before. This reaction is not atypical of pregnant women as they try to manage their own expectations of themselves at work. They will often go to great lengths to preserve their professional identities by documenting all of their responsibilities, trying not to take time off during pregnancy, and working up to the last days of their pregnancy.[2,5]

During pregnancy, women may also start to feel guilty about needing to rely on others who may have to take on more work because of their pregnancy and maternity leave. For women who face physical complications that require them to scale back before maternity leave, the sense of guilt and shame can be overwhelming. Janine, an older first-time mother, stated:

> I think it was very stressful because I felt quite guilty about turning over a large volume of patients to add to the workload of my colleagues who were already very busy. So that is why I was trying to help out as much as I could and be available by e-mail or phone . . . But physically there wasn't much I could do because I was on bed rest.

Thus, in addition to the pressure of feeling as though they may be "counted out" for having a child, pregnant women may also experience stress associated with not physically being able to work and pushing that burden onto others. As Janine's story illustrates, finding creative ways to stay engaged at work, supporting colleagues who may take on extra work, and maintaining your professional identity even if you are not physically present can often lessen the guilt for a pregnant working woman.

On a more positive note, pregnancy may become a time when women reflect upon and reestablish their priorities with regards to work. This may be the first opportunity pregnant women get to pause and reflect on what they want out of work and what values they bring to the organization and their work. Megan explained how pregnancy forced her to reflect on her career:

> What I think is so interesting is that some people never get this period to reevaluate themselves; not just their career but who they are. During pregnancy, you get this opportunity. We tend to put a negative tone on it because it is hard, but it can be a very positive experience too. If you can just take a step back and ask, what matters to me? Who am I? How much does my career matter to me? It matters a lot; it matters a little. I do not know, but at least

I get this chance to try to figure it out. Moreover, I just think some people could go their whole lives without getting that opportunity to evaluate themselves.

Megan's experience indicates how pregnancy can also provide a positive space for women to reflect on who they are, what they have done, and most importantly what they want from their future. Some women may realize they are not satisfied in their careers and may want to explore different career options. If women can learn to separate from societal expectations, pregnancy provides a precious space to uncover and hone in on their own values around work and motherhood.

PHYSICAL ADJUSTMENTS: FLATULENCE, FATIGUE, AND FULL FIGURES

There are countless pregnancy books that provide extensive detail and guidance on the physical changes that women may experience during pregnancy. While there is much advice about how women experience physical changes and symptoms of pregnancy, rarely discussed is how a woman can manage these physical changes at work. Most notably, the changing maternal body signals sexuality and procreation—topics avoided in most workplaces. There is only so long that a pregnant woman can hide her changing body under baggy clothes, and little that can be done to control a changing appearance that may feel uncomfortable when at work.

Managing physical changes at work is particularly difficult today, since the pregnant body is often seen as something to be glorified in the non-work realm. Photos of pregnant Hollywood stars, athletes, and even royals anoint magazine covers. Fashion for pregnant women has moved away from floral tent-like dresses to tight-fitting jeans and dresses that hug the body. The pregnant body is often depicted as something beautiful and natural. However, in the workplace, the pregnant body violates the prevailing culture of masculinity that still dominates most workplaces.[6,7] In the workplace, a symbolic form of professionalism is that of a slender, controlled, self-contained body.[6] A pregnant body is none of these things, and so it becomes a visible symbol of something forbidden or taboo.

Most pregnant women find the simplest way to manage one's changing body is to hide it for as long as possible. Eliza explained,

> You know, it is sad to say, but I try to hide my body as much as I can. I do not think I'm showing. There are days I feel like I am, so I will dress a little differently. I just am uncomfortable, so I just try to be as normal as can be, to get around the situation.

We find most working women will continue to conceal their pregnancy even after announcing it. Pregnant women are trying to avoid unwanted attention to their private life and physical body. They also are trying to preserve their professional image. Eliza wanted others to see her as a "normal" professional, and in her mind, her body violated that image. While coworkers are often trying to be supportive with comments about how good a pregnant woman looks, how much energy she has, or the favorite "you are all baby," even these seemingly positive comments may create discomfort. Frequent positive comments spotlight an identity that a pregnant woman is uncertain about and has not yet embraced.

Women also manage their changing bodies by hiding any physical symptoms they may be experiencing. For example, Lian explained how she carefully redirected conversations when she was asked about her pregnancy:

> I do not complain. Even if I am not feeling very good, I always say that I feel great. I always say I've had a great pregnancy so far. That is my canned response, even if in reality I slept poorly or just threw up in the bathroom.

While women who are in positions of power may feel comfortable with the limitations of their body, women who are less secure about their work position will engage in redirecting behaviors. Redirecting behaviors include deflecting conversations as Lian did, refusing help lifting heavy items, or continuing to take on excessive travel. Pregnant women often go to great lengths to manage their bodies, maintain their organizational status, and minimize the impact of their pregnancy.[8] The challenge is that this redirecting behavior further reinforces a pregnant woman's ability to "do it all" both in her mind and in her colleagues' minds, which can be difficult to reconcile once the baby is born.

A personal story comes to mind. When one of the authors (Jamie) was pregnant with twins during her graduate program, she went to her department chair to share the news. Because she had done such a good job deflecting her first pregnancy, when she told her department chair (an older man with no children of his own), he commented, "Two? Well, that is no big deal for you!" Yet this was a big deal: her symptoms were far worse than in her first pregnancy, and since she was carrying twins, her pregnancy was high risk. After working very hard for three years to show others that she was worthy of being in the program despite being a new mother, now she was confronted with what seemed like an insurmountable hurdle of trying to prove she could continue to do it all.

SHIFTING WORK RELATIONSHIPS

This brings us to the third major shift—interactions with colleagues, bosses, and clients. Many women carefully manage how much and with whom they discuss their personal lives at work. Conversations about the weekend, movies, politics, and local athletic teams happen without hesitation, yet professional working women may be more cautious when discussing more personal matters. Pregnancy crosses this boundary and women find themselves in conversations, or the subject of conversations, about their career, their work life, and their pregnancy itself. These interactions have the potential to positively and/or negatively affect a pregnant woman's life at work.

While the Pregnancy Discrimination Act of 1978 resulted in the elimination of the more overt biases against women in the workplace, it did not mitigate subtle forms of discrimination.[9,10] Subtle biases may arise from cultural assumptions and organizational practices that may inadvertently disadvantage women. This form of bias often comes up in conversations that send indirect messages that the only way to successfully integrate work and family is for a working mother to cut back at work. Even if an organization has generous maternity leave or other work/family policies, how managers think about and implement these policies can send very different messages to pregnant women. When discussing maternity leave, managers may communicate how other women's careers were derailed or roles were eliminated when they went on an extended maternity leave.[11] Beyond reviewing work/family policies, you may also want to examine how your colleagues, peers, and managers act toward working mothers. Subtle forms of discrimination may be garnered from comments directed toward pregnant employees. These covert biases can have psychological and emotional consequences for pregnant women as well as for the other women in the organization who overhear these comments and who may be thinking about having children.[10,12]

Sometimes these biases are subtle and seemingly supportive but in reality may pose a threat to your identity as a professional. For example, Hailey was frustrated by how her manager was approaching her work:

> He kept asking me if I could travel. And I kept saying, "Sure, I can travel." I just want him to treat me the same. I work hard to keep the perception out there that I am still here, still working hard, and I do not need special treatment.

Hailey's boss might have been trying to be supportive, but his assumptions about her limitations made her feel more concerned about her professional status. These types of interactions, which appear to be positive on the surface, reinforce gender stereotypes and workplace inequality.[13] Scholars label these types of interactions as "benevolent sexism"—a kinder, gentler form of prejudice.[14] Because of the elusiveness of this form of sexism, these comments can have an even greater effect on undermining a pregnant woman's confidence about her professional status and her eventual ability to combine work and motherhood.

While there may be times when it is appropriate for women to avoid these interactions with colleagues, some interactions can be helpful. Often coworkers, managers, and even clients share their own stories of pregnancy, integrating work and family, and returning to work. Learning what works and doesn't work for others may help you craft a clearer image of yourself and your future as a working mother.[2] We find that many women benefit from having a support network that can provide a range of advice and mentorship.[15] Interestingly, before pregnancy, you may find yourself left out of conversations related to parenting and family, but once you become pregnant, you will likely find you are now part of a "club" you may not have known existed. Whitney found herself mentioning her pregnancy because it helped her build connections with colleagues in a new job:

> I find I'm actually more prone to talking about my pregnancy and then to ask them about their own families. I am looking for that common ground, and it is a way to say, "Hey, we are friends."

While these psychological, physical, and interpersonal dynamics ebb and flow throughout pregnancy, there are two pivotal moments when all three transitional experiences intersect: (1) when disclosing pregnancy at work and (2) when negotiating maternity leave. Because of the intersecting personal, physical, and interpersonal experiences, these moments often help women begin to develop a clear picture of their future as working mothers. We discuss each of these moments in more depth next as we consider how women can successfully manage these experiences as they create their own work/life path.

THE BIG REVEAL: WHEN AND HOW TO DISCLOSE PREGNANCY

When to tell? Who to tell? How to tell? What to tell? These are the questions that often dominate a woman's mind as she considers how to announce her pregnancy at work, since pregnancy is often stigmatized in the workplace.[16] The process of disclosing a stigmatized identity at work can affect your psychological, physical, and emotional health.[17] Those who have a stigmatized identity may feel vulnerable and open to prejudice or discrimination. Disclosing your pregnancy at work is challenging in part because most pregnant women have not yet reconciled their own internal feelings about combining work and motherhood, as discussed earlier.

Delaying pregnancy disclosure is one way pregnant women actively manage their colleagues' impressions of their competence at work to avoid overt, or covert, discrimination.[18] For example, Kiara waited until she was almost halfway through her pregnancy before disclosing it to her manager:

> They were talking about promoting me, and I did not want that promotion to fall through, so I just didn't say anything about the pregnancy. I was not showing, and I wanted to wait until after the early risk assessment and level two ultrasound.

While Kiara stated she delayed pregnancy disclosure partially because of concerns about the pregnancy, the driving factor appears to be protecting her promotion. While she had no explicit indications that she would not be promoted if she were pregnant, her concerns about the implicit biases she perceived put her into a protective mode. The more importance a woman gives to her professional identity and the more time and energy she has invested in this identity, the more she is going to be concerned about the biases that may arise by revealing her pregnancy.[16]

While in theory putting off pregnancy disclosure is a good strategy if there are possible career implications, there are downsides to delayed disclosure. Some pregnant women who delay disclosure find it difficult to maintain an authentic sense of self at work. Further, delaying disclosure means that a woman will need to actively conceal her stigmatized identity, which is stressful and can have a negative impact on her well-being.[19] Constantly hiding doctor's appointments and concealing your excitement about the pregnancy may also further heighten your concerns about being able to integrate work and motherhood in the future. Delaying disclosure may also result in missed opportunities to begin to establish supportive relationships with others who can help you navigate pregnancy and begin to plan for your life as a working mother. For women who are having physical challenges, delaying disclosure may limit their ability to seek accommodations that would help them more easily integrate work and pregnancy.[19] Research has even shown that for some women, early disclosure of pregnancy alleviates stress and anxiety while at the same time enabling them to maintain authenticity.[16] While pregnancy complications mean that not all women get to decide how and when to disclose their pregnancy, when women can choose their disclosure process there are steps they can take to facilitate these conversations.

Some women find it useful to create a predisclosure process to better prepare for the consequences of disclosure. The first step in planning for disclosure is assessing how your organization, manager, and colleagues approach pregnant women and working mothers. Observing and listening to other pregnant women and working mothers, as well as to colleagues' interactions and reactions to these individuals, is a simple way to gather information. You should be prepared for how supportive your organization is explicitly, and implicitly, about employees' work/family balance. Many pregnant women we have spoken with also find it helpful to set up confidential conversations with other women at work who have managed a pregnancy and maternity leave. Having a confidential conversation with another working mother, or even several, can help you better understand the organizational setting as well as learn from others' experiences. These conversations can be particularly helpful for uncovering how flexible an organization is in accommodating different individual circumstances. The goal of these conversations is to learn from others' experiences and begin to get a more realistic understanding of how a manager and the organization respond to pregnancy, maternity leave, and reentry. This knowledge is essential for preparing for a disclosure conversation.

Once you feel you have some understanding of how your manager and organization may respond to your pregnancy, you can begin planning for your disclosure conversations. The first step of planning involves the sequencing of conversation. Who should you tell first—your boss, your project lead, human resources, or someone else? Deciding whom to tell first should be guided by the knowledge you gathered in the predisclosure phase. Most women find it best to tell their manager first, but if you have a tenuous relationship with your manager or if you are afraid of how your manager will respond, you may decide to tell human resources or a colleague first.

Planning what to tell each person is also important. While women tend to want to resolve all of the uncertainty associated with pregnancy and maternity leave in this first disclosure conversation, it is important to remember this is just that—a first conversation. Conversations about pregnancy and maternity leave will be ongoing, and plans will not be finalized in this first discussion. We encourage you to keep initial disclosure conversations short. At a minimum, sharing how far along you are in your pregnancy, your due date, and how you are feeling in general is a good starting point. If you are already experiencing physical complications that are affecting you at work, it is important to be honest about your health. While you shouldn't have to reaffirm your commitment to work and to returning after maternity leave, some women find comfort in setting expectations with their peers and manager to avoid assumptions based on societal expectations (i.e., they will fall in love with the baby and never return to work). There are many unknowns in pregnancy and childbirth, and in life in general, so of course there is no way to be 100% certain you will return. Nonetheless, you may find it helpful to set the record straight to avoid anyone setting those expectations for you.

A major goal of this disclosure conversation is to begin to alleviate any concerns a manager may have about your commitment to work, as well as to begin to build a support system for the transition to working motherhood. Diava did this by preparing for the concerns she thought her boss might have and developing a plan for managing them:

> I knew his worry would be the clients, so I wanted to explain to him how many months I had left, the different types of project roles that I thought I could be effective at given that I would have transitioned off the client and the project, and also explain that I planned to return fulltime.

When she did speak to her boss, the conversation went better than she expected in part because she was prepared for his concerns.

Some women find it useful to go so far as to script and role-play a disclosure conversation to prepare for the different reactions the other person may have. Scripting is an approach that is useful for managing any difficult conversations you anticipate with your manager or colleagues about work/life.[20] In advance of the conversation, you will want to write out what you will say, anticipate the other party's reaction, and develop a possible response. Scripting a conversation is not about ensuring the conversation goes as planned but about preparing for the unexpected. You can never prepare exactly for how your boss will respond when you reveal your pregnancy, but the scripting process can help you stay focused and respond more positively to unexpected behavior from the other party. In our experience we have found that scripting helps women more successfully manage these disclosure conversations.

PLANNING AHEAD: NEGOTIATING MATERNITY LEAVE

As has been well documented, the United States is only one of two countries left in the world that does not mandate paid maternity leave, despite the corresponding economic and behavioral benefits.[21] All that is required by the Family and Medical Leave Act (FMLA) is that organizations of fifty people or more provide twelve weeks of unpaid leave for the birth or adoption of a child. Consequently, only 12% of U.S. employees receive paid leave, with most resorting to using sick time or vacation time to supplement or fully fund a leave. Even if pregnant women are covered by more substantial leave policies, they need to understand that these U.S. policies communicate a cultural mindset that pregnant women are "on their own" when it comes to having a baby. This mindset is exacerbated by the fact that maternity leave is often seen as an accommodation and a disruption rather than as a normal period in a professional working woman's work history. The cultural norms we discussed earlier may prevent women from asking for a nonstandard leave or an adjusted work schedule, because they feel as if they are supposed to be able to manage the pregnancy on their own and avoid disrupting the workplace. These cultural assumptions may also affect how accommodating a manager will be when negotiating maternity leave.

On the positive side, many academics, policymakers, and business leaders are working to rewrite this cultural narrative. Cities and states are taking up the fight and instituting their own paid parental leave policies. In 2016, Washington, D.C. introduced a progressive leave policy, guaranteeing part-time and full-time employees sixteen weeks of paid family leave to care for a newborn child or an adopted child, or to tend to an ill family member or one's own health issues. While this plan has a salary cap, it is very different from what most pregnant women typically get across the United States. At the industry level, companies that are struggling to attract and retain workers are also expanding their parental leave policies. Some high-tech and consulting companies, such as Amazon, Netflix, Twitter, Deloitte, and Ernst and Young, are offering paid parental leave that ranges from sixteen to twenty weeks. Many of these organizations are also allowing customized, flexible, and/or prolonged return-to-work programs. In these organizational settings, pregnant women often feel more confident advocating for what they want and less concerned about the potential impact that maternity leave will have on their professional status.[12]

As you think about negotiating maternity leave, it's important to realize that you are not just negotiating the nuts and bolts of time away, salary, and benefits; you are also negotiating how you see yourself—and how others see you—as a professional in light of your new identity as a mother.[2] In managing these perceptions, we find that many pregnant women try to limit how much time they take off prior to their maternity leave. Stephanie talked about her maternity leave plans:

> My supervisor has said to me, "No, you will not take your laptop home, and you are going to need to take more than the minimum of six weeks off." I know I am trying to be protective of my role and I do not want to come back and find someone else has taken on my position and is doing it better than me.

Even with her manager's support, Stephanie still felt the need to protect her position at work. Beyond these external negotiations, maternity leave is also an internal negotiation about how a woman is beginning to define her life as a working mother and how to integrate professional life and motherhood. These interpersonal and internal negotiations are complex and emotional and can derail women from advocating for what they need out of fear for how their family needs may affect their own and others' views of them as professionals. The best way to manage these potential insecurities is again to plan for and actively manage the negotiation of your maternity leave, to the extent that it is possible.

Before any specific, detailed conversation about leave occurs, you will want to begin by researching your organization's policies regarding maternity leave, return to work, flexible work arrangements, and childcare benefits. While it is important to know the formal organizational policies, it is equally important to research how other women have adjusted these formal policies. Questions to consider include: To what extent can sick days or vacation days be used to supplement a leave? If you are physically able to work until delivery, will this enable you to take more time off after the birth? Has anyone else in your organization been able to use their maternity leave to return to work gradually, such as two days a week? Exploring these questions with other working mothers will enable you to begin to understand how much latitude you may have in negotiating something other than the formal policy. If the organization has been supportive of diverse work models or if other women were able to use flexible arrangements to return to work, you will likely have an easier time customizing maternity leave to meet your own personal needs.

It is essential to research state and city parental leave policies, which may be in the process of legislative change. For example, on June 28, 2018, Massachusetts Governor Charlie Baker signed into law a paid family and medical leave program that will be funded by a state payroll tax but won't go into effect until the beginning of 2021. Several different stipulations for employers are associated with this program, so it is important to familiarize yourself with pending laws to understand what your firm must offer. It may also be useful to research industry standards to see if an organization's policies are up to par. The point of gathering this information is to be informed about, but not constrained by, the formal policies that exist as a woman begins negotiating her maternity leave.

During pregnancy, you may also want to talk to your partner about your needs as a couple before negotiating maternity leave. Your partner also needs to gather information about his or her organization's formal policies and informal practices regarding family leave. Partner benefits can greatly influence how you negotiate your leave. For example, Ginger's company allowed her to take up to ten weeks of paid maternity leave and her husband's company allowed the non-primary parent to take four weeks of paid leave for the birth or adoption of a child. Ginger and her husband negotiated with their organizations such that he used vacation days when their baby was born and then had his paternity leave start when she returned to work at ten weeks. Ginger was more comfortable as she returned to work because she knew her baby was still at home with her husband. Couples who think creatively about their collective leave policies can often negotiate a return to work that better supports the transition.

While we are on the topic, conversations with your partner should also focus on each other's expectations around work, family, and career. Some questions to consider are: How will household and childcare responsibilities be shared? How satisfactory are each person's current work, compensation, and benefits, and where does each see his or her career going in the coming years? When Antonia got pregnant, she and her husband both had high-powered careers in professional services that required long hours and travel. As she and her husband spoke about their careers, they realized that neither of them wanted to adjust their work schedules to accommodate their expanding family. Rather than fight about whose career should take priority, they decided they would simply need to hire additional childcare. They used a combination of a daycare center and a part-time nanny to cover their long workdays.

For some couples, it can be hard to clarify their desires around work and family separate from traditional, societal, and family norms that still expect women to shoulder the majority of childcare responsibilities despite significant demographic shifts. According to the Bureau of Labor Statistics, 28% of wives earned more than their husbands in 2014, which is up from 18% in 1987. During almost the same period (1989–2012), the number of stay-at-home dads doubled from 1 million to 2 million. Overall, fathers are participating more in childcare and household chores than they did in the 1960s and 1970s.[22] All of this is good news for women. Without a doubt, an engaged partner makes it easier for women to integrate work and family successfully, and the changing norms make men more open to being equal partners at home. We discuss this in more detail in Chapter 9.

Once you have a better understanding of your work context and your partner's desires regarding work and family, you will want to begin the process of negotiating your maternity leave and return to work. First and foremost, you may have more power in these negotiations than you realize. This power comes from your years of hard work and being well regarded by your peers and your manager.[23] Professional status, social capital, and the value that you bring to the organization can be an advantage in drafting a maternity leave and return-to-work plan that meets your needs. You should not be afraid to use any advantages you have to ask for something that deviates from the standard policy. While the focus should be on advocating for yourself, it is important to keep your manager's needs in mind. In planning for maternity leave, managers tend to be concerned with how the work will get done. You might consider how you can help your manager solve this problem. While this is not specifically your problem to solve, it shows commitment to the organization. Finally, it is important to remember that maternity leave negotiations, like all negotiations, require patience and creativity. It will likely take multiple conversations, multiple iterations, and multiple people to create a plan that works for you and the organization.

A final reminder as you are managing your feelings, your interactions with colleagues, and your body during these pivotal moments is the need for flexibility. Up until this moment, you may have carefully planned your life out. Planning is good, and it is an important part of the transition to working motherhood. However, pregnancy and motherhood introduce new challenges for which you may not be able to plan. Feelings about work and family will change, health and well-being issues may arise, and childcare plans will break down. There is no shortage of unexpected changes that will come your way after a baby is born. Having a plan makes these adjustments easier, but reframing adjustments as simply part of the plan might help you to become more flexible and less stressed when these unexpected situations arise. Becoming more flexible during pregnancy can certainly ease the transition to life as a working mother.

GARNERING ORGANIZATIONAL SUPPORT FOR PREGNANT EMPLOYEES

Fortunately, organizations have become more attentive to the challenges pregnant women face and the advancement of women into top leadership positions.[24] *Working Mothers Magazine* and recent books provide excellent guidance on work/family benefits programs that support pregnant women and their transitions to motherhood. Here, we provide a few creative ideas beyond the standard benefits programs that can further support working women during pregnancy and as they begin to think about this transition.

Work/Family Coaching

One way some organizations are supporting pregnant women during this period is by providing work/family coaching for expectant mothers, and even for expectant fathers. While some organizations are providing coaching for women as they return to work, we believe coaching can be helpful to women early in pregnancy. As we have laid out in this chapter, throughout pregnancy women are navigating their feelings and their interactions at work as they begin to form expectations about their lives as working mothers. Even in early pregnancy, a coach can help a woman explore how she wants to integrate motherhood and work, how to negotiate maternity leave, and how to manage interactions with coworkers. Pregnant women often feel more comfortable having these conversations with a coach, as compared to a boss or an internal mentor, because a coach has no personal agenda and is solely focused on the pregnant woman and helping her craft her work/life path.

If you work for an organization that has the resources, we strongly encourage you to take advantage of them, or, if you are willing to use your own personal resources, you can find a coach on your own. Companies such as Talking Talent are contracted by some firms to provide pregnant women with a series of coaching sessions that are focused on navigating both work and home as they begin to shape their lives as working mothers. These firms employ individuals who are professional life coaches and often parents themselves and thus know how to help pregnant women develop the skills and confidence to advocate for what they need. Professional coaching has a long-term impact on working mothers' professional development, as it helps them work through internal and external barriers and develop realistic visions for integrating work and motherhood.[25]

If your organization does not have the resources to provide external coaching, you could suggest to senior leaders or human resources that the firm develop an internal coaching program. A team of senior managers can be trained in coaching skills geared toward pregnant women. Ideally, these individuals would be working parents, so they can share and draw upon their own experiences. Pregnant women can then be paired with a senior manager who is not directly connected to their work. In their capacity as a coach, the senior manager needs to be careful to provide unbiased, confidential support to the pregnant woman. Terry explained how her internal coach empowered her to advocate for herself as she went to negotiate maternity leave:

> We have talked very candidly about what my approach is going to be with the director when I go and ask for maternity leave. What I planned to do was ask for one day working at home when I come back. However, she encouraged me to ask for a longer leave and even more flexibility. She helped me realize that if I ask for more, we might settle somewhere in the middle, but I could get even more. She has been very empowering.

For an internal coaching program to work, a pregnant woman needs to feel comfortable sharing concerns, uncertainties, and questions she may be having in a judgment-free environment.

Modeling Behavior by Senior Leaders

As we discussed previously, when pregnant women begin to think about integrating work and motherhood, they look to others in their organization to understand how to integrate work and family effectively. What senior leaders do as they integrate work and family strongly influences how pregnant women begin to envision their lives as working mothers. Extended maternity or paternity leave policies and support for pregnant women have little value if senior leaders do not use these benefits. Senior leaders need to demonstrate that it is safe to use these benefits and show that they work. If you notice that senior leaders in your organization don't use these benefits, you may want to find out why that is the case. If cultural norms prevent women (and men) from taking advantage of work/family benefits or cause them to feel uncomfortable discussing their family situations with others, then that may be a signal of what to expect after the baby arrives and you return to work. If these are things that are important to you, it may be time to start exploring different career opportunities.

While organizations often are focused on women using maternity leave and alternative work arrangements to the fullest, we believe it is equally important for male managers to make use of paternity leave policies and alternative work arrangements, particularly men at the upper echelons of the organization. In so doing, men are helping to break the norms of the ideal worker and any stigma associated with taking parental leave, an issue we discuss in Chapter 9. One woman we spoke to expressed her confidence about going on maternity leave and transitioning to motherhood because she saw men and women on the senior leadership team manage this transition:

> There are ten to twelve people on the senior leadership team. One is seven months pregnant, and one just came back from a six-week paternity leave. He now works from home two days a week.

Customizable Policies

Does your organization provide women and managers the space to adjust work/family benefits to fit the varied needs of pregnant women and working mothers? This is an important question to consider as you begin thinking about your own unique needs and how to feel empowered to write your own work/life path. Managers need some flexibility in determining how to best support a pregnant woman and a working mother more broadly. For example, if an organization provides twelve weeks of paid maternity leave, a woman may want to return to work after eight weeks and use the remaining four weeks (twenty days) to return to work on a flexible arrangement of three days a week for ten weeks. If this arrangement works for the manager, he or she should have the flexibility to support this use of the maternity leave. At the same time, if managers have this level of individual discretion, they need to be encouraged to be open to diverse maternity leave options and to recognize that supporting women's individual needs with pregnancy and maternity leave can help women more confidently manage their transition to motherhood and the return to work. Monica explained how her company's customized policy helped her:

> You can split up your maternity leave; you can have a flexible return. It is not rigid. They try to work with us to determine what we need. You can even change your plans in the middle of your leave.

If we are to support the premise that there is no single work/life path, organizations need to find ways to empower managers and organizational members to adjust policies so they meet the needs of both working mothers and the organization.

CHAPTER TAKEAWAYS

1. Pregnancy involves physical, psychological, and interpersonal changes that can challenge positive feelings toward motherhood and the ability to balance work and future family demands.
2. Pregnancy is a time of transition. Managing your own expectations and those of others is an important way to navigate this period, particularly as you manage the disclosure process and negotiate your maternity leave.
3. Explore and advocate for creative ways that your organization can move beyond the laws that protect the rights of pregnant workers, such as customizing leave and return-to-work practices and developing coaching programs that help women begin to feel confident in their emerging roles as working mothers.

REFERENCES

1. Van Gennep, A. (2011). *The rites of passage*. Chicago, IL: University of Chicago Press.
2. Ladge, J., Clair, J., & Greenberg, D. (2012). Cross-domain identity transition during liminal periods: Constructing multiple selves as professional and mother during pregnancy. *Academy of Management Journal, 55*(6), 1449.

3. Hays, S. (1996). *The cultural contradictions of motherhood.* New Haven, CT: Yale University Press.

4. U.S. Department of Labor. (2016). *Employment characteristics of families: Summary.* Washington, DC: Bureau of Labor Statistics.

5. Williams, J. (2000). *Why work and family conflict and what to do about it.* New York, NY : Oxford University Press.

6. Haynes, K. (2008). Transforming identities: Accounting professionals and the transition to motherhood. *Critical Perspectives on Accounting, 19*(5), 620–642.

7. Haynes, K. (2012). Body beautiful? Gender, identity and the body in professional services firms. *Gender, Work & Organization, 19*(5), 489–507.

8. Gatrell, C. J. (2013). Maternal body work: How women managers and professionals negotiate pregnancy and new motherhood at work. *Human Relations, 66*(5), 621–644.

9. Sturm, S. (2001). Second-generation employment discrimination: A structural approach. *Columbia Law Review, 101*, 458.

10. Williams, J. C., & Cuddy, A. (2012). Will working mothers take your company to court? *Harvard Business Review, 90*(9), 94–100.

11. Halpert, J. A., & Burg, J. H. (1997). Mixed messages: Coworker responses to the pregnant employee. *Journal of Business and Psychology, 12*(2), 241–253.

12. Ladge, J. J., & Greenberg, D. N. (2015). Becoming a working mother: Managing identity and efficacy uncertainties during resocialization. *Human Resource Management, 54*(6), 977–998.

13. Hebl, M. R., King, E. B., Glick, P. Singletary, S. L., & Kazama, S. (2007). Hostile and benevolent reactions toward pregnant women: Complementary interpersonal punishments and rewards that maintain traditional roles. *Journal of Applied Psychology, 92*(6), 1499–1511.

14. Glick, P., & Fiske, S. T. (2001). An ambivalent alliance: Hostile and benevolent sexism as complementary justifications for gender inequality. *American Psychologist, 56*(2), 109–118.

15. Murphy, W., & Kram, K. (2014). *Strategic relationships at work: Creating your circle of mentors, sponsors, and peers for success in business and life.* New York, NY: McGraw Hill Professional.

16. King, E. B., & Botsford, W. E. (2009). Managing pregnancy disclosures: Understanding and overcoming the challenges of expectant motherhood at work. *Human Resource Management Review, 19*(4), 314–323.

17. Chaudoir, S. R., & Fisher, J. D. (2010). The disclosure processes model: Understanding disclosure decision making and postdisclosure outcomes among people living with a concealable stigmatized identity. *Psychological Bulletin, 136*(2), 236–256.

18. King, E. B. (2008). The effect of bias on the advancement of working mothers: Disentangling legitimate concerns from inaccurate stereotypes as predictors of advancement in academe. *Human Relations, 61*(12), 1677–1711.

19. Clair, J. A., Beatty, J. E., & MacLean, T. L. (2005). Out of sight but not out of mind: Managing invisible social identities in the workplace. *Academy of Management Review, 30*(1), 78–95.

20. Stone, D., Heen, S., & Patton, B. (2010). *Difficult conversations: How to discuss what matters most*. New York, NY: Penguin.

21. Gault, B., et al. (2014, January 23). *Paid parental leave in the United States: What the data tell us about access, usage, and economic and health benefits. Institute for Women's Policy Research Report*. Retrieved from https://iwpr.org/publications/paid-parental-leave-in-the-united-states-what-the-data-tell-us-about-access-usage-and-economic-and-health-benefits/.

22. Parker, K., & Livingston, G. (2016). *6 facts about American fathers*. Retrieved from https://fathermatters.org/6-facts-about-american-fathers/.

23. SHRM. (2014). *SHRM research spotlight: Strategic use of flexible work arrangements*. Retrieved from https://www.shrm.org/about-shrm/press-room/press-releases/Documents/14-WorkplaceFlexibility-StrategicUseofFWAs.pdf.

24. Hoobler, J. M., Lemmon, G., & Wayne, S. J. (2011). Women's underrepresentation in upper management: New insights on a persistent problem. *Organizational Dynamics, 40*(3), 151–156.

25. Edelman, J. (2015, February 18). Maternity coaching aims to support pregnant women in the workforce. *Huffington Post*. Retrieved from https://www.huffpost.com/entry/maternity-coaching-aims-t_b_6321070.

3

Becoming a Working Mother

Maternity Leave and Returning to Work

At work, I had been the star player. But after my daughter was born, I was thrown into the great equalizer of first-time motherhood and I felt like a failure. You are sleep deprived and everything is new and you are unsure of your instincts. It is very stressful. So when I returned to work after my maternity leave, I think I was surprised by how much I was able to fit right back into the groove of things. There was no moaning about being away from my daughter. I was still breastfeeding and I was pumping at work. I love my daughter, and I was thrilled to see her when I came home from work, but I was also happy to be at work. Society makes you think that you should always be crying, and I just wasn't. But that then made me feel guilty. What was wrong with me that I wasn't feeling that I want to stay home with the baby all the time and be a stay-at-home mom and dedicate my whole being to raising this tiny human the best way possible?

What also surprised me was how many times everybody assumed that it was an incredibly difficult transition to leave the baby. Instead of telling people this is so much easier than I expected, I would just lie a lot, so my challenge came when I interacted with everyone else. I believe I am a really good mother, and I love my daughter to pieces, and just because I choose to work doesn't mean I shouldn't have children. I also know I am really good at my job even if I leave at 5 to get my daughter. I have to say all this because I constantly feel defensive about feeling good.

—LAURIE, *marketing associate*

Up until the baby arrives (or babies, in the case of twins or more), women have mostly been thinking about, envisioning, and planning for life as a working mother. Among the more significant challenges at this point in time is navigating the onslaught of opinions from friends, family, and coworkers about how to parent and how to combine work and motherhood. Sometimes this advice can be empowering and help a new mother feel confident about integrating work and motherhood. Alternatively, it can have an adverse effect, especially if it deviates from your own feelings, thoughts, or decisions. Laurie's story at the start of this chapter illustrates how fearful women are when they are making choices or having feelings that contradict others' assumptions. These pressures can prevent women from feeling confident in their choices as they work to establish their own identities as working mothers.

In this chapter, we transition to the postnatal period. We focus first on the experience of maternity leave and some of the factors that help and hinder new mothers from becoming confident about being good mothers. We then turn our attention to the initial return to work and explore how women begin to integrate motherhood and work as they launch their lives as working mothers.

TWELVE MONTHS AND COUNTING: MATERNITY LEAVE

After the birth of your first child, you may be faced with the emotional and overwhelming question of "now what?" The first few weeks are intense, complicated, and exhausting for most new parents—even when the baby and mother are completely healthy. The emotional, physical, and life changes new mothers experience as they begin caring for their infant often leave them wondering "Am I doing this right?" and "How can I be a good mother?" From our research, we find there are three central issues that working mothers are encountering as they begin to establish their lives during their maternity leave: (1) finding your way as a new mother, (2) managing workplace separation, and (3) establishing a co-parenting strategy with your partner.

Finding Your Way as a New Mother

An immediate concern for all new mothers is feeling capable and confident. The pervasive myth in North America—and perhaps the world at large—is that women, simply because of their biological sex, are natural mothers and are born knowing how to take care of children.[1] Mothers are burdened further by the societal assumptions that women are responsible for childbearing and childrearing, and that a woman's identity is defined primarily by her maternal role.[1] The popular press feeds into this myth by drawing inaccurate conclusions from biological and neuroscientific research, such as "the blueprint for mothering behavior exists in the brain even before a woman has children."[2] Because of this rhetoric, new mothers are often shocked by how challenging it is to care for a newborn and how difficult it is to feel good about themselves as mothers. Several new mothers have told us that they find motherhood infinitely more challenging than work. The rhythms and rewards of work are straightforward. Bosses and colleagues provide frequent feedback, which a woman reacts to as she becomes more confident in herself as a professional. Caring for a child, particularly a newborn, does not come with such direct feedback, so assessing how well you're doing as a mother is not easy. As Brianna explained,

> I think I doubted myself a lot just in terms of caring for her. I was constantly wondering, "Am I doing things the right way?" Because I was doubting myself, I was afraid to show people what I didn't know. I didn't always want to pick up the phone and call someone; I thought my questions would probably sound stupid to someone

else. When I think back on those first few weeks, I can't think of
any aspect of caretaking that wasn't difficult for me. There were days
when there was more crying than others, but all days involved tears.

Brianna's story illustrates how difficult it can be to care for a new baby.
Brianna also explains the need that she, and many women, have to be seen
by others as someone who has figured out the mothering role. Her desire
to protect how others see her prevented her from asking for the help that
could have eased her transition.

Some women avoid asking for help because mothering advice is often
laden with societal lore regarding the virtues of intensive mothering. Take,
for example, one of the most controversial issues: breastfeeding. Intensive
mothering rhetoric suggests that breastfeeding is almost a requirement
for good mothering.[3] But many women are unable to breastfeed for an
entire year as is recommended by the American Pediatric Association.
Breastfeeding can be difficult and fraught with physical struggles for
both the child and the mother. Even if a workplace provides structural
and cultural support for lactation, individual job characteristics may
make it difficult for a new mother to combine breastfeeding and work.[4]
For women who travel frequently, share an office, or have limited time
for breaks, breastfeeding can pose a challenge. Janelle, an IT consultant,
brought her breast pump with her on a business trip to South America.
Forgetting about the voltage issue, she plugged her breast pump in only
to find that it shorted out and was unusable. Even pediatricians who advocate for breastfeeding recognize these challenges. After trying to follow
her own advice to breastfeed her child for one year, Perri Klass, a pediatrician, wrote, "The experience made me deeply aware of how much this advice [breastfeeding for a year] is asking of women and how hard it would
have been to do if my life were less privileged and well supported."[5] Not
breastfeeding, or not breastfeeding for a full year, becomes one more way
a working mother may feel like she is failing.

Unfortunately, this list of "shoulds" for mothers extends far beyond
breastfeeding. At every turn, a new mother may find herself confronting
judgment that diminishes her self-confidence. Often such "constructive"

advice starts at home with a woman's mother, grandmother, mother-in-law, sister, or close friend. While some advice can be quite useful, other advice can hamper a woman's confidence in herself as a mother, particularly when it centers on combining work and motherhood. Undermining comments can often be quite subtle and may unintentionally affirm stereotypes and demean a new working mother's self-esteem.[6,7] New mothers often hear comments that sound something like, "I am so impressed by how you are going to do it all! Taking care of a child was enough of a full-time job for me (or for my partner)" or "I don't know how you do it." These comments may not be so easy to brush off. If they recur, a new mother needs to let the person know how it is affecting her and how these comments only perpetuate gendered norms.

Connecting with supportive individuals can help to lessen the effects of negative stereotypes. A supportive network is critical to helping women begin to establish a unique identity as a working mother.[4] Rhea explained,

> It's like you are all alone, and then all of a sudden the world is so much bigger because you realize that all these other women have gone through the struggle. It's wonderful.

Hearing about other women's successes and struggles helps a new mother understand and accept the chaos and realities of motherhood. Some women find it particularly helpful to connect with other working mothers whose babies are a year or two older than their own. These women have recent experiences to draw upon that can be particularly helpful. In general, building relationships that are trusting and affirming of combining work and motherhood will help develop a woman's confidence in herself as a working mother.

For many women, new mothers' groups provide an easy way to start building these supportive relationships. These groups can be found through different community or professional networks and focus on everything from book discussions to parenting workshops to exercising with babies. Beyond simply providing you with supportive relationships, these groups can also help you recognize you are not alone in your parenting struggles. Additionally, new mothers can be a valuable source of feedback for helping you manage your unique circumstances. For example, Toni talked about how important her new mothers' group was to her confidence. Toni's baby appeared to have an extreme case of colic, and conflicting comments from her family were causing her to feel depressed and overwhelmed. She talked to her new mothers' group and got advice for how to respond to her mother-in-law's discouraging comments. Group members also prompted her to go back to her pediatrician to see if an underlying medical condition was causing her baby's distress. She took this advice and learned that her son had gastroesophageal reflux. With changes to her diet and some medicine, his crying was greatly reduced. By sharing her concerns with other new mothers, Toni took control of her situation and began to feel more confident and happier as a new mom.

When looking to join a new mothers' group, we encourage you to take your time to find a group that is right for you. Researching and even "trying out" different groups before committing to one is a good approach, as they are not all the same. Depending on the combination of women, how the group is organized, and the group's focus, the group may or may not be supportive in the way that you need. Describing the first new mother's group she joined, Kate said,

> I was intimidated by the other women in the group because most of them had no plans to go to work. It was not a group that resonated with me.

For Kate, a group of mostly stay-at-home new mothers did not provide the social support she needed and only fueled her anxiety as she thought about her return to work.

Managing the Workplace During Maternity Leave

The myth of maternity leave is that women will completely disengage from work with little to no contact and will return from maternity leave to jump back into their roles with ease and efficiency. This is far from reality: how a woman engages with work during her leave depends on her unique circumstances. One woman we interviewed told us that four hours after she gave birth she got on a conference call. Her work was so deeply embedded in her identity that she did not know how to let it go, even immediately after giving birth. Having a baby can be life-changing, but it does not mean that all individuals will experience that change right away. It takes time for some to ease out of their professional roles, particularly when those roles have been an integral part of their lives. Indeed, for many women, stepping into maternity leave can be difficult because of their emotional connections to their work.

Individuals differ in the extent to which they see work as a job, a career, or a calling.[8] Women who see work as a calling describe work as an integral part of their life, their identity, and their personal fulfillment. For these women, stepping away from work can be difficult irrespective of how excited they are about motherhood. For other women, particularly women who are older first-time mothers, work is such an important component of their identity they find it difficult to separate from their professional life—even for a short time.

Some new mothers have trouble disengaging from work because of explicit and implicit organizational pressures. As was discussed in Chapter 2, during pregnancy women begin to learn how supportive an organization is as they disclose their pregnancy, negotiate maternity leave, and simply watch and engage with colleagues, organizational leaders, and other working mothers. By the time you go on maternity leave, you will likely have a clearer understanding of the organizational norms regarding working mothers. If you are concerned about biases against working mothers in your organization, you may try to protect your role and professional identity while on leave and subsequently may have trouble disengaging from work during maternity leave for fear of negative repercussions. Unfortunately, these fears are often substantiated. Too many women have shared stories with us over the years of being passed over for promotions, having their work given to a less-qualified candidate, or simply being "benched" during or after maternity leave.

When considering whether and how much to disengage from work during maternity leave, it is important to remember that maternity leave is first and foremost about managing your health and that of your child. While some women and their newborns may be physically and emotionally stable enough to balance returning to work within days of giving birth, this does not represent the majority of women's experiences. Given that close to 40% of women in the United States give birth by cesarean section, many women must contend with the physical recovery from childbirth and from major surgery. Also, the Centers for Disease Control and Prevention reports that 11% to 20% of women will experience some symptoms of postpartum depression.[9] These women need space from work to focus on their own and their child's health and well-being. Most mothers also just need time to settle into their new role. Research shows it takes approximately four months for first-time mothers to embrace motherhood as part of how they see themselves and to become confident in their abilities as a mother.[10-12]

Still, we are not advocating that all new mothers need to disengage completely from work during maternity leave. While some women need, or simply want, a separation to adjust to their lives as mothers, others may choose to stay connected with work to ease the transition back to work later. Staying connected with work can help some new mothers stay grounded when so much of life is changing. For new mothers who have higher work-role involvement, a longer, disconnected maternity leave can decrease emotional well-being.[13,14] However, if your desire to stay connected is driven by negative emotions such as fear of retaliation or unrealistic work expectations, you should be cautious about succumbing to these concerns. A new mother who is driven to stay engaged at work needs to determine the best approach to do so without introducing additional demands into her life. Checking in regularly with a boss or coworker to stay informed on what is happening at work is reasonable. The ability to check in with a conference call or to stop by the office may be beneficial for a new mother, as it may ease her anxiety about what is transpiring at work. Also, regular calls can remind your manager that he or she needs to prepare for your return to work, which can help avoid career penalties from maternity leave. These conversations can also reinforce to the manager your continued commitment to—and engagement with—work. However, there is a difference between occasional calls and actually doing substantive work, and this distinction needs to be carefully managed.

Women who work during maternity leave may want to explore renegotiating the terms of their leave. For example, one of the authors returned to work after three weeks of maternity leave because the professor who took over her class could not complete the term. She worked part-time for the final weeks of the semester, meeting with students, evaluating final presentations, and grading exams. Before she did this, she negotiated her leave so that it would extend into the second semester, and she did this knowing she had much support at home. We suggest that if staying connected involves engaging in significant work during maternity leave, negotiating a different model of maternity leave guards against setting unrealistic expectations.

Launching a Co-Parenting Model

During maternity leave, new mothers may be so preoccupied with the work of caring for their newborn and developing their confidence as a mother that they forget to also focus on their partner and his or her development as a parent and/or as a working parent. The term *shared parenting*, or *co-parenting*, refers to how two parents decide to share caregiving responsibilities, which include organizing and being responsible for activities such as shopping, cooking, bathing/hygiene, laundry, cleaning, and housework, as well as the social-emotional work of raising a child. Most of the caregiving responsibilities continue to fall on women, even if they work outside of the home, and can create unending demands that make it more difficult for women to integrate work and motherhood.[15,16] As Sheryl Sandberg has rightly stated, making a partner a "real partner" is critical to a working mother's ability to thrive.[17]

During maternity leave, a new mother needs to start to empower her partner to be a "real partner." Establishing this model is not easy.

Traditional gender norms may influence how a couple thinks about work and parenting. Discussions of shared caregiving are laden with gender stereotypes such as: "The woman starts from her 'natural' position as a caregiver and the man from his 'natural' position as breadwinner."[18] New mothers may respond by trying to protect their role as caregiver. The term *maternal gatekeeping* describes new mothers' reluctance to relinquish parenting responsibilities to their partner. New mothers who are uncertain about their competence as mothers may begin to engage in this behavior to further validate their maternal identities.[19] A woman who takes on too many caregiving responsibilities during maternity leave may unintentionally sabotage herself. When women act as gatekeepers, they perform an average of five additional hours of house or childrearing work each week and divide labor around the home and children with their partner less equitably.[20] This inequitable distribution of caregiving can make it more difficult down the road for a woman to manage work and motherhood.

Men, like women, need the chance to interact with a child to establish their identity and confidence as a parent. When men have an opportunity to be active caregivers, they develop a "parental caregiving neural network," and, like women, they become more attuned to their infant's state, more emotionally connected to their infant's care, and more confident as a parent.[21] Studies show little difference in the nurturing behavior of mothers and fathers who are the primary caregivers.[22] Moreover, in co-parenting families, children's preferences often shift back and forth between parents, depending on who has taken care of them more recently.[23] Thus, when parents share infant care, it debunks myths about gender differences in caregiving. Co-parenting also benefits children's social, emotional, and cognitive development,[24] and couples who share in caregiving tend to stay married and have more sex.[25] Finally, when working dads are involved fathers, it increases their job satisfaction, which in turn further benefits the women with whom they are partnered.[26] We discuss the topic of fathers in greater depth in Chapter 9.

New mothers may need to work at sharing caregiving responsibilities and encouraging their partners to be co-parents. As this occurs, a mother needs to give her partner room to develop his or her parenting identity.

Kate, a data analyst on the West Coast, left for work very early to be ready when the financial markets on the East Coast opened. Initially, she thought about having extra childcare to cover these early mornings. However, she encouraged her wife, who could go to work later, to be responsible for morning drop-off, and Kate would do daily pickup. When Kate returned to work after her maternity leave, she struggled with leaving before her baby was awake, but she loved picking up her child and overseeing dinner and bath routines. She also talked about the ease with which she began her work day, not having to worry about getting her daughter to daycare and knowing that her wife was getting to connect with their child in her own way. By relinquishing control and empowering her partner, Kate began to build a co-parenting model that supported her identity as a working mother.

A final but important reminder: co-parenting is not about a 50/50 division of responsibility. Focusing on trying to make everything equal will likely make both partners miserable. Caregiving responsibilities ebb and flow. Sometimes clearly delineated responsibilities, such as those that Kate and her partner created, work for a couple. For other couples, work schedules may be less structured, so home schedules may need to be more fluid. Partners may find it useful to "meet" monthly or even weekly to manage a more flexible model of co-parenting. Sometimes, because of career demands or parenting desires, one parent will take on more responsibility at one stage of childrearing. In all families, co-parenting will need to evolve as family and work demands shift. By starting a model of co-parenting during maternity leave, a working mother will be better able to adjust to these shifts and to continue to manage work and motherhood effectively.

A co-parenting model works well for divorced and unmarried couples, but single mothers are left to their own devices as they parent on their own. There are pros and cons to going it alone. One on the hand, single mothers have the added pressure of not having another set of hands to help with caregiving (unless they have round-the-clock childcare). More careful planning is needed for single mothers, even for something as simple as running to the grocery store. On the other hand, developing a sense of confidence as a parent may come faster for a single mother, since she has to handle all aspects of childcare as compared to couples who may develop a childcare dependency on one another. For example, when Susan returned to work, she was well aware of the protocol at the daycare center, which had fairly strict guidelines on drop-off time and location, nap times, and food to pack. When a last-minute trip for work came up, her husband stepped in to do the drop-off and pickup. He did not know about any of the procedures for drop-off, including where in the building to drop off his son and which snacks were allowed. These kinds of scenarios can put undue stress on both parents. Single mothers do not experience these kinds of co-parenting strains. Decisions may also be made faster because there isn't another parent to run things by. This doesn't necessarily make things easier, just more efficient. Regardless of these differences, there is a growing population of women aged 35 and older who are having babies outside of marriage.[27] Like all working mothers, single mothers need to advocate for what they need from their family, friends, and workplace. Because of the differences between single and couple parenting, many people are unaware of the additional needs of a single mother. A single mother may need additional support and become comfortable asking for that help, particularly on the home front.

We now move into a discussion on the experience of transitioning back to work after maternity leave.

TRANSITIONING BACK TO WORK WITH EASE . . . OR AT LEAST WITH LESS ANGST

Like most aspects of life, and particularly anything related to children, maternity leave ends as soon as it begins. Before you know it, you will be back at work and managing the daily responsibilities of your job and motherhood. The good news is that you will not be alone, as nearly two-thirds of new mothers return to the labor force within a year of having a child,[28] so you will likely have other women around you who have been through or are going through the same transition. In returning to work, you will need to work through the logistical and emotional issues of integrating childcare schedules with demanding and sometimes unpredictable work schedules. In this section of the chapter, we first discuss the initial experience of reentry, including strategies for easing back in, integrating work and maternal identities, breastfeeding challenges, and establishing a childcare routine.

Initial Experiences in Reentry

What does it feel like to go back to work? Not as bad as you might think. Margie explained her feelings:

> I thought I would come back and have forgotten everything, but I was surprised by quickly I acclimated. It was as if I had never left. It's not like I didn't miss my daughter; I did. But I also enjoyed having adult conversations and using my brain again.

The popular press has taken great interest in highlighting the guilt and emotional anguish some women experience when returning to work.[29] Particularly for women who take short maternity leaves due to financial or work pressures, the process of returning to work and leaving an infant in someone else's care can be heartbreaking. However, not all new mothers singularly experience anguish when they return to work. Many new mothers experience more mixed emotions—difficulty leaving their child but excitement returning to a satisfying job. Some new mothers are simply looking forward to their return to work, even though they may be afraid to admit it. In talking about her return to work, Joan shared,

> This is awkward to say because I feel like there are so many societal ears listening if I were to answer this question truthfully. So let me preface this by saying I am not a horrible person. I am a good mother. I love my child to pieces, and she is everything to me. But if I didn't work, I would die. I love what I do, and I feel really great

about being back at work. I rarely admit what I admitted to you. I'd like my voice to be heard because I know there are more working mothers out there like me.

By overemphasizing the guilt women feel, we overlook the fact that women, like men, often have an internal drive to work and value the intellectual challenge of work. The social interaction and positive feedback at work can also build up self-esteem in a way that can't typically be experienced in the early stage of mothering.

You may find it helpful to remember that being happy at work does not mean being unhappy as a mother. Being excited about social interaction, handling intellectual challenges, feeling pride in earning a paycheck to support the family, and being a role model for your children are all positive emotions working mothers feel. As Joan shared, women can simultaneously love their job and love being a mother. For most working mothers, a love for work and a love for your family is not an either/or proposition. However, not all women love their jobs or their colleagues, so these experiences are likely to differ depending on their level of job satisfaction and commitment. Loving your job is also a function of workplace culture. If the culture at work is one in which gender equality is recognized and rewarded, new mothers may have an easier transition back to work. However, if gender inequities are prevalent or male dominance is overt, then this will create issues for new mothers as they return to work.

For example, some women may go so far as to hide pumping at work. We have heard stories of women pumping in their car, not only because they did not have the accommodations in their workplace but also because they wanted to keep their private lives separate and not be subjected to the comments of immature colleagues. In the novel *Opening Belle*, written by Maureen Sherry and loosely based on her own experiences as a former managing director at Bear Stearns, Sherry described the "walk of shame" when she would need to get up from her desk with her breast pump to go to the lactation room to expel milk. On her way there, she would often hear mooing noises coming from her male peers. These "frat-boy" behaviors may be a thing of the past in most organizations, but sadly they do still exist in some workplaces. Many women are fighting back and challenging these behaviors and others that stigmatize new mothers by becoming powerful advocates in their organizations and industries, and even considering legal action when necessary.[30,31]

As you transition back to work, you may want to consider different ways in which to ease back in and adjust to the management of work and child. For example, several new mothers have said that it is better to come back to work in the middle of the week rather than at the start of the week, allowing for a shorter first workweek. Other women may work half-days for a few weeks, or schedule compressed workweeks. Some women will put their children in daycare or have a nanny start working a few days or even weeks before they return to work. This way they can get comfortable with their childcare arrangement before adding in the return-to-work adjustment. Tye shared with us that before returning to work, she dropped her daughter at daycare, took the train in to her office, used the time to shop and connect with friends, and then took the train home at the time she would need to pick up her daughter at daycare. This trial run helped alleviate her concerns about managing her schedule.

There is not a shortage of reentry strategies. It's important to find the strategy that works best for you based on your needs as a mother, your financial situation, and your organization. Whatever choices you make, reentry will be easier when you carefully manage this process.

Intersecting Work and Mothering Identities

In returning to work, one of the biggest challenges for new mothers is determining how to best integrate work and motherhood into their overall self-concept. It can be useful to think about how important each identity is to your overall self-concept, as this can guide difficult decisions about how to manage your time and energy. Women whose professional identity is more central than maternal identity may choose to continue to pursue a highly demanding work role as they look for more childcare or have their partner engage in more caregiving. Other women see their maternal identity as more salient to their self-concept than their professional identity. These women may choose to hold off pursuing more demanding work roles or may even scale back at work to accommodate their caregiving demands in the short term. Jasmine worked in a highly demanding job, and while she continued to work full time, she was very conscious of how her professional goals had shifted—at least in the short term:

> I am not putting pressure on myself right now to become a VP. I really want to have time to be with my kids while they are little. When my kids are in school full time and older, then I will go back full force at work and pursue that leadership role.

Jasmine's example show how the salience of one identity over another can change as life and work shift.

A third approach a new mother may take is to place equal emphasis on both roles. In so doing, she may need to dial back her expectations of herself at work and at home. Katie explained,

> I am passionate about my job and about my baby, but I am coming to this realization that I can't be superwoman anymore. Maybe I used to be able to do it all and make it seamless and perfect, but now I can't. It's been a good lesson for me.

Actively thinking about the priority she places on work and motherhood and letting go of unattainable expectations of herself helped Kate more easily transition back to work.

As we think about the relationship between work and motherhood, we want to emphasize that being a good professional should not stand in opposition to being a good mother. This oppositional, or conflictual, perspective is based on the premise that a working mother has a fixed amount of resources and you must choose between work and motherhood as you determine how to divide your time and energy. This conflictual positioning of work and motherhood frequently leaves new mothers feeling they are either bad professionals or bad or reluctant mothers.[32]

To move past these feelings, we encourage you to look at the relationship between work and family from a different vantage point—that of enrichment. Feeling good about work and yourself as a professional can enhance your confidence and effectiveness as a mother. The same is true for the impact of motherhood on your professional life. The energy, engagement, and positive emotion that you experience in one role can spill over and lead to greater positivity in another role.[33]

Being connected to multiple roles, such as mother and professional, also leads to an accumulation of skills, knowledge, and relationships that can increase your effectiveness as a manager and leader.[34] When Regina returned to work after her daughter was born, she had to leave the office each day at 5 to pick up her daughter. Before her daughter's birth, she had always closely managed her team and had unconsciously assumed that people who were in the office more were highly productive. After her daughter was born and her work schedule shifted, she became more open to diverse work arrangements, trusted the members of her team more, and micromanaged them less. All of this made her team more productive and her a better manager.

Establishing Supportive Childcare

While our focus on reentry has predominately been on a new mother's experiences at work, our last point focuses on managing home— specifically, managing childcare. Unless your partner has chosen to stay home full time or both of you can work flexible schedules, you may need to solicit childcare support. Whether it is through the help of an extended family member, a nanny or au pair, home-based or traditional daycare, or some combination of these options, choosing a childcare arrangement that works for you and your partner is critical to supporting a positive return to work. While there are several books and websites that provide extensive guidance on this topic (i.e., *Here's the Plan* by Allyson Downey), here we focus more broadly on how you can reframe how you think about childcare to help ease your reentry experience.

New mothers tend to make better choices around childcare if they frame it as an investment rather than a cost. We are not saying childcare is not costly. We know how much of a paycheck goes to childcare—we both have paid years of daycare, nanny care, and after-school costs, and for many people those costs can be a significant financial burden. However, thinking about childcare as an investment in a child's development, his or her emotional well-being, and your own career is one way to help positively reframe the experience. For example, childcare is about investing in your child, and the importance of high-quality childcare is well documented. From the time a child is born to the age of five, a child's brain is experiencing its most rapid period of development. High-quality childcare provides young children with the emotional support, cognitive stimulation, and independence that is critical to their early development.[35] Children who receive high-quality childcare show better outcomes regarding socioeconomic, mental, and social-emotional health all the way into adulthood.[36] Furthermore, a new mother who is confident about her childcare feels less guilty about leaving her child when she goes to work.

Framing childcare as an investment also leads new mothers to evaluate childcare options differently. When Trisha returned to work, she thought she had found the ideal childcare arrangement. The daycare center she chose was close to her office and much less expensive than the childcare options near her home. Soon after returning to work, however, she realized this might not have been the best choice. She found the drive with her infant daughter to and from work to be stressful. She also had trouble managing her work responsibilities while also being solely responsible for all childcare drop-offs and pickups. Trisha and her partner decided to spend a little more for a daycare center closer to home so that her husband could share childcare responsibilities and she could use her commute time for conference calls and quiet time.

Another way to reframe childcare relates to backup childcare. The term *backup childcare* invokes the idea that it will only be used on rare occasions, but any working parent can attest that this too is a myth. Whether it be a sick child, a sick nanny, daycare closings for weather, or last-minute demands at work, women frequently find themselves missing work as a result of childcare breakdowns. These breakdowns cause anxiety and stress. Cecilia explained,

> There was one instance when there was a snowstorm. I do not remember exactly what happened; it was supposed to be a very, very bad snowstorm, and my nanny couldn't come. I had a bunch of really important meetings, and since I live less than a mile from my job, I really have to go to work regardless of the weather. So I had to have the meetings from home, and I pretty much couldn't because I had the baby here and that was challenging, and of course I felt really guilty about it.

If childcare breakdowns occur frequently enough, they can lead a new mother to question whether she wants to try to continue to integrate work and motherhood.

Instead of thinking about backup childcare, you may want to think about developing childcare *bench strength*. This is a term we adapt from athletic teams, which are strengthened by having multiple high-quality players who can substitute in during a game. Organizations also use this term to talk about the quality and number of employees who can easily step into a leadership role if it becomes vacant. Similarly, working families need childcare bench strength, and they need to create it before they have to use it. Your childcare bench strength may involve having extended family members on call or knowing about backup childcare options available in your community or workplace. Childcare bench strength may include other parents you may know or meet through work or daycare. Elise coordinated with a colleague so that they each always had an extra car seat and could easily help each other with childcare pickups if one of them was running late. Bench strength can also come from friends or family who are home full time. One working mother shared with us how she had a close friend who had chosen to stay at home after having children. This friend was available for backup childcare, and the working mother would reciprocate by providing care for her friend's children on the weekends.

Establishing bench strength before or early on when returning to work helps a new mother more successfully manage those moments when work and motherhood collide.

Seeking Support from Your Organization During Maternity Leave and Return to Work

When looking at how to provide support to working mothers, managers and human resources professionals frequently focus their attention on improving policies related to maternity leave, childcare support, and flexible work arrangements. Policies such as providing tax breaks for childcare and offering flexible work arrangements are instrumental in helping to ease reentry, which in turn supports the retention of new mothers.[28] While policies may signal to the wider organization expectations around integrating work and family, which can help build a more family-supportive culture, human resources professionals also need to consider how best to empower individual managers who are the gatekeepers of these policies. Indeed, many new mothers have shared frustrating stories with us about how their companies have extended maternity leave policies or flexible return-to-work options, but their managers—either through explicit statements or implicit behaviors—suggested that new mothers should not make use of those policies.

In many cases, managers may lack the training or knowledge as to how to support working mothers, which is where you can help—particularly if you are the first or one of only a few women who are planning a maternity leave and/or reentry. Managers may want to be more supportive of new mothers but are unsure of how to do so. With concerns about political correctness, gender bias, and sexual harassment, male managers in particular may avoid these conversations, yet they are so important to have so that you can feel confident and secure in your role and set expectations for both parties. If you have a manager that is reluctant to talk to you about these concerns, you may have to be the one to initiate the conversation.

This may not be a bad thing, as you can set the tone of the conversation and ask for whatever it is you may need based on what you may have learned from other women in your organization or your human resources department. If you work in a small organization, it may be necessary to find out what the industry standards are, as well as what other small businesses in your community offer in terms of support for maternity leave and reentry. Working together to come up with a solution that works for both parties will put each at ease and pave the way for more effective conversations in the future.

While it is not your job to educate managers about the needs of working mothers and fathers, you may suggest to your human resources department ways in which managers can provide support in meaningful ways. Doing so does not only help you and your fellow parents at your workplace; research provides ample evidence that increased managerial support for new mothers has a positive impact on the organization, as it leads to reduced absenteeism, fewer healthcare expenses, and reduced turnover.[37] Managers need to learn how to provide new mothers with the instrumental and emotional support they need to ease their return to work.[37,38] Instrumental support is about helping a new mother manage her workload when she returns to work. This may include checking in with women about their roles and responsibilities, their schedules, and/ or the extent to which they are being impacted by last-minute demands that cause friction at home. Managers may need to work with new working mothers to set limits, restructure work assignments, or intervene with a team. Managers also need to learn how to provide emotional support to new mothers during maternity leave through phone calls, visits, or gifts that are focused on acknowledging and supporting a new mother (obviously, there is a boundary to be managed here— baby books may be a perfect gift, while a breast pump may not). Once a new mother returns to work, a manager can provide emotional support through regularly scheduled check-in meetings, informal conversations about work and home, and connecting a new mother with resources or support within the organization. New mothers also mention they find the transition back to work easier when they have a manager who is modeling successful work/life integration. Regardless of whether one has children, having a manager who talks about his or her life outside of work, makes time for that life, and sees the benefits of having a personal life models for new mothers that their value at work is not diminished by their new role as a mother.

Lastly, it is also important to make sure that your manager (and coworkers) are honoring your negotiated maternity leave and your return-to-work plan. New mothers see a maternity leave not just as a formal contract but also as a psychological contract that demonstrates the organization's support for them as a new mother. Maternity leave and return-to-work plans are the basis for helping new mothers feel more confident and at ease when managing these transitions. When organizations or managers break these contracts by eliminating flexible work arrangements, gradual reentry, or lactation support, it can have a negative impact on a working mother's intention to remain in the workforce.[39]

CHAPTER TAKEAWAYS

1. Don't try to fit a mold based on outdated expectations. Your experiences and feelings during maternity leave and return to work may differ from what others have experienced. What may be exciting to you may be anguish for others, and vice versa.

2. Establish a collective support structure—including childcare arrangements, a predetermined co-parenting strategy, and initial schedule flexibility, if possible—to ease the emotional and logistical constraints of integrating work and family.

3. Seek support from your organization to facilitate your successful return to work by asking for modifications and adjustments as appropriate and letting managers and human resources know how best to provide emotional and logistical assistance during your reentry into your work role.

REFERENCES

1. Woodward, K. (2003). Representations of motherhood. In S. Earle & G. Letherby (Eds.), *Gender, identity & reproduction: Social perspectives* (pp. 18–32). New York, NY: Springer.

2. Lafrance, A. (2015, January 8). What happens to a woman's brain when she becomes a mother. *The Atlantic*. Retrieved from https://www.theatlantic.com/health/archive/2015/01/what-happens-to-a-womans-brain-when-she-becomes-a-mother/384179/.

3. Turner, P. K., & Norwood, K. (2013). Unbounded motherhood: Embodying a good working mother identity. *Management Communication Quarterly, 27*(3), 396–424.

4. Guendelman, S., Kosa, J. L., Pearl, M., Graham, S., Goodman, J., & Kharrazi, M. (2009). Juggling work and breastfeeding: Effects of maternity leave and occupational characteristics. *Pediatrics, 123*(1), e38–e46.

5. Klass, P. (2017, June 12). Practicing what I preached about breast-feeding. *New York Times*. Retrieved from https://www.nytimes.com/2017/06/12/well/family/practicing-what-i-preached-about-breast-feeding.html.

6. Chae, J. (2015). "Am I a better mother than you?": Media and 21st-century motherhood in the context of the social comparison theory. *Communication Research, 42*(4), 503–525.

7. Sue, D. W. (2010). *Microaggressions in everyday life: Race, gender, and sexual orientation*. Hoboken, NJ: John Wiley & Sons.

8. Wrzesniewski, A., McCauley, C., Rozin, P., & Schwartz, B. (1997). Jobs, careers, and callings: People's relations to their work. *Journal of Research in Personality, 31*(1), 21–33.

9. Centers for Disease Control and Prevention. (2017). *Depression among women*. Retrieved from https://www.cdc.gov/reproductivehealth/depression/index.htm.

10. Mercer, R. T. (2004). Becoming a mother versus maternal role attainment. *Journal of Nursing Scholarship, 36*(3), 226–232.

11. Mercer, R. T. (1986). *First-time motherhood: Experiences from teens to forties*. New York, NY: Springer Publishing Company.

12. Mercer, R. T., Kay, M., & Tomlinson, P. S. (1986). Predictors of maternal role attainment at one year postbirth. *Western Journal of Nursing Research, 8*(1), 9–32.

13. Hyde, J. S., Klein, M. H., Essex, M. J., & Clark, R. (1995). Maternity leave and women's mental health. *Psychology of Women Quarterly, 19*(2), 257–285.

14. Wiese, B. S., & Ritter, J. O. (2012). Timing matters: Length of leave and working mothers' daily reentry regrets. *Developmental Psychology, 48*(6), 1797.

15. Bianchi, S. M., Milkie, M. A., Sayer, L. C., & Robinson, J. P. (2000). Is anyone doing the housework? Trends in the gender division of household labor. *Social Forces, 79*(1), 191–228.

16. Bianchi, S. M., Robinson, J. P., & Milkie, M. A. (2006). *The changing rhythms of American family life*. New York, NY: Russell Sage Foundation.

17. Sandberg, S. (2013). *Lean in: Women, work, and the will to lead*. New York, NY: Alfred A. Knopf.

18. Slaughter, A.-M. (2015). *Unfinished business*. London, UK: Oneworld Publications.

19. Schoppe-Sullivan, S. J., Altenburger, L. E., Lee, M. A., Bower, D. J., & Kamp Dush, C. M. (2015). Who are the gatekeepers? Predictors of maternal gatekeeping. *Parenting*, *15*(3), 166–186.

20. Schoppe-Sullivan, S. J., Brown, G. L., Cannon, E. A., Mangelsdorf, S. C., & Sokolowski, M. S. (2008). Maternal gatekeeping, coparenting quality, and fathering behavior in families with infants. *Journal of Family Psychology*, *22*(3), 389–398.

21. Abraham, E., Hendler, T., Shapira-Lichter, I., Kanat-Maymon, Y., Zagoory-Sharon, O., & Feldman, R. (2014). Fathers' brain is sensitive to childcare experiences. *Proceedings of the National Academy of Sciences of the United States of America*, *111*(27), 9792.

22. Geiger, B. (1996). *Fathers as primary caregivers*. Westport, CT: Greenwood Press.

23. Deutsch, F. M. (2001). Equally shared parenting. *Current Directions in Psychological Science*, *10*(1), 25–28.

24. Pleck, J. H., & Masciadrelli, B. P. (2004). Paternal involvement by US residential fathers: Levels, sources, and consequences. In M. E. Lamb (Ed.), *The role of the father in child development* (pp. 222–271). Hoboken, NJ: John Wiley & Sons Inc.

25. Boushey, H., & O'Leary, A. (2009). *A woman's nation changes everything: The Shriver Report*. New York, NY: Free Press.

26. Mundy, L. (2013). *The richer sex: How the new majority of female breadwinners is transforming our culture*. New York, NY: Simon and Schuster.

27. Miller, C. C. (2015, May 8). Single motherhood, in decline over all, rises for women 35 and older. New York Times. Retrieved from https://www.nytimes.com/2015/05/09/upshot/out-of-wedlock-births-are-falling-except-among-older-women.html.

28. Laughlin, L. (2011). *Maternity leave and employment patterns of first-time mothers: 1961–2008*. Washington, DC: U.S. Census Bureau.

29. Holcomb, B. (2000). *Not guilty! The good news for working mothers*. New York, NY: Simon and Schuster.

30. Bird, R. C. (2016). Precarious work: The need for flextime employment rights and proposals for reform. *Berkeley Journal of Employment and Labor Law*, *37*(1), 1–41.

31. Williams, J. C., & Cuddy, A. (2012). Will working mothers take your company to court? *Harvard Business Review*, *90*(9), 94–100.

32. Garey, A. (1995). Constructing motherhood on the night shift: "Working mothers" as "stay-at-home moms." *Qualitative Sociology*, *18*(4), 415–437.

33. Greenhaus, J., & Powell, G. (2006). When work and family are allies: A theory of work-family enrichment. *Academy of Management Review*, *31*(1), 72–92.

34. Ruderman, M. N., Ohlott, P. J., Panzer, K., & King, S. N. (2002). Benefits of multiple roles for managerial women. *Academy of Management Journal*, *45*(2), 369.

35. Landry, S. H., Zucker, T. A., Taylor, H. B., Swank, P. R., Williams, J. M., Assel M., . . . Klein, A. (2014). Enhancing early child care quality and learning for toddlers at risk: The responsive early childhood program. *Developmental Psychology*, *50*(2), 526–541.

36. Heckman, J. (2015, October 15). Quality early childhood education: Enduring benefits. Retrieved from http://heckmanequation.org/content/quality-early-childhoodeducation-enduring-benefits.

37. Hammer, L. B., Kossek, E. E., Anger, W. K., Bodner, T., & Zimmerman, K. L. (2011). Clarifying work–family intervention processes: The roles of work–family conflict and family-supportive supervisor behaviors. *Journal of Applied Psychology*, *96*(1), 134–150.

38. Hammer, L., Kossek, E. E., Yragui, N. L., Bodner, T. E., & Hanson, G. C. (2009). Development and validation of a multidimensional measure of family supportive supervisor behaviors (FSSB). *Journal of Management*, *35*(4), 837–856.

39. Botsford Morgan, W. A., & King, E. B. (2012). Mothers' psychological contracts: Does supervisor breach explain intention to leave the organization? *Human Resource Management*, *51*(5), 629–650.

4

The Evolution of Work and Family

Growing a Family and a Career

Many of the senior leaders in my firm are women who have multiple children, so when it came time for me to think about having another, it didn't seem like a big deal. I already had some flexibility in my schedule that I had worked out with my boss, who also had two kids. She knew I was working hard and getting my work done, regardless of whether I was working from home one or two days a week. When planning for my second child, I didn't really consider how it would affect my career or that people would look at me differently, because the culture of my firm is not like other firms where women often must quit if they are denied flexibility or have inadequate work/family benefits. Right before I went on my second maternity leave, the company announced enhancements to their parental leave policy, which would now be fully paid leave as well as a month of paid paternity leave, signaling a renewed commitment to retaining mothers and fathers.

So, unlike some women who don't have these organizational perks, what I was thinking about was my own balance. My boss and I had been discussing succession planning and I knew I would be taking on more at work at some point, and I wondered whether I could juggle the additional responsibilities that go along with parenting two young children with a promotion. I considered talking to my boss about taking a career break, but then I decided not to because I realized it was going to be more time but it could mean more stress. I found that I became more efficient and prioritized my work better than I had before. I also learned how to say "no" to things, which gave me more credibility among my coworkers. This has made me more successful because people noticed it and recognized me for it. I've now become a "get to the point, no BS" kind of person.

As my children have grown, I have become a better manager. Motherhood has taught me how to guide people while letting them figure things out on their own. It also has helped me recognize and understand that people are motivated by different things. Most importantly, it has pushed me to help other women (and men) navigate maternity leave and return to work. In fact, all of the women and men on my team have come back after having children.

—SARAH, *insurance executive*

Up until this point, we have intentionally emphasized early motherhood, concentrating on the challenges and rewards of pregnancy, maternity leave, and the return to work. While this early transition into motherhood is particularly complex, it is not the only transition you will experience as a working mother. As you become confident in managing your work and family demands, that comfort level will likely change as your family grows and changes. These new transitions bring with them new questions, challenges, and opportunities.

In this chapter, we move beyond the first-time experiences of early motherhood to consider how life as a working mother shifts as a family structure evolves. We emphasize the work and family questions that surface for women as their family changes and ages. This next series of transitions differ from those of early motherhood because of the complexity associated with managing a household with multiple children. Increased work/family interruptions, nearly constant shuffling of time and resources, and navigating "big kid" problems versus "little kid" problems differentiate these transitions. In exploring these issues, we center on how relationships within the family, at work, and in the community impact a working mother.

GROWING A FAMILY

Two children are the norm for most American families, with American households averaging 2.4 children despite declining fertility rates. Most adults also believe that two children is the ideal family size—a number that is significantly smaller than in prior decades, when three or four children was the ideal.[1] This shift in perception of the ideal family size is likely a function of changes in workplace demographics and the rise of women in managerial and professional roles. Your own opinion of the ideal family size may likely be driven in part by your view of how more children will impact you at work and at home.

Many working mothers find there are career repercussions of having more than one child. As women have more children, their wage gap increases by 5% for each subsequent child.[2] Working mothers with three or more children are also less likely to stay in the workforce compared to working mothers who only have one or two children.[3] Together, these factors have given rise to a myth that suggests professional working women cannot have successful careers and large families. Stevie, a corporate lawyer, explained that when she told her manager she was pregnant for the third time, her manager assumed that this third pregnancy was unplanned. The manager continued by saying that rarely did women make partner if they had more than two children. In fields that are male dominated, such as technology and science, working mothers often choose to have fewer children than they desire in order to maintain their career progression.[4]

Having multiple children also translates to more work at home. Parents often find the stress level of moving from one child to two is more manageable than the stress of moving from two to three children.[5] With two children, parents can more evenly divide their time, but with three children or more, parents are outnumbered. There is always another child with another request to be filled. Think of it as going from a person-to-person defense to a zone defense. Increased family size can also lead to shifts in how parents share childcare responsibilities. In the previous chapter, we talked extensively about the importance of sharing infant care with your partner to set the stage for co-parenting.[6] Working parents who share childcare equally between themselves with their first child may revert to more traditional roles after the birth of a second child. Women often start to assume an even larger percentage of childcare responsibilities with the birth of each subsequent child.[7] This increase in home responsibilities and diminished shared caretaking explains why working mothers with larger families often experience higher levels of work/family conflict.[8] A final consideration on the home front relates to the increased childcare costs for more children. Working mothers may find that the cost of childcare for two or three children exceeds their earnings, leading them to stop working—at least in the short term.[9]

Before panicking too much about the negative effects of multiple children, it is important also to know that some of these effects seem to be short-lived. In looking at women's careers over a thirty-year career period, the impact of multiple children seems to be quite different. The same research that looked at drops in productivity for women with multiple young children also shows that over the course of a thirty-year period, working mothers with two or more children are more productive than working mothers with just one child, and even more than women who never had children at all.[2] Over time, women adapt to their larger family and develop additional skills in time management and multitasking to manage the additional demands of a larger family. These skills spill over to the workplace and may help working mothers increase their long-term productivity.[2] This becomes another way in which work and family enrich one another—a topic that was discussed in the previous chapters.

In determining the ideal family size, some working mothers are also affected by the norms of their culture and community. Hispanic American families tend to be larger, with 51% of families having three or more children.[10] Higher fertility rates coupled with cultural norms that place a high value on family over individual well-being partially contribute to these norms.[11] For Asian American working mothers, the cultural pressures may be quite different, since only 28% of families have three or more children.[10] Going against the trends of one's community—by having either more or fewer children—may generate more negative feedback from the community about how a working mother is approaching work and motherhood. These community pressures can give rise to work and family conflict.

Beyond racial, ethnic, and religious communities, norms about family size also arise in geographic communities. Terri and her husband had decided they wanted just one child, but in her upper-middle-class, predominately white suburban community, having large families was the trend.[12] She shared that it was always exhausting to be responding to comments like, "Is she your ONLY?" or "It must be hard not having more children." She interpreted these comments as the community suggesting that she had sacrificed motherhood for her career when in fact she was equally committed to both.

Social media can also become a source of pressure. Facebook and Instagram have become hotbeds for opinions and advice about seemingly everything related to parenting, often with little to no scientific evidence to back it up.

Once the decision has been made about having a second or even a third child, many working mothers turn to the question of timing. Some working mothers want to have their children close together, with less than 2.5 years in age difference. These women believe it will be easier to manage children who have similar developmental needs and similar routines.[13] For some women, managing two pregnancies that are close together seems more challenging, particularly with regards to work. Back-to-back pregnancies, maternity leaves, and reentries can make it more difficult for a working mother to reestablish her professional identity and build momentum in her career.[7] Additionally, it can take up to two years to begin to feel confident about yourself as a mother and feel physically back to yourself. By spacing children at wider intervals (i.e., between 3 and 5 years), working mothers may find it easier to replenish their emotional, physical, and cognitive capabilities and more fully establish their lives as working mothers before expanding their families further.[7]

Career changes such as a promotion, a geographic move, increased responsibilities, or switching industries are all decisions that introduce additional stress into life. Some women may find they want to delay having a second child if they are undergoing a major career transition. Infants who require less sleep, need more physical contact, or have health issues create more demands on parents. In these circumstances, some women may wait longer to have another child. For example, Larissa always thought she wanted three children. However, her two boys both had reflux, and neither slept well for the first year of their lives. The sleep deprivation was exhausting and affected her confidence at home and her productivity at work. She and her partner chose not to have a third child, and she did not regret the decision.

Our intention is certainly not to discourage you from having two or more children, or to instill fear in you if you have already expanded your family. In fact, both authors have three children, which certainly has not been the norm of women business school faculty. Our hope is that knowing the potential impact of family size and timing decisions on work and home may help you better manage, or at least worry less about, these dynamics. If you have or plan to have multiple children, you may just need to think about how you want to manage the additional demands at home in relation to your career. Hiring additional help, choosing not to take on greater responsibilities at work in the short term, or having one partner temporarily scale back may all be possible solutions if you find it challenging to manage these demands.

On the work front, you will want to keep a close eye on your compensation, career growth, and image at work. Some women will find they need to more actively manage any potential negative effects of a larger family. For example, Diane, a senior partner at a large public accounting firm with four children, actively managed her boss and her staff to ensure they were focused on her as a professional, not as a mother of a large family. When offered a challenging work assignment she wanted to accept, she would take time to sit down with her boss to consider how it might impact her career. Simultaneously, she would discuss with her husband how the new assignment might impact her family, but never did the two conversations intersect. At the same time, she did not hide her family at work, and she felt a sense of pride about herself as a working mother that had a positive impact on both her work and her children.

THE EARLY YEARS

When children are six years old or younger, caregiving demands are at their highest. Young children have little to no ability to do things on their own, limited patience to wait, and little ability to communicate their needs, and they are sick more frequently. When children are young and more dependent, the time demands, workloads, and pressures on parents are greater and less predictable. Because of this, working parents with younger children experience more interruptions at work and increased role overload compared to working parents with older children.[14]

During these early years, some women often express more guilt for not spending enough time with their children. However, according to a report in *Working Mother Magazine*, stay-at-home moms may carry as much guilt as working mothers. Fifty-one percent of working mothers expressed guilt about not spending enough time with their children, and 55% of stay-at-home moms expressed guilt about not working and not making an economic contribution to the family. These feelings of guilt also extend to household management. Working mothers and stay-at-home mothers express guilt over "domestic dishevelment."[15] Guilt over domestic life has increased in part because

We have ratcheted up what it means to be a good mother way above what our own mothers or grandmothers had to do . . . Even if you're staying at home, it isn't like Monday is wash day and Tuesday is baking day. You're ferrying junior to gymnastics and mommy-and-me activities.[15]

Most women, working or not, seem to be their own worst critics and would benefit from relaxing expectations of themselves both at work and at home. A perfect way to start is by moving away from un-realistic visions of a perfect home. For example, Leanne, a single mom of twins, started biweekly "crappy dinners" with a friend after reading about the idea in a blogpost. As she explained, crappy dinners involve having friends over without cleaning your house or shopping for food—you eat whatever you and your friends can cobble together. Crappy dinners enabled Leanne to have more of the companionship and sup-port she needed without the expectations of domestic bliss. (More infor-mation on crappy dinners can be found at http://www.thekitchn.com/5-rules-for-hosting-a-crappy-dinner-party-235815.)

The adage "the days are long and the years are short" is important to re-member during these early years. Children progress through stages in a pre-dictable pattern from newborn to preschool to school age to teenage years and beyond. Each stage comes with a unique set of demands, questions, and possibilities that create potential changes in roles, relationships, and responsibilities for a working mother.[16] Below we focus on two of these f-amily transitions that we feel mark the most significant next changes for working mothers: the transition to elementary school and the teenage years.

SCHOOL-AGE CHILDREN: NEW ROUTINES

The transition to school may generate a sigh of relief for many working mothers: the guilt and struggles over childcare die down when children are in school for most of the day. As children age, you may feel more adept at managing work and family demands and experience less stress and role overload at work and at home.[17] While there are certainly ways in which life eases up as children begin school, this transition also brings with it new issues to manage.

Navigating the Care Gap

One of the most startling changes you may experience as children age is the change in the rhythm of home life. Working mothers with young children typically structure childcare so that it matches the demands of their work schedule. Whether it be in-home care, daycare, or onsite care, working mothers usually establish a childcare schedule that is consistent year-round. However, once children enter school, working mothers now need to respond to a home schedule that is anything but consistent. As Brianna explained,

> I loved my daycare, as they were open every day except Christmas and Thanksgiving. My daughter is now 6, and I cannot keep track of all the days her school is closed. They are even closed on Halloween for a "clerical day." What is a "clerical day," and why does a school need to be closed?

In the United States, the school calendar runs from August/September to May/June with a school day of six to seven hours. This schedule leaves working parents with significant care gaps. First, there is a daily care gap. The standard workweek for working professionals in the United States is now forty-seven hours, with 40% of workers saying they work more than fifty hours a week on average.[18] Given the length of the school day, most families need ten to fifteen hours of after- or before-school care every week.[19] Then there is the issue of school closings and vacations. Schools close for national holidays, winter breaks, and weeklong breaks in February, March, and/or April. There are professional development days and often historical days off that have nothing to do with school, such as the opening day of deer-hunting season. During the ten months in which school is "open," schools are typically closed for twenty-nine days. If two working parents use all of their vacation and sick days, they may be able to cover these closings. Now add on the eight weeks of summer vacation and perhaps a few days when a child is home sick, and even a dual-career couple who have generous sick and vacation time will need to find weeks to months of alternative care for their school-age children.[20] This childcare gap is worse for single parents, professionals who have little vacation time, and professionals who have significant commutes. The public school calendar increases the stress working parents experience as they try to manage their commitment to their families with their commitment to their work.[20]

Parental after-school stress, or "PASS," refers to the worry parents have about the welfare of their school-age children during non-school time. These concerns center on children's safety, the reliability of after-school care, and productive use of children's time.[21] This stress can be costly for both parents and companies. Parents who are concerned about their children's after-school care are three times as likely to experience job disruptions and 4.5 times as likely to experience lower psychological well-being compared to parents who do not experience PASS.[22] With regards to job performance, parents with PASS miss on average five days more of work a year, are more likely to make errors at work, are more likely to miss meetings and deadlines, and rate their work quality as lower than parents who are not concerned with after-school care.[22] When working mothers find that the school schedule, their out-of-school care arangements, and child transportation plans meet their needs, they are more confident at work and at home.[23] When Jackie moved to a different town, she was thrilled to learn her children's school offered both a before- and after-school program. This made her life easier, as she often needed to be at work by 7:30 a.m. Although she did not need to drop her boys off early every day, the reassurance of knowing she could eased her anxiety. Similarly, an after-school program that was located at her children's school meant she did not have to manage the logistics of researching and finding transportation to an offsite after-school program. All of this diminished her guilt, alleviated much of her PASS, and elevated her productivity and performance at work.

One way you can reduce these stressors is by beginning to think about out-of-school care well before your children enter kindergarten. Out-of-school care can be managed through camps, vacation-week programs, part-time sitters, and after-school programs. It may be helpful to reach out to working mothers with older children to get advice on the advantages and disadvantages of different childcare arrangements in the same way that parents research infant or preschool care. Working mothers are sometimes surprised to learn the financial costs of out-of-school care. When looking at these costs, we encourage you to remember our discussion in the previous chapter about framing care as an investment rather than a cost. Given the personal, family, and career costs of PASS, working mothers may need to make more of an investment to ensure they have reliable, safe, and high-quality out-of-school care.

Some working mothers find technology can be very helpful for managing a busy household with two working parents' schedules, children's schedules, and activities. There are many software packages available in which parents can share calendars, track and remind each other about carpool or childcare duties, and manage grocery shopping and to-do lists. (For reviews of shared family technology, see http://www.momof6.com/mom-organization/the-6-best-family-calendars/ and https://www.wsj.com/articles/SB10001424052748704250704576005380226320262.) With a shared family calendar, working parents can more easily plan how to manage potential conflicts between schedules and calendar changes. A shared calendar and shared household lists can be helpful for maintaining a co-parenting model, as both parents own these responsibilities. As children get older, teaching them how to access and review the shared family tools also becomes a way to help them become more independent and responsible for their lives, which further eases home pressures.

Shifting Work/Life Schedules

We tend to focus on the need for flexibility when children are younger, but the schedule shifts and emotional needs of older children leads some working mothers to reconsider their work schedules. As Arielle explained,

I had been doing direct service work with teenagers for almost 20 years, and I loved what I did and was good at it. But the nature of the work meant there were few boundaries and my schedule was not traditional. I regularly worked evenings and weekends, and then there were the occasional crises. When my kids were little, it was great because I could spend time with them during the day and early evening and my husband took over when I had to work at night and on the weekends. I thought I had the best arrangement because I often went back to work when my kids were getting ready for bed. But once they were both in school, weekends, evenings, and no boundaries no longer worked for me. The issue was, I knew that type of work couldn't be changed. I left the organization and direct service work and took on a different role in the same general field. I am happier because my schedule aligns better with my kids and I still love my work.

Work arrangements differ in the extent to which schedules can be flexible and work/family boundaries crossed to manage unexpected crises. For some working mothers, work cannot be shifted or adapted to align better with a school calendar. Working mothers may find themselves needing to make difficult choices about this misalignment. Some women, like Arielle, may decide that a work schedule in which a majority of work occurs when children are at home does not match how they want to integrate work and family. For other women, this type of arrangement may work well, particularly if they have a partner who has a more flexible schedule. Working mothers need to pay attention to their feelings about the intersection between their work schedule and their children's schedule. If this intersection is out of alignment, they may need to make adjustments that better support how they want to design this work/life chapter.

Building high-quality connections with other parents in the community can also be helpful for managing the new challenges that arise as children move into elementary school and beyond. For example, Kerry Healey, the first female president of Babson College and the first female lieutenant governor of Massachusetts, has spoken about the importance that her supportive network of friends, teachers, and family members played when her children were young. Her "close-knit group of North

Shore mothers" who pitched in with childcare, provided one another meals, and counseled one another's children about college and work were central in supporting her as she managed work and family while building her political career.[24] When another working mother, Martha, moved to a new city, she no longer had her extended family to help with after-school care. Through her religious community, she developed a relationship with another working mother whose children were close to hers in age. Over time, the two working mothers began to function like one extended family, helping each other manage school pickups, drop-offs, after-school activities, and even dinners. By working together, the two families could better manage the cost, time, and complexity of out-of-school care during the elementary and middle school years, and it created an enriching home life for Martha and her children.

Finding a Community That Fits Your Needs

As children transition to school age, working mothers often sharpen their focus on where they want to raise a family. As working mothers make this decision, they likely are weighing issues such as the cost of housing with school quality. Rarely do working mothers consider community support as part of this decision-making process. Community support refers to the extent to which the resources in the community support a working mother's work/family needs. While there are many different communities to which a working mother belongs, here we are referring to the geographic community in which a working mother resides.[25] Communities can provide working mothers with diverse resources ranging from public transportation to high-quality daycare and after-school care to well-priced summer and vacation camps. Having more community support leads to lower job disruptions, lower psychological stress, and higher job quality for working mothers.[26] Greater community support also increases a family's resilience to the conflicts and overloads of managing paid and unpaid work.[27]

We encourage you to think about community support as part of the decision-making process of where to raise your growing family. The primary factors to consider in assessing community support are childcare resources, working parents' culture, and transportation. When evaluating school districts, parents may want to look beyond test scores, teacher-to-student ratios, and reputation to also consider school schedules and school-sponsored childcare. Does the school have full-day kindergarten? Is there an after-school or before-school program, where is it located, and how much is it used? What does the school schedule look like, and how will that affect work schedules? Does the town offer reasonably priced vacation and summer camps? For example, Deliah was evaluating a few different towns to move to as her daughter transitioned to kindergarten. As she researched towns, she initially focused solely on housing affordability and quality schools, but in a chance encounter, she learned the town she was most interested in had a half-day kindergarten program and a little-used after-school program. Concerns about managing this schedule and finding quality after-school care led Deliah and her wife to rent a house in a different town.

The lack of well-used after-school care also raised concerns for Deliah about how many working mothers lived in this town. Having more working mothers in a town increases the likelihood that school and recreation programs are compatible with the schedules of working families. This makes it easier for parents and their children to be involved in these activities, which makes a working mother more confident about her choices.[28] A higher percentage of working mothers in a town also increases the likelihood that a working mother will be able to build the support network she needs to feel confident about herself as a working mother.

A third aspect of community support to consider is that of transportation needs for both commuting adults and children. As Yun looked to buy a house, she focused on the importance of the bus program to her and her son. She shared,

The bus drops him and picks him up at the end of the driveway. If I have to be at work for an early meeting, I do not worry about leaving and him getting to school. I can leave him alone until the bus comes. I cannot give that up.

In Yun's case, the bus was a benefit she learned about after her son started school, but it quickly became an important resource that helped her manage work and family. Beyond just school buses, working mothers may also want to consider whether public transportation or ride sharing is available, reliable, and safe for older children.

We recognize it is not always easy to research community support. It also may not be easy to assess whether the community resources match your specific needs. In the short term, it may feel easier to ignore the community and just focus on finding the best house in the best school system. However, in the long term, you will find that it is much less stressful to move houses within a town or add that much-needed family room than it is to switch to a new town in a new school district. Furthermore, for a child's development and well-being, a proud, engaged working mother is far more important than a big backyard.

TWEENS AND TEENS: BALANCING CARE, WORK, AND GROWING INDEPENDENCE

While after-school care and summer camps can meet the care needs for elementary school children, as children advance to middle school and beyond working mothers are confronted with a significant decline in school-based care resources. While 45% of public schools in the United States offer before- or after-school care for elementary school children, the number of after-school programs drops significantly for children after fifth grade.[20] Furthermore, tweens and teens often have their preferences for how they spend out-of-school time and may be reluctant to participate in such programs. Janna shared,

When my son was in elementary school, he loved after-school. However, as he entered middle school, it became a battle. He would say, "I hate it there! Only losers go to middle school after-school." Of course, this only made me feel even more guilty.

This conflict is not unusual, since middle schoolers are naturally beginning to assert their desire for greater autonomy. The difficulty is that few
middle schoolers are fully prepared or able to manage their time out of
school independently.[29] Knowing that this conflict is developmentally appropriate does not necessarily ease a working mother's feelings of guilt
and stress.

The lack of age-appropriate after-school care for tweens and teens
translates to a large percentage of teenagers managing themselves
after school while their parents are at work. While different families,
neighborhoods, cultures, and communities have different cultural
assumptions about self-care for older teens, most parents have some
concerns about teens being unsupervised for too much time. Adolescents
who are on their own too much after school are more likely to develop
various problems such as low academic performance, low self-esteem,
depression, and substance abuse,[30] whereas teens who have some out-of-
school support and services have decreased instances of self-destructive
behavior, better academic development, and greater workplace read-
iness.[31] Even without out-of-school care, these negative effects can be
substantially mitigated when parents are monitoring their adolescent's
comings and goings and are available emotionally.[32] This is particularly
good news for working mothers of teenagers, who may not be able to be
physically present every day but can find ways to be emotionally available, whether by phone or video conference, occasionally working from
home, or having regularly scheduled one-on-one time. Finding ways to be
emotionally present can help reduce a working mother's concerns about
her ability to support her teen during this confusing and complex stage of
development.

The unpredictable, variable nature of teenagers' schedules also
introduces new strains for working mothers. During middle and high
school, teenagers are likely to participate in one or more weekday activities such as sports, clubs, religious and volunteer activities, and paid work,
which can vary from week to week. When these activities are either highly
inflexible or constantly changing in terms of start times, end times, or
locations, last-minute driving demands, changing carpools, or teens being

penalized for being late can produce parental insecurity. For example, Mary Kathryn described the new tensions that arose as her daughter transitioned to high school and took up rowing:

> I am thrilled she is so passionate about this, but I cannot believe the stress it creates for me. We have to figure out a ride or carpool for her every day, and there are not many kids from our town who row at her club. The club makes last-minute changes to the schedule in response to the weather, and here in Seattle our weather changes by the hour. I feel like I am constantly caught at work searching for a ride for her when they change the practice schedule. We have had times when I am on a conference call, and she cannot find a ride, and there is nothing I can do.

Beyond the shift in schedule, these after-school activities frequently come with expectations about parental support, be it in the form of coaching, booster club participation, attendance at games or meets, and team coordination. The more collective activities that children are involved in in a household, the more work and strain it can create for working mothers at home.[33] In discussing the challenge of integrating teenagers and work, Hannah confessed that she was secretly pleased that her daughter was not elected senior class president because she did not want the responsibility that would fall on her to host social events for senior class parents, raise money, and solicit parent volunteers for the senior class activities. As Hannah's story illustrates, these new home responsibilities produce the same feelings of work and family conflict and role overload that a working mother may have experienced when her children were younger. Working mothers may start to feel a renewed sense of angst about not living up to the expectations of "intensive mothering" ideals. These pressures may also be experienced at the couple level, as many working parents often "keep score" of how much each partner participates in their children's activities.

To be responsive to the fluctuations and increased parental demands of a teenager's schedule, you may need to be more creative in how you think about after-school support for your teens. Tai, an obstetrician, felt she had the "ideal" childcare arrangement when her children were young: she had the financial resources to hire a woman who worked for her full time from the time her children were born until the oldest was in middle school. However, as her two boys transitioned into middle and high school, her childcare provider left. Tai was devastated. As she took stock of what she and her family needed in light of her children's ages and her recent divorce, she realized her needs had shifted. Now her boys needed a role model and driver, and she needed more help around the house and with meals. Her boys also articulated they wanted some more independence and felt comfortable being home alone some of the time. As a family, they came to a compromise, and she hired a male house manager to work three afternoons a week. He helped with minor repairs around the house, cooked meals, and drove and mentored her teenage sons. What started as a potential crisis turned out to be an opportunity to create a new arrangement that better met her family's childcare and financial needs. Being open to change can provide exciting new after-school options.

Tai's story also points to how working mothers may want to think beyond traditional childcare arrangements as they consider the needs of their older children. If children are self-directed and just need to be shuttled to activities, perhaps all that is needed is a driver or a driving service that is designed specifically for children. Kidskruiser.com in Ann Arbor, Michigan, is an example of a driving service focused on kids. They explain, "Our drivers are not just hired chauffeurs. We interact with your children and build a relationship with them, just as we did in our former jobs as nannies, teachers, and school bus drivers." If children need academic and organizational support for homework and time management, a local teaching assistant may be a perfect after-school sitter. Jada's children were old enough to walk home after school, but they both needed extra learning support. Rather than hire an expensive tutor and a separate afterschool provider, Jada hired a local teacher who would arrive at her house after the children came home from school. The teacher provided homework support and drove the children to an occasional activity. For older teens who are looking for more independence, the local library, coffee shop, or even a parent's office can provide a safe space for after-school homework while also providing the desired level of independence.

Even though parenting demands are still high at this stage, organizations and coworkers may forget that working mothers still have caregiving responsibilities. Research has shown that while access to family-friendly policies is associated with increased work/life satisfaction for working mothers with younger children, these programs and policies have little impact on working mothers of school-age and teenage children. Lack of organizational support partially explains why working mothers with older children still experience quite a bit of stress and work/family conflict even though they may have fewer home demands.[34] You may need to advocate more for your continued work/life needs as your children age. Toni, a wealth advisor at a bank, had always worked full time while relying on a variety of childcare and after-school arrangements to support her family. As her children entered high school, she found herself wanting to be more available to attend athletic events, go to performances, and help with the college search process. She used the power she had created for herself based on her years of experience and high levels of performance to advocate for having the control to adjust her schedule on an ad hoc basis during her children's teenage years. In this way, she could be present for her older children while continuing to work full time. In the process, she found herself educating her organization about the care demands for working mothers of older children.

THE BENEFITS OF ACCUMULATED WORK/FAMILY EXPERIENCE

As your children age, you may find the experience of managing work and family eases in part because of the experience you have accumulated. By the time your children become teenagers, you will have likely navigated countless work/family conflicts and developed a set of skills for managing these situations. Some women even find that over time this accumulated experience increases their confidence as working mothers. Isabelle shared,

At some point, you realize that you have been able to do it all, just differently and not without challenges along the way. You see that your children are happy and doing okay and you are happy at work. I feel more of a sense of pride now because I realize the tough choices I have made and how much work it has been. When certain thresholds are passed, it is like, "Wow, I cannot believe that I was able to do that."

Another tension that eases over time is the quest for balance. We loathe the term *work/family balance*. It dominates societal rhetoric around work/family and often leads people down an unattainable path. Working women are often consumed by constantly wondering when they will achieve this mythical balance. Will it happen after the next promotion, when their children enter school, or when they are grown and out of the house? The word *balance* implies that there can be an equilibrium between work and family, but these two aspects of life are never static and therefore never in equilibrium. Balance also assumes that work and family are on opposite sides of a spectrum, which can prevent people from seeing how work and home life are intertwined and even enriching. The balance metaphor can blind individuals from seeing the possibilities that arise from being deeply engaged in both one's professional and family life.[35]

We encourage you to relinquish the quest for balance and to develop your own definition of what it means to successfully integrate work and family. Despite the negative rhetoric that assumes work and family are always in conflict, being engaged in multiple roles can have positive outcomes for working mothers in a number of ways. First, it leads to the accumulation of more positive experiences, which has an additive effect on overall well-being. Second, participation and satisfaction in one role buffers stress in another. Lastly, experiences in one role can lead to the development of new skills, knowledge, and capabilities that have a positive effect on another role.[36]

Supreme Court Justice Ruth Bader Ginsburg shared how motherhood had a positive impact on her law school experience:

My success in law school, I have no doubt, was in large measure because of baby Jane. I attended classes and studied diligently until four in the afternoon; the next hours were Jane's time . . . After Jane's bedtime, I returned to the law books with renewed will. Each part of my life provided respite from the other and gave me a sense of proportion that classmates who only focused on law studies lacked.[37]

Justice Ginsburg's quote supports the notion that home life can provide a working mother with renewed energy and interest that enables her to be more focused and productive at work.

Carla, a researcher, shared that as a working mother she often felt guilty about the time she spent away from her lab to be with her family. She worried that her male colleagues were "getting ahead." Over time, she started to realize that the time away enabled her to distance herself from her research and return with new perspective. Having a family, and its corresponding distractions from work, made her a more innovative researcher. And work can provide a much-needed break from the struggles and worries associated with raising children, particularly teenagers. Working mothers are more open to the opportunity that work affords family and family affords work if they abandon the quest for balance.

Finally, as children age, you may also start to realize the important role modeling you are providing for your children. All parents serve as role models for children—sometimes positive and sometimes negative—and help to shape children's understanding of how things are and can be. As was discussed in Chapter 1 about how women form visions of their lives of working motherhood, working mothers shape children's understanding of what is possible in combining work and family.[38] Maya recognized this:

I am proud to show my children that women can be successful and can have lives outside the house, and I feel in some ways like a role model in that respect.

Women whose mothers worked outside the home are more likely to work themselves, are more likely to hold managerial roles, and earn more than women whose mothers stayed at home full time. Men who are raised by working mothers are more likely to be involved co-parents and share the responsibilities of household chores and caring for children.[38] Working mothers have this impact on their children regardless of whether they worked continuously or had intense professional careers. Even as early as high school, teenagers start to articulate more egalitarian expectations around work and family when they have been raised by a working mother.[39] Undoubtedly, some mothers will still get pushback from their teens, as Fiona shared:

> I am divorced and work full time. When I ask my son to help with laundry, he says, "When I grow up I am going to marry a woman who stays home and takes care of everything." I have to remember that is just typical teenage behavior and mostly he is proud of my work.

Remembering that you are a positive role model for your children can be helpful when navigating challenging parenting moments. After reading about the positive impact of working mothers on their adult children, Amy shared:

> One consoling thought for me is that, hopefully, I am setting a positive example for my daughter and for my sons about how they may support their partners and families someday as they see how much their dad does at home to make my career possible. It is a good reminder when you head to work with a double-sided to-do list, an unmade bed, and promising that you will get to bed at a reasonable hour tonight.

Amy reminds us that remembering this long-term perspective may be particularly helpful to new working mothers or moms with younger children as they get caught in the everyday struggles and stresses of managing work and family.

GETTING ORGANIZATIONAL SUPPORT AS YOUR
FAMILY EVOLVES

As we have already mentioned in this chapter, organizational efforts to build policies and a culture that is supportive of work/family management frequently focuses on the early years of parenting, as new mothers return to work and manage the intense early years of integrating work and family with young children. However, parents of older children still need support, and there are different forms of assistance you can explore with your organization as your family evolves over time.

Some organizations may partner with an agency or web-based childcare service to help parents of older children with backup care for the days that schools are closed. Care.com offers a service for organizations called "care@work" in which they help families with backup childcare needs and with finding childcare during out-of-school time. Campseekers.com contracts with companies to provide employees with childcare support during school vacations and summers. You may want to consult your firm's Employee Assistance Programs to explore whether these programs are offered and whether any financial assistance is provided. If not, you can try to make the case to offer such programs to your human resources department by explaining the research that shows that PASS costs companies $50 billion in healthcare and lost productivity annually (e.g., http://www.brandeis.edu/barnett/research/docs/PASS_Findings.pdf, Community, Families and Work Program Report of Findings on parental afterschool stress project [April 2004]). By reducing PASS, organizations may find that employees miss fewer workdays, experience less work/family conflict, and stay engaged and productive.

Another form of support services some organizations offer are those that help working mothers manage the stresses of parenting older children. Issues about drugs and alcohol, teenage sexuality, and the college search process are paramount for parents of teenagers. Many working parents miss school programs on these topics because they occur during the workday. If your organization doesn't already do so, you might suggest bringing in experts to provide seminars, workshops, or even one-on-one coaching to help working mothers navigate the difficult issues associated with parenting teens. Some large organizations have even developed programming for middle school children on staying safe when home alone and for teenagers about career development skills. There is no shortage of programs and coaching support that organizations can provide. They just may need to begin with you championing such efforts.

A final point to consider when thinking about the kind of support you may need when parenting older children pertains to control over your work hours. Working mothers with older children often need flexibility to manage after-school care and to be available to their teenagers on an as-needed basis. While we will discuss formal workplace flexibility in detail in Chapter 6, we note here the importance of finding ways to gain more autonomy over your work schedule. This autonomy may pertain to control over how, when, and perhaps even where work gets done. Some working mothers may want to shift their work hours to be more available in the afternoons, while others simply want greater autonomy to be available to their children for an occasional afternoon or school event. This can be challenging if your manager tends to focus more on schedules than on results. However, research suggests that manager support can have a significant influence on reducing work/family conflicts and increasing positivity with regards to parent–adolescent relationships—both of which affect employee well-being, retention, and productivity.[40]

CHAPTER TAKEAWAYS

1. Schedules, routines, expectations, and demands will evolve as your children grow in number and move from infancy into the school years. Covering childcare gaps, managing multiple schedules and activities, and identifying community and school resources can alleviate feelings of guilt and stress during these transitions.
2. As a parent of older children, your work/life demands will change but not necessarily decrease. Seek out support from family members, friends, fellow parents, and your workplace.

3. Surrender the quest for the mythical "work/life balance." Instead, welcome the benefits of being a working mother, such as increased confidence, a greater focus and productivity at work, and a recognition of yourself as a role model for your children.

REFERENCES

1. Gao, G. (2015, May 8). *Americans' ideal family size is smaller than it used to be.* Retrieved from http://www.pewresearch.org/fact-tank/2015/05/08/ideal-size-of-the-american-family/.

2. Krapf, M., Ursprung, H., & Zimmerman, C. (2014). *Parenthood and productivity of highly skilled labor: Evidence from the groves of academe. Journal of Economic Behavior & Organization, 140,* 147–175.

3. Stampler, L. (2011). Working moms: Women with three children less likely to have jobs that those with two, study says. *Huffington Post.* Retrieved from https://www.huffingtonpost.com/2011/07/12/women-three-children_n_895517.html.

4. Ecklund, E. H., & Lincoln, A. E. (2011). Scientists want more children. *PLoS ONE, 6*(8), e22590.

5. HuffPost Mom's Blog. (2013). Having three children is most stressful for mom, survey finds. *Huffington Post.* Retrieved from https://www.huffpost.com/entry/three-children-is-most-st_n_3229032.

6. Deutsch, F. (1999). *Halving it all: How equally shared parenting works.* Cambridge, MA: Harvard University Press.

7. Daniels, P., & Weingarten, K. (1982). *Sooner or later: The timing of parenthood in adult lives.* New York, NY: Norton.

8. Eby, L. T., Casper, W. J., Lockwood, A., Bordeaux, C., & Brinley, A. (2005). Work and family research in IO/OB: Content analysis and review of the literature (1980–2002). *Journal of Vocational Behavior, 66*(1), 124–197.

9. Newman, S. (2011). *The case for the only child: Your essential guide.* Deerfield Beach, FL: Health Communications, Inc.

10. Livingston, G. (2015). *For most highly educated women, motherhood doesn't start until the 30s.* Retrieved from http://www.pewresearch.org/fact-tank/2015/01/15/for-most-highly-educated-women-motherhood-doesnt-start-until-the-30s/.

11. Wight, V. R., Bianchi, S. M., & Hunt, B. R. (2013). Explaining racial/ethnic variation in partnered women's and men's housework. *Journal of Family Issues, 34*(3), 394–427.

12. Baskin, K. (2014, July 2). With affluent parents, "Four is the new three." *Boston Globe.* Retrieved from https://www.bostonglobe.com/lifestyle/style/2014/07/02/for-some-parents-one-child-gratitude-tempered-twinge-defensiveness/zJiFyV7AzejnnTKxBqTP1L/story.html.

13. Collins, G. (1982, January 25). Timing of the second child. *New York Times,* p. A20.

14. Grzywacz, J. G., Almeida, D. M., & McDonald, D. A. (2002). Work-family spillover and daily reports of work and family stress in the adult labor force. *Family Relations, 51*(1), 28–36.

15. Working Mother Research Institute. (2011). *What moms choose: The Working Mother report.* Retrieved from http://www.workingmother.com/research-institute/what-moms-choose-working-mother-report.

16. White, J. M. (1991). *Dynamics of family development: A theoretical perspective.* New York, NY: Guilford Press.

17. Higgins, C., Duxbury, L., & Lee, C. (1994). Impact of life-cycle stage and gender on the ability to balance work and family responsibilities. *Family Relations, 43,* 144–150.

18. Saad, L. (2014). *The "40-hour" workweek is actually longer—by seven hours.* Gallup. Retrieved from https://news.gallup.com/poll/175286/hour-workweek-actually-longer-seven-hours.aspx.

19. Gareis, K., & Barnett, R. C. (2006). *After-school worries: Tough on parents, bad for business.* New York, NY: Catalyst.

20. Brown, C., Boser, U., & Baffou, P. (2016). *Workin' 9 to 5: How school schedules make life harder for working parents.* Retrieved from https://www.americanprogress.org/issues/education/reports/2016/10/11/145084/workin-9-to-5-2/.

21. Gareis, K. C., & Barnett, R. C. (2002). Under what conditions do long work hours affect psychological distress? A study of full-time and reduced-hours female doctors. *Work and Occupations, 29*(4), 483–497.

22. Barnett, R. C., & Gareis, K. C. (2006). Parental after-school stress and psychological well-being. *Journal of Marriage and Family, 68*(1), 101–108.

23. Barnett, R. C., Gareis, K., & Brennan, R. (2010). School and school activity schedules affect the quality of family relations: A within-couple analysis. *Community, Work & Family, 13*(1), 35–41.

24. Gehrman, E. (2016, October 27). Secrets of the top women execs: Some of Greater Boston's most accomplished women share their strategies for success. *Boston Globe.* Retrieved from https://www.bostonglobe.com/magazine/2016/10/27/secrets-top-women-execs/qhSPHefkyGAuRs65J7bWkM/story.html.

25. Bookman, A. (2005). Can employers be good neighbors? Redesigning the workplace–community interface. In S. M. Bianchi, L. M. Casper, & R. B. King (Eds.), *Work, family, health, and well-being* (pp. 141–156). New York, NY: Routledge.

26. Gareis, K., & Barnett, R. C. (2008). The development of a new measure for work-family research: Community resource fit. *Community, Work & Family, 11*(3), 273–282.

27. Sweet, S., Swisher, R., & Moen, P. (2005). Selecting and assessing the family-friendly community: Adaptive strategies of middle-class, dual-earner couples. *Family Relations, 54*(5), 596–606.

28. Stobbe, M. (2017, May 17). *Women in 30s now having more babies than younger moms in U.S.* CNBC. Retrieved from https://www.cnbc.com/2017/05/17/women-in-30s-now-having-more-babies-than-younger-moms-in-us.html.

29. Polatnick, M. R. (2002). Too old for child care? Too young for self-care? Negotiating after-school arrangements for middle school [Abstract]. *Journal of Family Issues, 23*(6), 728.

30. Mahoney, J. L., & Parente, M. E. (2009). Should we care about adolescents who care for themselves? What we have learned and what we need to know about youth in self-care. *Child Development Perspectives*, *3*(3), 189–195.

31. Partee, G., Brand, B., Pearson, S., & Hare, R. (2006). *Helping youth succeed through out-of-school time programs*. American Youth Policy Forum Inc. Retrieved from https://www.aypf.org/resource/helpingyouthsucceed/.

32. Richardson, J. L., Radziszewska, B., Dent, C. W., & Flay, B. R. (1993). Relationship between after-school care of adolescents and substance use, risk taking, depressed mood, and academic achievement. *Pediatrics*, *92*(1), 32–38.

33. Lareau, A., & Weininger, E. B. (2008). Time, work, and family life: Reconceptualizing gendered time patterns through the case of children's organized activities. *Sociological Forum*, *23*(3), 419–454.

34. Craig, L., & Sawrikar, P. (2009). Work and family: How does the (gender) balance change as children grow? *Gender, Work & Organization*, *16*(6), 684–709.

35. Thompson, J. A., & Bunderson, J. S. (2001). Work–nonwork conflict and the phenomenology of time. Beyond the balance metaphor. *Work and Occupations: An International Sociological Journal*, *28*(1), 17–39.

36. Greenhaus, J., & Powell, G. (2006). When work and family are allies: A theory of work-family enrichment. *The Academy of Management Review*, *31*(1), 72–92.

37. Ginsburg, R. B. (2016, October 2). R.B.G.'s advice for living. *New York Times*. Retrieved from https://www.nytimes.com/2016/10/02/opinion/sunday/ruth-bader-ginsburgs-advice-for-living.html.

38. McGinn, K. L., Ruiz Castro, M., & Lingo, E. L. (2015, July 2). Mums the word! Cross-national effects of maternal employment on gender inequalities at work and at home. *Harvard Business School Working Knowledge*. Retrieved from https://hbswk.hbs.edu/item/mums-the-word-cross-national-effects-of-maternal-employment-on-gender-inequalities-at-work-and-at-home.

39. Davis, S. N., & Greenstein, T. N. (2009). Gender ideology: Components, predictors, and consequences. *Annual Review of Sociology*, *35*, 87–105.

40. Davis, K. D., Lawson, K. M., Almeida, D. M., Kelly, E. L., King, R. B., Hammer, L., . . . McHale, S. M. (2015). Parent's daily time with their children: A workplace intervention. *Pediatrics*, *135*(5), 875–882.

5

Older, Wiser, But Still a Working Mother

As my kids began to leave for college, graduate school, and began to establish their own lives, I looked down the road and realized I didn't want to keep working fifty or sixty hours a week. I had been with my current employer for over ten years, and I had achieved a lot and was proud of that. At the same time, I recognized I had many goals outside of my profession that I wanted to achieve, but I never had the bandwidth to do so because the focus was always on the children and family and work. After twenty years in ful-filling, exciting senior leadership positions, I started to realize that I wanted things to be different. I wanted more of my own life and wasn't sure I wanted to keep making personal sacrifices to continue climbing in my career. I started to think about what I wanted, and I realized I had achieved what I set out to do. I owned a home, owned other property, put my children through college, and did not have any debt. At about that time, I went on a trip to Colorado with other women I had never met. It was an amazing and empowering trip and probably one of the first things I did for "me" in a very long time. I realized that while I wanted to keep working, I wanted to do it differently, with more time for "me." I started to spend more time with my husband and travel because I now felt greater flexibility to do so. That is something we had not been able to do because of my work schedule and because of the time and financial priority of raising our family. I don't regret any of my choices that I made. It is just now I am really enjoying this other part of life.

—WENDY, *retired senior VP of human resources*

The term *working mother* typically evokes an image of an early- or mid-career woman balancing the demands of a young family and a career. Think about the women we see in movies like *I Don't Know How She Does It, The Intern*, or *Baby Boom*. Rarely do we think about working mothers at a later age, family stage, and career stage, as well as the transitions of this period. Even if a professional woman waits until her thirties to start her family, there will be a time in her late forties or fifties when her children do leave home. The years of juggling carpools, school drop-offs and pickups, participation in school activities, and ensuring time for the ever-important family dinner will end. While this transition may bring with it feelings of loss and anxiety about what comes next, it also can be a generative time for a working mother. For most working mothers, the stresses and time pressures of daily parenting ease up as children move into adulthood and (hopefully!) begin to cultivate their own, more independent lives. As the opening story suggests, this easing up of life may provide working mothers with an important opportunity to pause, reflect, and reestablish priorities for the next phase of life.[1] For working mothers, whose career and work decisions for the past eighteen to twenty-five years have been made in conjunction with children's needs, this next phase of life can offer a welcome chance to focus more on themselves and what they want from their careers and their lives.

Given the length of women's careers today, this next work/life phase is far more than just a holding period between raising children and retirement. Life expectancy for American women is currently around eighty years.[2] Furthermore, women are working longer. The percentage of women who remain in the workforce in their later years has increased more quickly than the percentage of men. In 1992, just 23% of women aged fifty-five and older were working; by 2012, the figure was 35%. By

2022, the Bureau of Labor Statistics expects women to account for 82% of the over-fifty-five workforce.[3] While these changes are partially a result of shifts in mandatory retirement and economic pressures, they also may be a result of working mothers' desire to "lean in" later in life. As women age and children leave home, working mothers may find they have new energy and interest in their careers. In fact, at this later career stage women report higher levels of work engagement and fulfillment compared to men.[4]

In this chapter, we address how working mothers navigate work and family as they move from the daily responsibilities of raising children to parenting adult children to retirement. As Jolene explained,

> When your kids leave the house, you don't stop being a mom, but the role does change. Being a mother to adult children is about being an advisor and a guide, while for younger children it's more likely to involve housework and chauffeuring people around.

As working mothers experience this role shift along with other life changes of middle age, they may begin a process of career recalibration as they consider what they want to do that is meaningful and engaging in this next life phase. The varied ways working mothers approach this issue is a key focus of this chapter. We go on to discuss some of the late-stage transitions women may experience, including grown children returning home and leaving paid work permanently. Each of these experiences presents women with new choices as they shape the final chapters of their work/life paths.

A quick note for new working mothers: although it may be difficult to envision this later-stage life phase, we encourage you to read through this chapter. The pressure that early-stage working mothers experience around progressing in their careers while responding to the demands of raising young children may be somewhat alleviated by remembering that working mothers are working longer and experiencing great joy in their work and lives at this later stage. It can be helpful to know that Vera Wang, the famous designer, did not start her career as a fashion designer until she was forty. Viola Davis did not land her first movie role until she was forty-three; by forty-nine, she became a household name for her role in ABC's *How to Get Away with Murder* and her award-winning role in the movie *The Help*. Pleasant Rowland launched the American Girl doll company when she was forty-five; twelve years later, she sold it to Mattel for $700 million. Careers are likely to extend well into a woman's sixties and seventies. Knowing this may help new working mothers feel more confident about pacing and structuring their careers to fit their circumstances. So read away—even while nursing a new baby!

WORKING MOTHERS AND MIDLIFE

Midlife is typically defined as the years from forty-five to sixty-five, sandwiched between early adulthood and older age.[5] For most working mothers, two simultaneous shifts are happening at this life stage. From an aging perspective, working mothers are experiencing all of the normal cognitive, emotional, and physical shifts that accompany this life stage. From a family perspective, they are also adjusting to a shift in identity as their children leave home. We discuss both of these shifts and what they mean for working mothers' paths.

From an aging perspective, midlife is neither the onset of the decline of life nor a period of magical transformation where individuals leave behind their old lives and adopt an entirely new identity.[6] For most women, midlife is a time when one is cognizant of one's time horizon. This can lead a working mother to reflect on her past life experiences and how they inform her future choices. For women, midlife reflections can result in deeper awareness of their values and in letting go of constraining societal norms about life as well as critical self-evaluations. As Nadine shared,

I always had my work and my family to think about, but as I am getting older, I am thinking about work/life differently. Now I am asking the question, "What do I want to do to have a full and satisfying life?"

Women in midlife may find themselves clarifying their values and goals and becoming inspired as they consider this life stage. Women may also find the choices they are making at this stage are driven by questions about how they want to contribute or how they want to learn, rather than by what they have not yet accomplished.[6] For many working mothers, the freedom and reflective aspects of midlife can lead to a positive, powerful affirmation of their future.[7] For these reasons, women are less depressed, less anxious, and even less suicidal in midlife than at any other life stage.[8]

The generative nature of midlife applies in particular for working women, whose midlife experience often differs significantly from women who are not in the paid workforce. Working women often experience greater physical and mental well-being during midlife than women who have not been in paid work.[3] Working women also often experience midlife as a time when their confidence and assertiveness increase, along with their feelings of competence and self-efficacy.[9] Unlike men, whose midlife experience may lead to radical shifts in work and home, for women midlife often results in more incremental changes.[10] All of this is good news for working mothers.

Beyond the natural shift of aging, working mothers may also be experiencing the transition of their children leaving home (although for some working mothers, this transition may align more with the end of the midlife phase). Children leaving home is a process that happens over time depending on family size, age spread of children, and children's developmental needs. While separating from parents is a natural life cycle change, it too is surrounded by complex psychosocial and emotional dynamics. This process frequently is referred to as the "empty nest period." This term arose in the 1960s to refer to the feelings of stress, anxiety, and depression that mothers are assumed to experience when children leave home.[11] The negativity evoked by this term perpetuates the myth that women's lives are defined primarily by their relationship with their children. The assumption is that mothers will be emotionally distraught and lost when their children begin the process of leaving home. From our perspective, "empty nest" becomes one more societal myth of motherhood that can lead working mothers to feel guilty if their reactions do not align with these expectations. As Gena explained,

> When my son left for college, everyone kept saying, "Oh, you must really miss him." I didn't feel right saying, no, I didn't really miss him. He was thriving at college, and we talked or texted every day. I loved my new freedom, but I couldn't really say that.

Many women, particularly working mothers, respond as Gena did when their children leave home. While this parenting phase is always a transition for working mothers, it is not always, or solely, the depressive state that is implied by the term *empty nest*.

Similar to the arrival of a child, the leaving-home process can lead to changes in how a working mother defines herself and her life. At the point when children begin to leave home, a working mother's identity as a mother is well established and ingrained in her understanding of who she is. She has built her pathway of how to combine being a professional and being a mother. Being a mother is also a role from which women tend to derive satisfaction and meaning. As children begin to leave home, this role changes. Motherhood no longer occupies the same amount of physical and mental time, and a working mother may find it is no longer as central to her self-definition.[12] This role change may also lead to transitions in her social and community relationships. Ingrid explained,

> In high school, my children had always been involved with the theater program, so I participated with all the productions. Everyone knew me as their mom. When my youngest graduated, I lost those connections and the volunteer work that went along with it. At first, that was very hard.

As one's role as a mother and the related social connections shift, it can trigger feelings of loss and sadness that extend beyond the loss of the child at home. At the same time, this change in identity can be positive as it provides working mothers with the psychological and emotional freedom to engage with work differently or to explore other interests in a more significant way.[12]

Children leaving home also alters the daily responsibilities and pace of life. With fewer people in a house, there are fewer activities to manage, fewer competing demands to negotiate, and far fewer household chores. This decrease in household responsibilities and strains can lead to a reduction in the daily stresses and interruptions to manage and issues to be negotiated with one's partner. All of this positively affects a working mother's well-being.[13] These shifts also enable a working mother to pursue her career, or other interests, in a more significant way.

Reflecting and Recalibrating at Midlife

The combination of aging and shifting home responsibilities often prompts mothers to engage in an internal recalibration process as they reexamine their current approach to work and career.[10] Working mothers now have the space and flexibility to attend to their interests, motives, and passions with regards to work rather than consider work relative to their families' demands and interests. For example, at first Joan was devastated when her daughter left for college. She was older when she had her daughter, and being a mother was central to her identity. While she worked full time, she structured work around her family's needs. When her daughter left home, it took time to recreate her life and her identity. Eventually, she became more engaged in her art (her career) and added a new dimension to her work—teaching. To fill the sense of loss, Joan sought new employment opportunities that enabled her to grow. With increased clarity about their own wants and needs, working mothers may feel empowered to adjust their work so that they continue to find meaning in this next chapter of work and family life.[10]

For some working mothers, this recalibration process leads to decisions that are continuous with their prior work experiences. For example, some women may adjust their lives by making incremental shifts at work. Joan's story from the previous paragraph is an example of this. As her life changed after her daughter left home, she continued on the same career path, just adding new responsibilities to create greater meaning for herself at work. Other working mothers may find themselves choosing to become more deeply engaged at work and pursue new opportunities that can enable them to advance further in their careers. As Miriam explained,

> I could stay late and take on more intense projects without feeling the guilt. I became more focused on my career goals and was able to identify ways to achieve these aims without feeling pressure because of the kids.

During midlife, working mothers may find themselves wanting to accept more significant leadership roles or new responsibilities that require more time and psychological energy. Using the time and energy that is unleashed by the shifts at home is one way of creating a new work/life chapter that is meaningful and purposeful.

Other women find that while they are still engaged and active at work, they want to use this space for themselves. As Heather explained,

> After my children went off to college, I didn't change employers. I worked at the same place for twenty years and liked the stability that gave me. I didn't want to move into something where I had to learn new things or take on additional responsibilities. I wanted balance and time for me and some of the interests I had put on hold. Now, I am in the best physical shape EVER, and I get to ride horses every morning as opposed to only on the weekends. I'm traveling as much as I can—accompanying my husband on business trips, weekends away with girlfriends, and I went on my own to Berlin.

After navigating work and family for so many years, some women decide that they want to use the next phase of life to explore their non-work interests further. Of course, they must have the financial resources to make these choices. Neither Heather nor Wendy, from our opening story, stopped working. They both continued to work full time; they simply used their non-work time to further explore personal interests in a way that they could not when they were involved in hands-on daily parenting.

A third approach to this reflection and recalibration process is to become more deeply engaged in community work. Most working mothers tend to be involved in community work that directly relates to the lives of their children. At this new stage, women may start to think about issues that are broader and more meaningful to them such as poverty, hunger, or social justice. Bettina's story is an example of this type of shift. After focusing solely on her work to ensure that she and her family were financially secure, Bettina wanted to turn her attention to helping others after her children left home. Because of her childhood experiences with food insecurity, Bettina became deeply involved with her local food bank, volunteering weekly and eventually serving on the board. Many working mothers find that these experiences bring meaning to their lives in a way that is different from being a parent or a professional. In explaining why she joined a nonprofit board, Lucia shared,

> I started looking for a way that I can give back that really takes advantage of my other skills.

Rather than focusing on strengthening their identity and engagement at work to create meaning in midlife, these women find meaning by expanding their identities to pursue new interests and new affiliations.

While there is no "right" way to recalibrate during this phase, there are actions women can take to more effectively manage these life changes rather than be managed by them. Working mothers may find it helpful to pay attention to the stereotypes of the midlife crisis and the empty nest syndrome and remember that these are, in fact, myths that can diminish the validity of their own experiences. Gena's quote earlier in this chapter is a perfect example of how disconnecting your own midlife parenting experiences from societal myths about desperately missing one's children when they leave home can reduce feelings of guilt and empower you to be confident about your own decisions.

Working mothers may also want to begin to think about and prepare for midlife and their children leaving before the time comes. Preparing for this phase helps avoid surprises and mitigates feelings of loss. Working mothers may want to consider what they find meaningful about their work and their lives and what adjustments they ought to make to better center career and life on what is most meaningful to them. Rarely will this thinking and reflecting lead women to quit their jobs and completely transform their lives, but it may inspire a woman to consider how she may want to change her work and life to fill the newly available space. By asking these questions before reaching midlife, working mothers can begin to think about what learning opportunities to pursue or lifestyle changes to initiate to set these shifts in motion.

Changing Family Relationships

During midlife, some women find that their relationships with their spouse or partner, their parents, and their children change dramatically. As daily connections with children lessen, it allows for other relationships to strengthen. For married working mothers, empty nesting may become a period of marital renewal. Couples may travel more together and find ways to reconnect now that time is not spent negotiating pickups, drop-offs, and endless lists of daily household management tasks. Reconnecting with your partner after years of managing work and family may require effort.

After years of conversing about household logistics, some couples may wonder what they will talk about or whether they still have things in common. Rebuilding and creating these connections may require directed effort. Partners may want to invite one another to become involved in activities they might have pursued individually when the children were home. Other couples jointly pursue interests that they did not have time for previously. Wendy explained that when her children left for college, she and her husband reconnected by traveling to places they had not been to because of the previous time and economic priority of raising their family. As she said,

> I don't regret what we did then, but I am now really enjoying the time we have together.

The goal for a couple at this stage is to find ways to reconnect during this transition.

As children leave home, working mothers may also chose to focus more on extended family relationships. Working mothers may use their time to connect more with their parents, their in-laws, or other extended family members while these relatives are still healthy. In more challenging situations, working mothers may find that new caretaking responsibilities emerge as parents age and face health crises, a topic we will discuss in greater depth in Chapter 8. Jody's parents and in-laws all faced health crises just after her youngest son left for college. In less than a year, three of the four parents died. While this was a sad, draining period, Jody was grateful she had the extra time to help; she realized this might not have been possible if her son was still at home. Taking the time to care for her dying parents also shifted her perspective on midlife. As she said,

> I realized the importance of putting family first. Their deaths brought clarity to what my priorities were going forward.

Shifts in family relationships can also lead to changes in how working mothers construct this work/life chapter.

Finally, relationships with children can also change during this time. Clare explained,

> As your kids get older, you worry about different things—sex, drugs, and alcohol. When they head off to college, there is another set of concerns, and beyond that, the worries are about wanting them to have happy and fulfilled lives. My kids are now married, and my

daughter is expecting her first child. These relationships morph and change. Some women may feel as though their job is done, and they are not needed anymore, which is a difficult adjustment. However, many mothers come to realize they are still needed, but in a different way. The role shifts to one that is more peer-like in nature.

Clare's story reflects the idea that when your children are in adolescence, you are often fired as a parent. Your goal is to be rehired as a coach as your child moves into adulthood. Navigating this new parent–adult child relationship is not always easy and requires knowing how much guidance is appropriate without overstepping boundaries. Madeline Levine, the acclaimed clinician and author, advocates that to parent grown children well, parents want to begin the separation process before their children leave. She suggests, "We must learn to be quieter, to give fewer answers, and to ask more questions."[8] In other words, a working mother needs to shift to a coaching relationship with her teens to ensure this trend continues as they grow and establish their own lives.

A particularly challenging issue working mothers may have with their adult children is how to support them as they build their own work/ life paths. It is not uncommon for working mothers, particularly those with daughters, to meddle in their children's work and family decisions. Whether it be choices around staying in the workforce or taking time off, taking an extended parental leave or not, or how to manage childcare, it can be difficult to see an adult child construct a work/life path that is radically different from one's own. While they can guide and provide perspective, working mothers need to let their grown children construct their own paths, just as they did. Clarice explained how she navigated this tension:

I have fascinating and enjoyable conversations with my daughter all the time about work and family. I can provide useful insights into her career. I think it helps that she and her brother have a mother who works and is very supportive of their careers and their decisions, even when they are different from mine.

ADULT CHILDREN RETURNING HOME

Working mothers may also find that midlife includes another transition that prior generations did not contend with: the return of adult children. For previous generations, a stigma existed regarding grown children who had not succeeded in becoming fully independent, living on their own, and making their own way in the world. However, a less secure job market, an increase in housing costs, unprecedented levels of student debt, and delays in marriage have resulted in more adult children choosing to live at home for extended periods of time. Many adult children are making this choice in order to save money, attend graduate school, and pave the way for a more stable and secure future.[14] In fact, the number of young adults living at home is at an all-time high since 1950: close to 40% of young adults between the ages of eighteen and thirty-four are expected to live at home for an extended period at some point.[15]

While not akin to the responsibilities that arise with children under the age of eighteen, having an adult child at home does introduce new demands on a working mother. At the most basic level, there are logistical issues of having another person in the house who has a unique schedule, needs, and laundry. Depending on where adult children are in their career, they may require significant financial and emotional support. A working mother may feel resentment, anger, and sadness due to the impact that these new pressures have on the midlife work/life path she has so carefully constructed. This, in turn, may spawn old feelings of guilt and regret. Simultaneously, working mothers may feel that their child's return home is a sign of their failure as a mother, and in particular that their work is partially to blame for their child's current situation.[16]

On the flip side, having adult children back at home can be rewarding. Spending time with adult children is very different than spending time with young children. A new connection can emerge, and support is as likely to flow from child to parent as it is from parent to child. An adult child at home can provide working mothers with the opportunity to form a different relationship in which women are learning from their child about work, life, and career. Having an adult child at home can also provide working mothers with instrumental support, as there is another person to cook meals and take on household responsibilities.

To ensure that having an adult child at home is a positive experience for both parents and children, working mothers and their partners need to create some ground rules for this new arrangement. One of the most important of these rules pertains to the financial relationship. Some parents choose to charge an adult child rent; according to many financial advisors and psychologists, this is a must.[17] Obviously, paying rent may or may not be an option given an adult child's financial circumstances. At the same time, paying some rent can help the adult child feel more independent and gain confidence in his or her ability to reestablish a more independent life. If paying rent is not an option, parents may consider charging rent on a sliding scale, bartering for household chores they might have previously outsourced, or even charging rent that gets banked into a savings account to facilitate the adult child moving out.

Parents also need to consider the financial impact on themselves of having an adult child at home. Financial advisors estimate that an adult child at home can cost between $8,000 to $18,000 a year, depending on how much parents pay for incidentals.[17] A working mother who previously felt empowered to make work choices around her own needs and desires may find herself resentful if she must change these plans to adjust to the new financial pressures caused by her adult child. Working mothers need to decide how much fiscal responsibility they can and want to take on for this adult child, given where they are in their own lives and careers.

Beyond responding to the change in financial demands, working mothers will also want to think about how an adult child at home may impact daily life. As was discussed in the previous section, as children leave home the number of family chores diminishes, as does the pressure of needing to be physically at home. Many women may have filled this space by adjusting their personal and professional lives. When adult children return home, it creates new stresses, as there is no longer space for their demands. Working mothers can find themselves quickly slipping into old patterns of taking on household responsibilities for this adult child or feeling an instinctive pressure to be home. To address these issues, you will want to have explicit discussions about who is responsible for what and how household responsibilities can be shared between parents and children. For example, parents and children should decide how they will approach laundry, food shopping, cooking, and cleaning. What household responsibilities can the adult child take on? While nightly dinner might have been important in the teenage years, maybe biweekly dinners are more appropriate now. Discussing these issues will help to ensure that this returning adult child enriches, rather than depletes, your current work/life path.

PHASING OUT OF PAID WORK

For all working mothers, there will come a time to step out of full-time employment. Exactly when this occurs or what it looks like will vary depending on financial circumstances, family events, and the interests of each woman. Indeed, retirement today does not resemble the retirement of past generations. The traditional view of retirement as a one-time exit from full-time employment to full-time leisure is replaced by the idea of a third, or encore, stage. During the third stage, individuals continue to be engaged in meaningful activities made possible by improved heath and aging. This stage is more open and fluid as people use the shift away from full-time paid work to pursue educational interests, community engage-ment, or more informal and temporary paid work with organizations.[18] Short-term, project-based work enables women to have more control over when, where, and how much they work, which allow them to explore other interests in a more significant way. We explore the topic of project-based work in more depth in Chapter 7. While many working mothers choose when to move into this third stage, some find themselves pushed into it as their organizations manage difficult economic times through layoffs, buyouts, and incentivized retirement packages.[19]

Just as working mothers must contend with shifts in their identity as a mother when their children leave home, they now have to make sense of shifts in their professional identity when they leave paid work. Working mothers who have established their identity based in part on their work and career may find it difficult to shed this identity. Additionally, the identity of being a retiree may be unappealing and may not aptly describe the level of engagement and meaning working mothers are creating through either short-term work, community involvement, or commitment to their families. Leaving paid work also changes the daily pace of life, as working mothers suddenly find they have less structure and more free time. Working mothers who lived by carefully defined routines to effectively manage work and home demands may find the lack of structure paralyzing rather than freeing. Finally, working mothers with life partners also are considering the shifting work relationship of that partner, which may or may not be in harmony with their own. Not surprisingly, in heterosexual couples, working mothers will often mold their retirement plans to those of their husbands.[20]

Working mothers frequently turn to public service and community engagement to rebuild their professional identity after leaving paid work. Having developed particular competencies and skills through a lifetime of paid work, working mothers may thrive on the opportunity to use these skills to support a nonprofit that connects to their passions. Whether it be through nonprofit board work or direct volunteering, nonprofit service enables working mothers to continue to "work," but in a way that fits their new life and provides a different type of meaning. Strongly identifying with volunteer work and a nonprofit organization can help women reestablish meaning in their lives and contribute to feelings of self-worth—and, of course, benefit the community.[21] It is not surprising that women over sixty-five spend an average of two hours a day engaged in some form of unpaid work in the community.[19]

While full-time work may be left behind during the third phase, children are often not. Working mothers may decide to use their newfound freedom, and honed skills, to support their children and families in new ways. Some women find meaning by assuming caretaking responsibilities for their grandchildren. Upon retiring from her project accounting position, Olivia, who had raised her son on her own, decided to spend one day a week taking care of her granddaughter. Her son and daughter-in-law both worked. By taking care of her granddaughter, she could help ease the financial and emotional burden of childcare for her children. As she said,

That one day a week started as a gift to them, but it is a gift to me. I get to do what I couldn't as a single working mother, and I still have plenty of time for me.

Julia, who had retired from her senior operations position, moved closer to her daughter and son-in-law to help them with their farming business. She used her skills to help them build a marketing strategy and better manage the operations and finances of selling their produce at local farmers markets and to local chefs. Whether it be through caretaking or professional skills, working mothers can find it satisfying to use their talents to support their adult children further as they establish their work/ life paths.

FINDING ORGANIZATIONAL SUPPORT FOR LATE-STAGE WORKING MOTHERS

Let's begin with a bit of harsh reality. Many older women are forced out of the workforce by younger workers who do not know how to "manage up" (i.e., doing what it takes to manage your manager by making his or her job easier).[22] Older women report receiving harsher performance reviews with unrealistic expectations placed upon them. Many older women are also passed over for leadership opportunities, citing the double burden of gender and age-related bias. Even with a long career history, older women tend to earn less, are given low-level job responsibilities, and tend to have weak prospects for upward career mobility. This burden is carried more heavily by women who try to reenter the workforce after their children go to college. Just as women want to revitalize their careers, they may be hindered by a lack of acceptance of aging women in the workplace. Researchers have found that age discrimination of women is worse than men with regards to recruitment and selection.[23] We surmise that aging women may face greater discrimination due to the scrutiny of their physical appearance. You may find yourself needing to guard against such biases in the workplace, and you may also find yourself needing to educate others on what these stages of life represent and how they may be affecting you at work.

It's important to be aware of what organizations do offer to working mothers at this stage in life. Some organizations offer programs and learning opportunities to explicitly reflect on the transition that later-stage working mothers are experiencing and begin to set in motion a plan for their next phase of life. These programs can help women clarify what they want from their careers and establish the building blocks they need to achieve these goals. In doing so, some women may identify new skills they need to learn, internal training they want to take advantage of, or relationships they need to build to achieve what they desire in their careers.

Retention of older workers has become a critical issue for many employers. Referred to as the "brain drain," the loss of the baby boomer generation is a serious issue for many organizations. In California alone, more than half of all managers (220,000 employees) working for the state government are nearing retirement age.[24] Many older working mothers want to stay employed; they just may want greater flexibility in where, when, and/or how much they work. Some organizations are creating un-usually creative flexible work arrangements to retain older workers. For example, CVS Caremark offers older workers a "snowbird" option so that they can work in the warmer states in the winter if they are from the north. Other organizations may offer older workers unpaid sabbaticals so they can pursue outside interests while continuing to work. Still other organi-zations are offering health and wellness programs and training to upgrade skills to retain late-stage working mothers.[25]

In the chapters that follow, we move away from focusing on par-enting stages to closely examine other types of transitions and deci-sion points women may experience throughout their lives as working mothers. We focus on the ways work or family circumstances can create new transitions. Some of these circumstances include job and career flexibility, life interruptions, and the role of men in working mothers' lives. While we have touched upon some of these issues in the first half of the book, we now take a deep dive into exploring how working mothers construct their work/life paths around expected and unexpected transitions.

CHAPTER TAKEAWAYS

1. Making the transition into parenting adult children can open up new opportunities for both career and personal growth as home demands lighten and relationship dynamics shift.

2. The "empty nest syndrome" and "midlife crisis" stereotypes perpetuated in today's society should be taken with a grain of salt. The new freedoms and space in working mothers' lives that come along with children leaving home can result in emotionally challenging but ultimately positive experiences and can allow women to recalibrate their personal and professional goals.

3. Phasing out of paid work can be a highly rewarding experience, even for working women whose identities were heavily based on their careers. Transitioning into project-based, part-time, or more community-focused work, such as in the nonprofit sector, can offer enriching and rewarding work opportunities that also allow women the time and space to pursue personal passions and interests.

REFERENCES

1. Ryff, C., & Seltzer, M. (Eds.) (1996). *The parental experience in midlife*. Chicago, IL: University of Chicago Press.
2. Kochanek, K. D., Murphy, S. L., Xu, J., & Tejada-Vera, B. (2016). Deaths: Final data for 2014. *National Vital Statistics Reports, 65*(4), 1.
3. Baruch, G. K., & Barnett, R. C. (1986). Role quality, multiple role involvement, and psychological well-being in midlife women. *Journal of Personality and Social Psychology, 51*(3), 578–585.

4. Miller, C. C. (2017, February 11). More women in their 60s and 70s are having "way too much fun" to retire. *New York Times*. Retrieved from https://www.nytimes.com/2017/02/11/upshot/more-women-in-their-60s-and-70s-are-having-way-too-much-fun-to-retire.html.

5. Whitbourne, S. K., & Willis, S. L. (Eds.) (2014). *The baby boomers grow up: Contemporary perspectives on midlife*. London, UK: Psychology Press.

6. Strenger, C., & Ruttenberg, A. (2008). The existential necessity of midlife change. *Harvard Business Review, 86*(2), 82.

7. Howell, L. C., & Beth, A. (2002). Midlife myths and realities: Women reflect on their experiences. *Journal of Women & Aging, 14*(3-4), 189–204.

8. Levine, M. (2013, May 11). After the children have grown. *New York Times*. Retrieved from https://www.nytimes.com/2013/05/12/opinion/sunday/after-the-children-have-grown.html.

9. Clark-Plaskie, M., & Lachman, M. E. (1999). The sense of control in midlife. In S. L. Willis & J. B. Reid (Eds.), *Life in the middle: Psychological and social development in middle age* (pp. 181–208). San Diego, CA: Academic Press.

10. Gordon, J. R., Beatty, J. E., & Whelan-Berry, K. S. (2002). The midlife transition of professional women with children. *Women in Management Review, 17*(7), 328–341.

11. Deykin, E. Y., Jacobson, S., Klerman, G., & Solomon, M. (1966). The empty nest: Psychosocial aspects of conflict between depressed women and their grown children. *American Journal of Psychiatry, 122*(12), 1422.

12. Thorn, E. K. (2012). *Mothers' transitions to the empty nest phase*. University of Maryland, College Park. ProQuest Dissertations and Theses, 140. Retrieved from http://search.proquest.com/docview/1314825257?accountid=14872.

13. Dennerstein, L., Dudley, E., & Guthrie, J. (2002). Empty nest or revolving door? A prospective study of women's quality of life in midlife during the phase of children leaving and re-entering the home. *Psychological Medicine, 32*(3), 545–550.

14. Clay, R. A. (2003). Researchers replace midlife myths with facts. *Monitor on Psychology, 34*(4), 36–38.

15. Parker, K. (2012). *The boomerang generation: Feeling OK about living with Mom and Dad*. Pew Research Center. Retrieved from http://www.pewsocialtrends.org/2012/03/15/the-boomerang-generation/

16. Umberson, D., Pudrovska, T., & Reczek, C. (2010). Parenthood, childlessness, and well-being: A life course perspective. *Journal of Marriage and Family, 72*(3), 612–629.

17. Grind, K. (2013, May 3). Mother, can you spare a room? *Wall Street Journal*. Retrieved from https://www.wsj.com/articles/SB10001424127887323699704578326583020869940.

18. James, J., & Wink, P. (2007). Introduction: The third age: A rationale for research. In J. James & P Wink (Eds.), *The crown of life: Dynamics of the early postretirement period* (pp. xix–xxxii). New York, NY: Springer Publishing Company.

19. Moen, P., & Flood, S. (2013). Limited engagements? Women's and men's work/volunteer time in the encore life course stage [Abstract]. *Social Problems, 60*(2), 206.

20. Moen, P., Sweet, S., & Swisher, R. (2005). Embedded career clocks: The case of retirement planning. *Advances in Life Course Research, 9*, 237–265.

21. Warburton, J., & McLaughlin, D. (2006). Doing it from your heart: The role of older women as informal volunteers. *Journal of Women & Aging, 18*(2), 55–72.

22. Rikleen, L. S. (2016, March 10). Older women are being forced out of the workforce. *Harvard Business Review.* Retrieved from https://hbr.org/2016/03/older-women-are-being-forced-out-of-the-workforce.

23. Neumark, D., Burn, I., & Button, P. (2015). *Is it harder for older workers to find jobs? New and improved evidence from a field experiment.* National Bureau of Economic Research Working Paper No. 21669. Retrieved from https://www.nber.org/papers/w21669.

24. Wiltz, T. (2016). *Beating the brain drain: States focus on retaining older workers.* Pew Charitable Trusts. Retrieved from https://www.pewtrusts.org/en/research-and-analysis/blogs/stateline/2016/05/11/beating-the-brain-drain-states-focus-on-retaining-older-workers.

25. Greenhouse, S. (2014, May 14). The age premium: Retaining older workers. *New York Times.* Retrieved from https://www.nytimes.com/2014/05/15/business/retirementspecial/the-age-premium-retaining-older-workers.html.

PART TWO

The Unexpected Path

6

Making Workplace Flexibility Work

Over the twenty-one years I have been with this company, I have negotiated several different flexible work arrangements to balance out my changing home situation. The first was in 1990 when I had my son. While no one was talking about flexibility then, I negotiated returning to work part-time at twenty-five hours a week. Years later, as the pressure at home eased up and my son transitioned to school, I asked to return to full-time work but only work four days a week. At that time, they had just introduced a flexible schedule policy, so I was able to fill my work hours in a way that worked for me, my role, and my department. More recently, when I injured my back and needed to be on bed rest and reduce my driving time, I took only a few weeks off and was able to return to work full-time by working from home for six months. There was no way I could have managed the 1.5-hour drive, so without the work-from-home option I would have had to take an extended leave. Frankly, my manager was thrilled to see me work from home. I have been with this company a long time and they really value what I do, so past performance, loyalty, and commitment all come into play in my situation. However, the company and my manager have also made it easy for me to adjust my work arrangement, as they are very flexible and therefore not much negotiation is required when I need a change. When I talk to friends in other companies, I realize how lucky I am to have these arrangements.

—JADE, *accounting and payroll*

Workplace flexibility is a broad term that refers to any work arrangement where an employee has some ability to adapt when, where, and/or how much he or she works. The desire for greater workplace flexibility is not a new topic, nor is it one restricted to working mothers. In the United States, nearly 80% of workers reported they would like more access to workplace flexibility, and 61% would even prefer to formally reduce their work hours.[1] While we have mentioned workplace flexibility in previous chapters, this topic is so important to working mothers' paths that it warrants a more focused discussion.

Workplace flexibility is a broad topic in part because working mothers' flexibility requirements often differ greatly depending on their financial resources, community and family support, and children's ages and stages. Some working mothers want to adjust their work hours or work from home on a permanent basis. Others want a more ad hoc arrangement, so they can be available to stay home with a sick child, attend a school event, or manage a household issue. Regardless of the type of flexibility a working mother desires, what is consistent is the benefits flexible work can have for a working mother. Workplace flexibility can reduce a working mother's feelings of stress, burnout, and work/family conflict.[1] Working mothers who have greater access to workplace flexibility are more engaged at work, more satisfied, and more productive. This in turn benefits the organization, as it leads to lower absenteeism and lower turnover.[2]

The good news is that more and more organizations are introducing formal policies regarding workplace flexibility. Organizations recognize that workplace flexibility is critical to their ability to attract and retain top talent, particularly the talent of working mothers.[3] Recent studies suggest that nearly 80% of organizations allow employees some flexibility.[4] Job placement companies such as Werk.com have even emerged to assist organizations in recruiting working mothers for flexible positions.

Despite these advances in organizational policy, it still can be difficult for a working mother to gain access to the flexibility she needs. Some jobs cannot be easily adjusted to accommodate greater flexibility. Sometimes the type of flexibility the organization supports doesn't match a working mother's needs. Most frequently, we hear from working mothers that their managers won't approve a flexible work arrangement even if the organization has a corresponding policy. For these reasons, working mothers need to better understand the different types of workplace flexibility and learn to negotiate for the flexibility they desire.

This chapter helps women develop a more comprehensive understanding of workplace flexibility. We start with an overview of the different types of flexibility and some of the benefits and challenges women have experienced with these varied work arrangements. We go on to introduce some of the unforeseen challenges women will need to manage if they take advantage of a flexible work arrangement. Finally, we discuss strategies for effectively negotiating workplace flexibility so that you don't trade flexibility for compensation.

SO WHAT IS FLEXIBLE WORK REALLY?

With a formal flexible work arrangement, a working mother has negotiated an agreement with her manager or employer that gives her the flexibility she desires. Once a flexible work arrangement is created, it becomes a new standard schedule for a working mother. To change that schedule typically requires another negotiation. As Bea explained,

> In the past ten years, I've worked with two Fortune 100 companies and have negotiated three separate, distinct flexible work arrangements.

For some working mothers, adapting and renegotiating flexibility as their family shifts becomes a standard component of their work/life path. In the following, we discuss three types of formal flexible work arrangements, as well as a more informal arrangement.

Flexible Schedule: Shifting When One Works

As we discussed extensively in Chapter 4, many working mothers find the standard American workweek is out of sync with their children's and family's schedules. With a flexible schedule, a working mother can adjust her work hours so that they are better aligned with her home and family responsibilities. This was the story Elise shared with us when she explained what drove her to negotiate a shift in her work hours:

> My daughter started kindergarten last fall. Her bus comes at 8:20 a.m., which made it almost impossible for me to arrive at work by 9 a.m., particularly when the bus was running late. I spoke with my manager about starting my day at 9:30 a.m. and shortening my lunch break. If she had denied my request, I would have had to find a job closer to home.

As a single mother, Elise could not have continued with her job if her manager hadn't accommodated her request. Once she began working the new schedule, Elise found the later start time eased the morning stress she had felt and enabled her to arrive at work on time, less tense, and more ready for her day. The schedule shift helped her be more present at work and at home.

Another way for working mothers to shift their hours is to move to a compressed workweek. In this arrangement, a working mother typically works a full workweek but over four ten-hour days rather than the standard five eight-hour days. Another common compressed workweek is to do ten days of work in nine days, leaving the tenth day free for home and family responsibilities. The compressed workweek has grown in popularity since the economic crisis in the 1980s, as this model helped create more jobs.[5] The advantage of this schedule is it provides working mothers with weekday hours to attend to family responsibilities. As Amber explained,

> I have two children now, ages five and one. When my oldest moved to kindergarten, it meant they were attending two different schools.

I now had two communities to stay connected to and more doctors and teacher meetings, since my son has special needs. I shifted my work schedule to four days a week. I could keep one weekday for all the appointments related to my children and take care of some household chores. I really needed time during the week, not the weekends, to do all this.

With a flexible schedule, Amber was able to minimize family interruptions to, and conflicts with, her work, which eased her anxiety about managing work and home. Scheduling work in this way can be particularly beneficial to women who like to maintain boundaries between work and home responsibilities.

These stories illustrate that slight shifts in a work schedule can have a dramatic impact on a working mother's optimism toward managing work and family demands. For Amber, shifting her schedule enabled her to stay connected with the parents and teachers at her children's schools, which strengthened her connections to her community. Being connected in this way increased her confidence that she could take care of her family and still succeed in her career.

Remote Work: Flexibility in Where One Works

Twenty years ago, we still assumed that most work had to occur in a traditional office environment. While there are still some jobs that require employees to be in their office, more and more work is being done wherever one can access the internet—be it at home, in a coffee shop, or in a co-location space. Working mothers are using these shifts to their advantage as they negotiate flexible work arrangements that enable them to work remotely. Some working mothers may want to work remotely one day a week. Others work remotely five days a week, perhaps even working for a company or office in a different geographic location.

One of the most frequent reasons working mothers give for a desire to work remotely is that it frees up valuable commuting hours that can then be used to attend to work and home responsibilities. Lydia was working as a consultant when she approached her manager about working remotely. She had a long commute and wanted to work remotely four days a week. She explained:

> 75% of my work is alone at a computer, on a conference call, or at a client site. I live 60 miles from the office, so the commute during high-traffic hours is one to two hours each way, depending on when I leave. I approached my manager to see if I could work from home four days a week when I wasn't at a client's site. I convinced him that working from home was no different than working at a client's site.

Added benefits of telecommuting include fewer workplace interruptions and better control over the workday. Without interruptions, remote workers are able to focus more and complete their work with a higher degree of quality and efficiency.[6] Working mothers may find their work productivity actually increases by working remotely, which enables them to feel more optimistic about managing work and family.

Finally, working remotely can also enable a working mother to be more available for children and home responsibilities. Janelle began working remotely when her company moved to another city. She and a number of other workers kept their jobs and just began to telecommute. At first Janelle missed the interaction with her colleagues, but as time went on she found that working remotely enabled her to be more productive with her time. She also began to use the time she had spent on lunches and breaks with colleagues to attend parent/teacher conferences or school functions. Being available for these activities increased the optimism she felt about integrating work and family.

Janelle's story is not unusual. In fact, because remote work often reduces feelings of work/family conflict and eliminates commuting time, remote workers often work as much as a half-day more per week without experiencing increased difficulties in managing work and home demands.[7]

Job Sharing and Part-Time Work

With remote work or flexible scheduling, a worker's job responsibilities and the general number of hours worked do not shift. Nor does a working mother's compensation. Some working mothers may find that they simply want to shift the balance between time at work and time at home. If a working mother has the financial security, she may decide she wants to keep working, just not full-time. Depending on the nature of the job, one's manager, the organization, and even one's negotiating skills, a part-time or job-share position may be a viable option.

With part-time work, a working mother reduces the overall number of hours a week she works, and her salary is adjusted accordingly. In the United States, a part-time worker refers to any employee who works fewer than thirty-five hours a week.[8] We use the term more broadly to refer to any individual who has chosen to work less than a full-time schedule and has adjusted his or her compensation and responsibilities accordingly. The reduction in compensation and job responsibilities is what makes part-time work distinct from other types of workplace flexibility. Some women may make this choice for a few years when their children are younger and their home demands are often the greatest. Other women may want to shift to part-time work as their children move into school in order to manage the tension between school and work schedules.

Pursuing a part-time work arrangement is rarely as easy as pursuing a flexible schedule or a remote work arrangement. Organizations may not be as supportive of part-time work, or they may not be aware of how to restructure a job to accommodate a part-time schedule. Working mothers have to creatively advocate for what they want. One of the authors did this when she negotiated moving her tenure-track faculty position from full-time to part-time when her three children were younger. Her university had a course buyout policy that was for faculty when they secured external grants. She used this established policy to negotiate a reduction in teaching responsibilities and a reduction in pay. Her tenure clock was stopped while she was on this reduced teaching load, but she remained a tenure-track faculty. While the financial reductions in salary were significant during this period, the shift enabled her to remain as a tenure-track faculty and thus not veer off course in her career. After four years, she returned to full-time and her tenure clock was resumed.

To make part-time work feasible, a working mother needs to be vigilant that her responsibilities are reduced to match the reduction in work hours. Too frequently, we hear stories of women continuing to do a full-time job but in part-time hours with part-time pay. As Nina explained,

> While I was allowed to reduce my job to three days a week, no one was ever hired to work the other two days. So now I do my full-time job in three days but am only paid for three days of work.

One of the ways to avoid the situation Nina found herself in is to explore whether a job-share situation is possible. With job sharing, two employees share the work responsibilities of a single full-time employee. For example, Emi entered into a job-share arrangement with a colleague, Sheila, the year after her twins were born. Emi and Sheila co-taught a third-grade class, with Emi teaching Mondays, Tuesdays, and Wednesdays and Sheila teaching Wednesdays, Thursdays, and Fridays. By both working on Wednesdays, they could coordinate and share updates on the class. The teachers and the parents of the children were very positive in how the job-share arrangement worked. Emi worked this way for ten years until she decided to return to full-time teaching. Similar to other forms of workplace flexibility, the benefits of these alternative work arrangements for working mothers are quite high. Working mothers who enter job-share arrangements are typically happier and more satisfied with their work/home situation, experience less stress, are more satisfied with their career overall, and are more likely to stay in the workforce.[9]

Ad Hoc Flexibility

Not all working mothers want, need, or can make a formal adjustment to their work arrangement. Some working mothers simply want the option to adjust when or where they work as the occasion arises. We refer to this type of workplace flexibility as *ad hoc flexibility*. Marla worked for a pharmaceutical company and did not have a job that enabled her to work remotely or make a permanent shift to her work schedule. As a scientist, her work was primarily done in the lab with other scientists. However, as her children got older, she became increasingly frustrated by her inability to be a part of their school lives. Marla finally spoke to her manager about creative ways to accommodate her home demands:

> I spoke to my manager about having the flexibility to sometimes take time out of the day to get my children to a doctor's appointment or to attend a school function. He completely supported me because he knows I will make sure I am getting my work done.

Having a little more flexibility in her schedule boosted Marla's optimism about managing work and family. It also had the added benefit of making her even more committed to her work and her organization.

Because ad hoc flexibility is frequently a one-off, unwritten agreement that is not supported across the organization, a working mother may be uncomfortable mentioning her situation to her colleagues. Some working mothers have told us they go so far as to leave their computers and lights on in their offices to make it seem as if they are there but in a meeting. Hiding one's family responsibilities can create new tensions for a working mother, as this behavior can ignite concerns about her ability to be both a good mom and a good professional. We encourage working mothers to think more about emulating the behavior of working fathers. Research on fathers suggests that men rarely negotiate formal flexibility; rather, they use it in a "stealth" fashion. When men need to leave work early or come in late, they simply do so. Some men may also fake the number of hours they work to hide the fact that they engage in flexible work arrangements.[10] We discuss this in more depth in Chapter 9 but mention it here because women need to realize they may not always need to be as transparent and formal in how they approach workplace flexibility.

BEING ATTENTIVE TO THE DARK SIDE
OF FLEXIBLE WORK

Unfortunately, there are hidden challenges to flexible work arrangements that working mothers need to attend to. Organizational norms and gendered assumptions create additional biases against flexible work that women will need to manage. Furthermore, flexible work blurs the boundaries between work and home and can generate additional stress for a working mother. Below we discuss some of the challenges that can arise, as well as explore ways that working mothers can successfully manage a flexible work arrangement.

Flexibility Bias and Other Flexible Work Challenges

We have already spoken extensively about gender biases that working mothers can face—specifically that being a good mother conflicts with being a good worker. Working mothers who make use of workplace flexibility frequently face a second bias, referred to as the *flexibility bias*. Here, the assumption working mothers must contend with is that by choosing a flexible work arrangement, they are putting their family priorities ahead of their career, and therefore they are not as driven or committed to their careers. The term *mommy track*, which emerged in the late 1980s, is indicative of this bias.

The flexibility bias has arisen in part because flexible work arrangements are positioned as a deviation from the traditional work arrangement of an "ideal worker." As we have previously discussed, workplaces privilege those who fit the model of an ideal worker and are unencumbered by caregiving responsibilities.[11] By moving to a flexible work arrangement, a working mother is unknowingly reinforcing the bias that she is incapable of fulfilling her work obligations because of her family demands.[12] Working mothers who move to a flexible work arrangement are typically judged as being less motivated and less committed and as having lower career aspirations in the context of their careers.[13]

These biases can create an added burden for a working mother as she forges her work/life path. Women who take advantage of workplace flexibility may find they are not being considered for promotions or challenging career opportunities. When Tina's children were in elementary school, she decided she wanted to work part-time in order to be more available for her children. She kept her same role, but her job responsibilities and salary were reduced slightly to match her 75% work schedule. At first Tina was thrilled with the new work/life path, but over time she found she was not receiving the same career opportunities as she had previously:

> I feel as though I have been passed over for advancement opportunities due to my arrangement. I also feel like my manager doesn't take my compensation seriously. He assumes I don't care anymore because I have chosen to sacrifice salary for more time at home.

Tina's story shows how quickly a manager's perceptions can shift even when nothing about the working mother's commitment has changed. Even when working mothers with flexible work arrangements are still perceived as high performers, they may be passed over for promotions; their managers may assume they are less likely to complain or push back because they already are being accommodated. Research has shown that working mothers who make use of flexible work arrangements suffer wage penalties, receive lower performance evaluations, and are devalued as professionals.[4]

Beyond career opportunities, some working mothers also find that moving to a flexible work arrangement can lead to shifts in important work relationships. When making use of workplace flexibility, women may simply be less available for more informal interactions with colleagues. Over time, working mothers may find their colleagues are less likely to solicit their feedback or involve them in strategic conversations about the direction of the department or the organization. Sylvia, who worked from home two days a week, found that over time she began to feel marginalized by her department. She was being left out of important conversations, and junior colleagues were not seeking her out for support and mentorship:

> No one said anything directly, but it was obvious that they perceived that my commitment to my work responsibilities and career was diminished.

These shifts in work relationships can lower a working mother's satisfaction with her job, jeopardize her ability to manage work/family demands, and increase her intention to leave a job or even opt out of work entirely.[14]

Finally, remote workers may face unique challenges. Some managers worry that working from home enables an employee to engage extensively in non-work activities during work hours. Some of these concerns are justified: we spoke with one manager who eliminated remote work in her division after a working mother conducted a confidential client call while at the playground with her children. Debates around remote work have intensified in recent years, particularly after Marissa Mayer, then the CEO of Yahoo, had a nursery constructed next to her office for her infant after banning remote work for all of Yahoo's employees; she believed it was adversely affecting the company's culture. More recently, companies such as Best Buy and IBM have also begun restricting remote work.

While this may feel a bit like gloom and doom, we also want to point out that not all working mothers experience these flexibility biases. Many women have shared experiences of continuing to advance in their careers when they would have otherwise had to quit their jobs. Women have shared stories about "being promoted and given more responsibility and staff over the years despite my four-day-a-week schedule" or finding that "my job continued to become more critical, and my responsibilities were greater and more unique." By being aware of these potential biases, working mothers can think about how to manage actively their work situations to ensure that they have a positive experience with a flexible work arrangement.

Countering Flexibility Bias and Overcoming Flexible
Work Challenges

To manage potential biases, women can start by inventorying their specific work context to evaluate the likelihood that they will experience these biases. The first thing a working mother will want to assess is her organization's culture and the extent to which her manager and colleagues seem open to flexible work arrangements. When organizations provide open and equal access for all employees to flexible work, working mothers do not experience as many negative career repercussions, nor do they feel like "second-class citizens" or "low-impact employees."[5] Job autonomy can also reduce the negative bias of workplace flexibility.[15] When working mothers have a high degree of autonomy, they have already established their work commitment and shown their manager that they do not need to be micromanaged to be highly productive. If you have proven you are capable of self-managing your work and your career, managing a flexible work arrangement will be no different.

Even if when an organization and job are not aligned toward workplace flexibility, there are still actions working mothers can take to manage against flexibility bias. Working mothers on a flexible arrangement often find it particularly useful to become more proactive and vocal as they ensure that their colleagues and manager are aware of their work successes and commitment. By visibly demonstrating their hard work, demonstrating initiative with new projects, and showing some flexibility to unexpected workplace demands, working mothers can demonstrate their ongoing commitment to their organizations.[15] Alisha, a project accountant, used these strategies to ensure that she was successful in working remotely a few days a week, even when two other women in her department had faltered. As she explained,

> I always demonstrated a very strong work ethic, even for the work I did not enjoy. This way my employer never had any concerns about what I was doing. He knew the job would get done regardless of where or when I worked.

By taking steps such as providing weekly updates, participating in meetings remotely, and making visible the additional work she was doing even when it wasn't asked of her, Alisha demonstrated her continued dedication to her work, her career, and her organization. These actions likely reduced the biases her manager may have had and enabled her to successfully transition to a remote work arrangement.

When working mothers feel they have a lot of power in their organizations, they may want to highlight how they are invoking workplace flexibility in order to support the importance of work/family integration. Women leaders may want to use this approach to try to shift an organizational culture to become more open to flexible work and work/family integration. Connie, a tenured professor, shared,

> I used to try to hide the fact that I am a mother and work remotely after 3 p.m. most days. But I don't do that anymore, and I feel a lot better about myself. Once I was tenured, I wanted to show others that I am still a good researcher and teacher while being the best mother I can be. Everyone needs balance in their lives. If I can pave the way for that and influence others in my organization, that is an accomplishment in and of itself.

Another approach women often take to manage flexibility bias is to consciously dedicate time to building workplace relationships. When working mothers move to a flexible work arrangement, they sometimes become hyper-focused on the work that needs to be done and on being productive. They consequently lose track of maintaining and managing relationships, which is part of their work. Working mothers often need to be more conscious of setting aside time to informally connect with colleagues over lunch or coffee breaks, or simply stopping by someone's office. When possible, it's important to schedule informal lunches or coffee dates to ensure you are building relationships with new colleagues and potential sponsors and mentors. Actively building relationships ensures that your colleagues and organization know that your commitment to your career and the organization are the same as anyone who is working a more traditional work arrangement.

To build their credibility when working flexibly, working mothers may also find it useful to shift their schedules if unexpected demands arise. For example, a client meeting may require a working mother to come to the office on a day she is normally off or on a day she normally works remotely. If you do find yourself shifting your flexible schedule, you want to make sure your organization and manager are aware of how you are responding to their needs. Kiki, who worked for a public relations agency, worked remotely two days a week. While her colleagues tended to be attentive in scheduling face-to-face meetings on the days she was in the office, they also knew that, if it was necessary, Kiki would come in on a day she was supposed to be working from home. By being flexible, Kiki found her colleagues were even more respectful of her schedule, as they understood how committed she was to her work. On the other hand, you also need to be watchful for excessive requests to adjust your flexible schedule, and you need to negotiate these with your manager or your coworkers. Tia explained,

> When I went to a four-day-a-week schedule, my boss told me the burden of making the arrangements work fell on me. She indicated that work still needed to move on through the proper timelines and client responsiveness, and that I shouldn't expect anyone in the team to make any accommodations because of my schedule. The result is I made myself too accessible, and my day off ended up being just another workday.

While Tia's manager was not particularly helpful, she might have advocated further with colleagues and clients to ensure that she was better able to protect her day off.

In general, women need to be careful that they are not so appreciative of a flexible work arrangement that they find themselves being taken advantage of. Sometimes women are so grateful for workplace flexibility that they do not advocate enough for themselves. As previously mentioned, stories abound of working mothers moving to a part-time schedule and part-time pay but continuing with full-time job responsibilities. Chelsie, a doctor, had negotiated with her clinic's partners that she would work part-time. When reviewing the monthly patient reports, she discovered she was seeing more patients per hour than her full-time counterparts. As a result, she was seeing on average the same number of patients per week as the full-time doctors. While she was grateful to be working part-time, she was not willing to do so and be unfairly compensated. She carefully documented patient records and used the information to show the inequity to the group's partners. Her work and compensation were adjusted.

Beyond work, women also need to attend to potential increases in home demands when they move to a flexible work arrangement, which can create new boundary issues. When a mother shifts to flexible work, heterosexual couples are likely to revert to a more traditional pattern of home responsibilities divided by gender.[16] These added home demands can negate the potential benefits of increased control and time for work and home responsibilities that result from flexible work arrangements.[17] One way to avoid taking on those added responsibilities is to work a flexible arrangement for a few months before making changes at home. You can "test" how the new arrangement is affecting your work/family path and then evaluate what additional changes you might want to make.

For example, when Linda moved to a four-day workweek, she planned to move her daughter to four days a week in daycare, but her partner encouraged her to leave her daughter in full-time daycare at least initially. Linda found that having some time without her daughter enabled her to take care of home responsibilities, run errands, and take care of her appointments. She would then pick her daughter up after a half-day of daycare. Linda was fortunate in that with a compressed workweek her salary had not shifted, and she and her partner had the financial bandwidth to keep her daughter in daycare. While your circumstances may be different, you still can follow Linda's lead and be careful not to overwhelm yourself with additional household and community responsibilities as you shift your work responsibilities.

IS FLEXIBLE WORK A GOOD CHOICE FOR YOU?

When considering the possibility of a flexible work arrangement, we encourage working mothers to think about who they are and how they like
to work as they determine if flexible work will help them on their work/
family path. Flexible work arrangements tend to work best for those who
are self-motivated and organized self-starters with strong interpersonal
skills. These traits are essential to successfully manage the complexity of
flexible work.[15] Working mothers also need to consider how much human
interaction they need during the day and if they may find certain types
of flexible work de-energizing. For example, working mothers who are
high on the extrovert dimension may find full-time remote work isolating.
If there is a possible misalignment between your work style and flexible
work, you will simply need to find creative ways to ensure that you are
successful when working flexibly. One working mother, Nomah, accepted
a new job for a small nonprofit in which she would work remotely full-
time. Since her entire organization was scattered across the country and all
worked from home, she was not worried about a flexibility bias. However,
as an extrovert she was worried about the lack of human interaction. To
combat potential feelings of isolation, she connected with other women
in her geographic area who were working remotely for other organizations. They would meet and work side by side in coffee shops, libraries,
and homes. This group helped Nomah be more productive as she worked
remotely. It also provided her with a support network she could rely upon
for backup child care, career advice, and work/life counsel.

Another factor to consider when pondering flexible work is how you
prefer to manage boundaries between work and home. The term *boundary
management* refers to how individuals manage the relationships between
work and home. Our work and home lives can be separated by physical,
time, and mental boundaries. Working mothers differ in how they prefer
to manage these boundaries, with some preferring to keep work and home
separate and others preferring to integrate their work and home life. For
instance, think about what happens if you need to call your child's teacher.
You are likely to prefer to handle it in one of two ways: (1) an integrated

approach, in which you make a phone call while at work, or (2) a segmented approach, in which you send an email at night and ask to schedule
a call for another evening or during your lunch hour. While jobs and organizations differ in the extent to which they enable a working mother to
be integrated or segmented, individuals also differ in how much integration or segmentation they want in their lives.

Shifting to flexible work can alter how work/family boundaries are
constructed and controlled, which can introduce new pressures. Working
from home, for instance, eliminates the physical separation between
work and home and can result in more frequent traversing across the two
domains.[18] For women who prefer greater separation between work and
family, this structure may not work. When Fatima began working from
home two days a week, she thought it would greatly reduce the pressure
she was feeling at work and at home: she could eliminate the long commute on those two days, which would provide her more time to manage
family and work demands. However, she soon found she had trouble
tuning out her family while working from home. While she had complete confidence in her nanny, she found she was constantly distracted
by the daily activities of her children. She eventually shifted to working
remotely just one day a week and worked in her local library rather than
at home.

Working remotely can also be challenging if you are trying to manage
your work around your children's schedule. Jennifer, a journalist, did not
hire childcare when her infant was born because she assumed she would
be able to structure her work time around her daughter's nap and feeding
schedule. However, she quickly learned infant schedules are anything but
predictable:

> While I would plan to structure my work time around Lucy's naps,
> if on any given day she decided not to take her nap or take a shorter-
> than-normal nap (this happened, like, ALL THE TIME!), my work
> day was shot, and my stress rose. It also affected my relationship
> and bonding with my daughter, because I would find myself mad
> at her and resentful that she wasn't sleeping. I thought I was doing

something wrong as a mother by having a baby who wasn't taking the nap she was "supposed" to be taking, and then I was upset with myself that I wasn't able to get this work done that I had planned on doing, and I knew I would have to do it that night after she went to bed when my husband came home. I was exhausted by the time evenings came around, so it was hard for me to work then.

Considering in advance what your home situation is and how flexible work can affect work/life boundaries can help a working mother ensure that the flexible arrangement she negotiates is one that matches how she works best.

NEGOTIATING A FLEXIBLE WORK ARRANGEMENT

In most organizations, decisions regarding flexible work arrangement requests are left to the discretion of managers. As a result, most working mothers will find they need to negotiate with their managers if they want to move to a flexible work arrangement.

Preparation is the foundation for these negotiations. These discussions will be easier to navigate when there are clear workplace policies, when there is support for these policies from managers, and when others have already negotiated similar arrangements.[19] Therefore, learning what policies are available and who has used them can help you better plan for how to approach your manager. Working mothers can determine this information by reviewing organizational policies and by talking to other working mothers who have made use of workplace flexibility. If your organization does not have formal flexible work policies, you will want to consider how the organization approaches work and family more broadly. Is there a culture in which employees are encouraged to have full lives outside of work and where employees feel comfortable talking about non-work passions? How do managers respond when employees need time for a doctor's appointment or to attend to a sick child? In organizations where the culture is more family friendly in general, women find they have an easier time negotiating a flexible work arrangement, even if there are no formal policies specifically focused on flexibility.[19] Other cultural norms can also be helpful in determining how receptive the organization will be to a flexible work arrangement. For example, if a manager or organization is focused more on work results than on when and where work is done, a flexible work arrangement may be easier to negotiate.[20]

As you prepare to negotiate a flexible work arrangement, you also want to be conscientious of the power you do or do not have in your organization. For instance, if the work you do is critical to the organization or if the work cannot easily be done by others, this may strengthen your bargaining power. Neela had been concerned about how open the small family foundation she worked for would be to her request to work remotely. At the same time, she knew that the foundation

> needed my knowledge and expertise. No one else knew how to perform my job, and I knew it would be difficult to train someone else to do it.

Even though there were no policies or precedents for flexible work, Neela was confident in approaching her manager because she knew her manager could not afford to lose her.

Other factors, such as having a reputation as a high performer, holding a longer organizational tenure, and being well respected, can also help in successfully negotiating a flexible work arrangement. Take, for example, Tania's experience negotiating her flexible work arrangement. Tania was a full-time working mother with three children under the age of six. She was working for an investment firm that was concerned about gender equity. The company had little to no family benefits beyond a basic maternity leave policy. Tania's job could be categorized as an extreme job that demanded a full commitment to the organization. However, Tania knew she had power because of the company's focus on gender equity as well as her outstanding performance. She strategically thought about this as she negotiated a new work arrangement:

Since I joined the firm, the assets under management in my area had grown from $200 million to $1.7 billion in three years. I was a super-star performer, so I had a lot of credibility built up. When I requested a flexible full-time schedule, it also made everyone reconsider my load and the fact that we needed to hire at least one additional analyst to take on some of my work. Thus, at the end of the whole process, not only was my flexible work schedule need met, but a recruiting process started for another analyst. Honestly, I expected that and was hoping for that outcome because I started the negotiations aware of our equal bargaining power.

Being aware of and advocating for your power can help you even when your organization's policies or culture do not overtly support workplace flexibility.

In these negotiations, you want to advocate for your position and for the flexibility you desire, but you also want to be attentive to the needs of your organization. In other words, the goal is to find a win–win solution that will give you the flexibility you need, support the productivity of your department and organization, and be perceived as fair by your coworkers. When a flexible work arrangement is negotiated that does not meet the needs of both the organization and the working mother, then the deal is likely unstable. Too frequently, working mothers have shared stories of how they negotiated a flexible work arrangement only to find a few months later that they are facing one of the following types of predicaments: (1) they are overloaded with work and are not being compensated for it; (2) their manager has decided the flexible work arrangement is not working and wants them to return to full-time work; or (3) they have a new manager who will not honor the agreement. More likely than not, these negotiations were incomplete and neither party thought through how the new arrangement would work in the context of the group and the organization. Thinking through implementation issues is necessary to ensure that a flexible work arrangement is sustainable for the long term.[19]

One way of ensuring that you achieve a win–win flexible work arrangement is to be open to different work arrangements. You may want to brainstorm various options in advance so you can be responsive to suggestions your manager proposes. Carola explained how she considered different options in her negotiation:

> Even though my company has a telework arrangement, it is still up to the first-level supervisor's discretion as to whether to support the arrangement, so, in advance, I thought about different options before my supervisor even got a chance to ask. Eventually, we settled on a situation where I requested to work one day a week from home temporarily. This worked so well that I moved to telecommuting two days a week, which is what I do now, but I needed to establish the trust with my supervisor before I could get what I wanted.

By contemplating the impact of different arrangements before and during the negotiation with her manager, Carola showed her commitment to making sure this new arrangement worked for her as well as for her department. Carola wanted to work remotely more than one day a week from the beginning, but she remained open to her manager's need to try out the arrangement before committing. A multiphase approach to implementing a flexible work arrangement can be a particularly useful strategy when negotiating with a reluctant manager. Making an arrangement temporary and setting a timeframe to evaluate it can be an ideal way to prove that a flexible work arrangement can work.

GARNERING SUPPORT FOR FLEXIBLE WORK ARRANGEMENTS

What should be clear by this point is that supporting workplace flexibility is one of the strongest actions an organization can take to attract and retain working mothers. Working mothers who have access to workplace flexibility willingly take on work that is outside of their normal jobs, and they have increased loyalty and increased job satisfaction. Job flexibility helps working mothers manage the stress of demanding jobs and thereby reduces negative outcomes such as missing work, being distracted, and making errors due to stress.[21] Although many firms have formal policies for job flexibility, such policies tend to be instituted at the manager's discretion.[22] Organizations and managers can be inconsistent and even unfair in granting access to workplace flexibility. As Adeline shared,

> My company has flexible work options, but the inside "joke" is we have them, you just can't use them. We've lost a lot of excellent working mothers in our department because of the inability to use these options. Our senior vice president just does not believe in them, so he doesn't support requests for any type of flexibility. However, there are a few "favorite" employees that have been granted flexible work arrangements. When a number of us approached human resources about this, we were told it's a case-by-case basis and it's up to the manager's discretion. Does that seem like having flexible work options?

Flexible work policies that are not supported by managers or are not applied fairly across the organization can be more harmful than if the organization has no policies at all. If organizations are truly going to support workplace flexibility, they need to move beyond simply having policies to considering how to evolve the organization, and the managers, so that the culture truly supports workplace flexibility and all employees have access and feel comfortable using it. Training and mentoring can be particularly helpful to educate managers. At present, only 46% of employers provide training for managers on workplace flexibility.[1] Just as organizations are increasingly conducting diversity and inclusion training to confront racial and gender biases, training and education regarding work structures may be important to confronting the flexibility bias.

To more fully embrace flexibility, you can encourage your organization to consider a flexibility audit. Organizations need to ensure that the flexible work policies they have in place match the needs of their employees, particularly those of their working mothers. For example, the managers of a consumer product company in New York City believed they were supportive of working mothers because the firm had a policy that allowed employees to work a flexible schedule. The organization was surprised to find that few working mothers made use of the policy. When the organization conducted an internal survey, they learned that what mattered most to employees, particularly working mothers, was a flexible work policy that supported remote work. The greatest work/family and economic stress came from women's hour-plus commute and expensive parking costs. By shifting the policy to include diverse types of flexibility, the policy became more widely used and resulted in increased employee productivity. Similarly, flexible work policies may not be used because they do not match the type of work done in the organization. For example, in a client-centered business that requires hourly appointments, flexible scheduling may not be possible if other schedules are not shifted. Analyzing how work is done and how work might need to shift to support flexible work policies may yield greater access and use of these policies.

To fully embrace flexible work and move these arrangements away from being seen as a "deviant" alternative to traditional work, organizations will need to reimagine how work is done. A transformative approach to flexibility is for an organization to shift how its work is done, which reduces the potential for work/family scheduling conflicts to arise. One transformative approach that has been particularly successful is labeled the STAR intervention—support, transform, achieve, results.[2] Such an intervention begins with providing all employees control over when and where they do their work. Managers are trained in helping employees manage their schedules and in providing support for work/life issues. By reexamining how work is done, organizations can find ways to eliminate unnecessary meetings and facetime requirements and streamline the remaining work so that it is focused on results. Simple changes, such as considering who needs to be in a meeting rather than inviting everyone in a group, or changing project updates from long face-to-face meetings to electronic check-in documents, are ways to enable more employees to make better use of workplace flexibility. Managers are also encouraged to model their support by making use of workplace flexibility themselves. Embarking on these types of workplace transformations can dramatically shift employees' use of flexible work arrangements and can significantly improve employees' well-being, which further enhances organizational productivity.[2]

CHAPTER TAKEAWAYS

1. *Workplace flexibility* is an expansive term encompassing many different types of flexible work arrangements. You need to think about what type of flexibility will best match your unique work and family situation. You also need to be prepared that your needs will change over time, and you will likely want to shift your flexible work arrangement.

2. Workplace flexibility has many benefits for working mothers and can help build maternal optimism. However, it is not without its potential challenges, not the least of which is flexibility bias. Working mothers need to proactively manage these challenges at work and at home.

3. Working mothers need to plan for and actively negotiate the workplace flexibility they desire. You need to approach these negotiations with the same planning and structure that you would approach any negotiation related to your job responsibilities and compensation.

REFERENCES

1. Matos, K., & Galinsky, E. (2014). National Study of Employers. New York, NY: Families and Work Institute.
2. Kossek, E. E., Hammer, L. B., Thompson, R. J., & Burke, L. B. (2014). *Leveraging workplace flexibility for engagement and productivity*. SHRM Foundation's Effective Practice Guidelines Series. Retrieved from https://www.shrm.org/hr-today/trends-and-forecasting/special-reports-and-expert-views/Documents/Leveraging-Workplace-Flexibility.pdf.
3. Kossek, E. E., & Michel, J. S. (2011). Flexible work scheduling. In *Handbook of industrial-organizational psychology* (pp. 535–572). Washington, DC: American Psychological Association.

4. Munsch, C. L., Ridgeway, C. L., & Williams, J. C. (2014)., Pluralistic ignorance and the flexibility bias: Understanding and mitigating flextime and flexplace bias at work. *Work and Occupations*, *41*(1), 40–62.

5. Noback, I., Broersma, L., & Dijk, J. (2016). Climbing the ladder: Gender-specific career advancement in financial services and the influence of flexible work-time arrangements. *British Journal of Industrial Relations*, *54*(1), 114–135.

6. Kurland, N., & Bailey, D. (1999). Telework: The advantages and challenges of working here, there, anywhere, and anytime. *Organizational Dynamics*, *28*(2), 53–68.

7. Hill, E. J., Erickson, J. J., Holmes, E. K., & Ferris, M. (2010). Workplace flexibility, work hours, and work-life conflict: Finding an extra day or two. *Journal of Family Psychology*, *24*(3), 349–358.

8. Bureau of Labor Statistics. (2017). *Labor force statistics from the current population survey*. Retrieved from https://www.bls.gov/cps/lfcharacteristics.htm#hours.

9. HR Daily Advisor Editorial Staff. (2013, July 30). Job sharing: The advantages and disadvantages. *HR Daily Advisor*. Retrieved from https://hrdailyadvisor.blr.com/2013/07/30/job-sharing-the-advantages-and-disadvantages/.

10. Humberd, B., Ladge, J. J., & Harrington, B. (2015). The new dad: Navigating fathering identity within organizational contexts. *Journal of Business and Psychology*, *30*(2), 249–266.

11. Williams, J. (2000). *Unbending gender: Why family and work conflict and what to do about it*. New York, NY: Oxford University Press.

12. Williams, J., Blair-Loy, M., & Berdahl, J. (2013). Cultural schemas, social class, and the flexibility stigma. *Journal of Social Issues*, *69*(2), 209–234.

13. Ashford, S. J., George, E., & Blatt, R. (2007). Old assumptions, new work: The opportunities and challenges of research on nonstandard employment. *Academy of Management Annals*, *1*(1), 65–117.

14. Cech, E. A., & Blair-Loy, M. (2014). Consequences of flexibility stigma among academic scientists and engineers. *Work and Occupations*, *41*(1), 86–110.

15. Lee, M. D., MacDermid, S. M., Williams, M. L., Buck, M. L., & Leiba-O'Sullivan, S. (2002). Contextual factors in the success of reduced-load work arrangements among managers and professionals. *Human Resource Management*, *41*(2), 209–223.

16. Moen, P., & Roehling, P. (2005). The career mystique: Cracks in the American dream. *Journal of Marriage and Family*, *67*(4), 1099–1100.

17. Hammer, L. B., Neal, M. B., Newsom, J. T., Brockwood, K. J., & Colton, C. L. (2005). A longitudinal study of the effects of dual-earner couples' utilization of family-friendly workplace supports on work and family outcomes. *Journal of Applied Psychology*, *90*(4), 799–810.

18. Kossek, E. E., Lautsch, B. A., & Eaton, S. C. (2006). Telecommuting, control and boundary management: Correlates of policy use and practice, job control and work-family effectiveness. *Journal of Vocational Behavior*, *68*(2), 347–367.

19. Greenberg, D., & Landry, E. M. (2011). Negotiating a flexible work arrangement: How women navigate the influence of power and organizational context. *Journal of Organizational Behavior*, *32*(8), 1163–1188.

20. Stone, P., & Hernandez, L. (2013). The all-or-nothing workplace: Flexibility stigma and opting out among professional-managerial women. *Journal of Social Issues*, *69*(2), 235.

21. Karasek, R., & Theorell, T. (1990). *Healthy work: Stress, productivity, and the reconstruction of working life.* New York, NY: Basic Books.

22. Kelly, E. L., & Kalev, A. (2006). Managing flexible work arrangements in US organizations: Formalized discretion or a right to ask. *Socio-Economic Review*, *4*(3), 379–416.

7

Career Paths that Twist and Turn

At the time, I was working for a very innovative marketing consulting firm. I had joined a few years earlier after working at a Big Four firm. I had just been promoted, and my new position would require more evenings and client cultivation. At almost the same time, our nanny quit and my husband started a new job. I was emotionally overwhelmed. After a lot of discussion, I resigned and began my next phase.

I spent close to a decade at home raising our three children. During that time I became very involved in our community. I was a PTO president; I led a number of strategy and assessment initiatives for the school, including a controversial overhaul of high school athletics. I also served as a deacon for our church, during which time we doubled in size and significantly increased our youth outreach.

As my youngest daughter transitioned to high school, I knew I wanted to return to paid work. The problem was, I didn't know what I wanted to do and didn't know how to do it. I spoke with people I had worked with as a volunteer, I spoke to colleagues I had known from my prior life, I spoke to friends at dinner parties—basically, I talked to everyone. I started to realize I had a passion for education and was not so interested in returning to general consulting. I also began to realize that through my volunteer work I had developed an expertise and skillset around analysis and recommendations of strategic initiatives in public education.

Through my contacts in our school system, I was introduced to the director of an education-related think tank. He happened to have someone heading out on maternity leave and had a short-term assignment to continue the work on two evaluation projects. This was a perfect match to the skills I had developed as a volunteer and in my prior paid work. The think tank eventually received another grant and my short-term position became permanent.

—DEIRDRE, *educational research consultant*

One of the most forgotten but empowering realities for a working mother to remember is that everything does not have to happen now. Careers are long: they can span forty to fifty to sixty years. This gives working mothers plenty of time to explore different work options outside of continuous, full-time employment with a single company. Yet we still talk about career choices for working mothers as if they are either/or decisions. Either you are going to go back to work or you are going to stay home. Either you are going to stay on the "fast track" to promotion or you are going to move to the "mommy track." Either you are going to continue to pursue the corner office or you are going to drop out and start your own venture. We frame working mothers' work choices as permanent decisions, with the implicit assumption that any varied work or life choices are less legitimate than the more traditional, hierarchical career progression.[1] In addition, the increased attention on increasing gender parity in the corporate suite and boardroom may have the unintentional consequence of further undervaluing the diverse, meaningful career choices working mothers may be making that do not necessarily lead to such roles. While organizations need to address the biases that are preventing women from obtaining these higher-level positions, we also need to be more fully embracing the other legitimate, and impactful, ways that mothers choose to chart their work/life path.

Motherhood can be a trigger for assessing the importance of family and career. Some women will use this assessment as an opportunity to leave an unsatisfactory career, not just with the goal of focusing on family but also to move into a more meaningful career path.[2] Working mothers' careers may include any number of nonlinear choices such as industry changes, entrepreneurial pursuits, time away from paid work, and nonprofit board or volunteer work. Deirdre's opening quote certainly describes a varied career journey with twists and turns, all of which involve consistent, meaningful work engagement. Her story also underscores that few working mothers, even the elite ones profiled in the popular press who were said to be part of the so-called "Opt Out Revolution", truly opt out permanently.

This chapter moves beyond workplace flexibility to consider career flexibility for working mothers. *Career flexibility* refers to the varied career choices working mothers make as they pursue their work/life path. We begin by introducing a different metaphor of careers beyond the career ladder. The holistic career model provides a more expansive view of careers that encompasses work, family, and community interests and activity. This career metaphor more accurately fits the reality of today's workplace. It also gives working mothers authority to consider something beyond the next promotion as they construct their careers. We then take a deep dive into two of the more prominent twists working mothers make: taking time off from paid work and starting their own business. In introducing these choices, we focus on the tactics working mothers can use to ensure that these options fit with their work/family interests. The chapter concludes with a discussion of how we can ensure that organizations become open to women's diverse work and family paths.

A HOLISTIC APPROACH TO A CAREER

A career is actually a very broad idea, as it refers to the sequence of work experience that evolves over one's lifetime.[3] In North America, we have narrowed this concept to assume a career involves a series of linear, hierarchical moves; a career unfolds as individuals work their way up the hierarchy, taking on more prestigious positions that command a higher salary. Career success is defined by the increase in compensation, status, and title that come as employees move up this hierarchy. To achieve this success, individuals must be fully devoted to the organization with few, if any, outside distractions.[4]

While some people's careers may still follow this traditional model, for most individuals—men or women, with children or no children—this model does not align with the realities of today's workplace. Few individuals will spend their entire careers in a single organization, and they may not follow a linear career path. As individuals move between functional areas, companies, and industries, they are not necessarily taking on higher-status positions.[5] For dual-career couples, this model is also out of sync, as it assumes that one partner can be solely focused on his or her career while the other partner attends to family and home responsibilities.[6] Few individuals have the family structures that support this career approach, and even fewer want to be solely focused on their career. More likely, individuals—particularly working mothers—are interested in making career choices that enable them to build a meaningful life.[4]

With this more holistic view, careers are depicted as self-managed and boundary-less. The individual, not the organization, is in charge of his or her career, and the pursuit of a career includes work, family, and community experiences.[7] A working mother has the freedom to build the career she wants by crossing functional boundaries, organizational boundaries, and profit and nonprofit boundaries.[8] To successfully chart a path through these expansive career opportunities, working mothers must rely on their values, needs, and preferences to guide their decisions rather than on normative societal and organizational expectations.[9]

One of the advantages of contemporary careers is that they allow, and even encourage, working mothers to construct a career that will have twists and turns. As children age, as life shifts, and as interests change, women may want to make different choices about what work they do, how they work, and even if they work. Working mothers may explore nontraditional employment opportunities that are short term and dynamic, such as contract or project work.[9] Career choices are made by focusing on your own work interests as well as on personal and family needs.[10] With these varied career options, working mothers can no longer rely on salary and title to evaluate their careers. Instead, they need to attend to more personal measures of success such as confidence, meaning, purpose, work/family integration, and impact.[4] For some working mothers, this holistic shift can be difficult because it requires them to be more introspective as they craft their own professional identity and create work arrangements that enable them to live that identity.[11]

For working mothers, a holistic career perspective can be enriching as it mirrors how they have constructed their careers, even if they have not been conscious of it. Adopting this holistic career model does not preclude pursuing a promotion or accepting a job that may require substantial hours or travel. In fact, this model encourages and supports these choices as long as they are driven by a working mother's career desires and not by organizational demands. Becoming aware of your own career interests is essential to your ability to become your own career agent. Working mothers who take ownership of their careers and the decision-making process can make choices that fit their work/family desires.[10] Proactively charting a career path in this way is generative as you can embrace, rather than hide from, your professional and personal interests. The key is to be thoughtful and informed as you make these choices. On this note, we discuss two frequent choices we see women making: taking time off and pursuing entrepreneurship.

TAKING A BREAK FROM PAID WORK

Approximately 37% of college-educated women will choose to take some time off to serve as the primary caregiver for children or aging relatives.[12] On average, working mothers take 2.75 years off from paid work. However, as our introductory story illustrates, some working mothers may find their break from paid work spans a decade or two.[12]

Before detailing why and how to proactively take a break from paid work, we want to acknowledge that this choice does not align with the lived experience of most working mothers. While many articles written in the popular press have reinforced the myth that women are opting out of successful careers in droves after they have children, this choice is a luxury frequently reserved for white, upper-middle-class women in professional roles and dual-career partnerships. Single working mothers rarely have the option to "opt out." Even for most dual-career couples, taking time off is not possible, as both incomes are needed to cover the basics of family life. The myth of "opting out" also does not fit the reality of many women of color. African American mothers have historically worked, so they face a different bias if they take time off. Furthermore, women of color face greater career risks and challenges in returning to work than white women if they choose to take time off.[13]

When working mothers do take time off from paid work, they may actually be using motherhood as a way to gracefully exit an unsatisfying job, a difficult boss, or an overly demanding organization. For instance, extreme jobs with long hours and unexpected demands create structural barriers that make it more difficult for working mothers to successfully manage work and home.[14] In these organizational contexts, working mothers are more likely to feel conflicted about work and family if they are unable to put in the hours necessary for work or work-related social activities. Working mothers often start to feel guilty that they are letting their colleagues down, and they begin to question their value to the organization.[15]

Another common reason working mothers give for taking time off is an unsupportive manager and/or coworkers. When Bea, a university administrator, was pregnant, she found herself surprised by the subtle, and not-so-subtle, comments her female manager would make about work and family. Continual comments such as "You are not going to be one of those women who has children and can't give it your all, are you?" led her to conclude her boss was not going to be supportive of, or accommodating to, her work/family needs. Bea decided that she would not return to work, even though she loved what she did and planned to continue in the future in another organization. Comments like these, even if they are well meaning, often feel like a threat to a working mother's identity. If a working mother frequently experiences these identity threats, it may prompt her to take time off to escape what feels like a toxic environment for working mothers.

Even if the organization is supportive of work and family, working mothers may find the financial and career benefits of work do not balance out the complexities and costs that arise from trying to manage work and home.[16] This is particularly true for women who are in professions with lower salary structures. Riya was an elementary school teacher who stopped working after her second child was born. The financial costs of having two young children in daycare far exceeded her salary. She also knew she could take a few years off and easily transition back into teaching when her children were older. Ultimately, she stayed home for four years until it was financially viable for her to return to work.

The previous paragraphs detail some ways in which working mothers may be pushed to take time off due to organizational pressures and limitations. But working mothers may also find they are pulled to take time off because they simply want to have more time to care for their families. As women progress through their careers, they may find that their priorities shift, and having time to care for their family becomes an increasingly important priority.[17] Nonetheless, we find working mothers are often quite torn when deciding whether or not to take time off. Joan, who worked in the fashion industry, had her children later in life. She was passionate about her work and never questioned returning to work. Yet, as she aged and her children moved into elementary and middle school, she found her priorities shifting:

Making the decision to stop working was hard. I loved my work and my career. I was on the fast track and I had already passed the early years of newborns and toddlers. However, I had this desire to be home more. Making the decision to leave my job really came down to asking what I wanted to do at this point in time.

Joan's story illustrates the importance of being aware of your own desires and values as you chart a path through work and motherhood. Cori reiterated this perspective as she reflected on the five years she took off from paid work:

> I didn't take time off because I thought my kids would be better off if I were at home. I know many women who have worked full time all through and have great kids. I took time off because I wanted to be there when my kids were little—it was how I wanted to spend my time.

While we tend to assume working mothers take time off solely when their children are young, Joan's story illustrates that women make this choice at diverse points along the work/motherhood path.

Working mothers may also take time off to care for elderly parents or to manage their own or their partner's health issues.[16] Maggie took a break from paid work to care for her mother after her stroke:

> It is a gift I can give someone who inspired my career and the life I created. I don't want to look back and feel as if I didn't do everything I could for her.

Maggie loved her work and planned to return to her career, but she saw this as a short time away from work in an otherwise long work career. Taking a long-term approach to career and life, as we discussed in detail in Chapter 5 concerning aging working mothers, can be helpful as working mothers confront difficult choices about stepping away from paid work.

Understanding the Career Impact of Time Off

The unfortunate reality is that regardless of why or how long an employee leaves paid work, there are typically negative financial repercussions. While the most obvious loss comes in the form of lost income, there are other long-term financial implications for women to consider, and working mothers often forget to consider these when they are evaluating the costs of continuing or stopping work.

For instance, Devorah focused solely on the high cost of childcare when deciding to take time off:

> As an administrative assistant, my salary barely covered my childcare and commuting costs. I was tired, and my partner and I were constantly fighting over whose turn it was. The added income didn't seem worth the stress, so I quit.

However, there were added financial losses Devorah did not consider in this calculation, including salary increases, retirement income, health insurance, and other benefits. While it still might have made financial and emotional sense for Devorah to stop working, it is best to consider both short- and long-term financial implications when making this decision. Working mothers can use online resources such as financial calculators (e.g., https://interactives.americanprogress.org/childcarecosts/) that measure the impact on salary, wage growth, and retirement savings over time for every year a working mother is out of the workforce On average, working mothers can expect to lose three to four times their annual salary for every year they are out of the workforce.[18] For highly trained professional women, even an absence of less than a year leads to significant compensation penalties.[19] Considering these long-term financial implications may lead a working mother to evaluate the short-term financial and emotional impact of taking time off differently.

Time off from paid work also may have a negative effect on women's future career opportunities. Rapid changes driven by technology and globalization mean that working mothers who take time off may find their job skills, their industry knowledge, and their technical proficiencies are quickly outdated. This may limit their career options when they decide to reenter the workforce. Hiring managers may also have biases against working mothers who have taken time off from paid work. Skepticism about a mother's ability and commitment to reenter the workplace may lead a hiring manager to negatively judge a working mother's organizational commitment and motivation. Such skepticism may even prompt managers to ask illegal questions about a working mother's future family plans. These biases create additional barriers that can make it more difficult for working mothers to return to work when they are ready.

Making the Most of Time Off from Paid Work

Despite these potential career and financial penalties, many working mothers experience profound benefits from taking time off to focus on family needs. They may find that taking time off enables them to develop new skills, build new relationships, and increase their self-confidence. When women return to paid work, this increased self-confidence has a positive impact on work performance and career success.[20] Other working mothers use the time at home to plan for a new career that is more meaningful. Being at home can alter a working mother's outlook and help her begin to consider new avenues for establishing a more fulfilling career. This was Trisha's experience after staying at home for close to a decade:

> Staying at home changed what I found fulfilling professionally. I didn't want to go back to accounting, even though that option was open to me. I wanted to use what I knew about helping children with special needs to create a new career.

Other working mothers find that time away from paid work simply reinforces how much meaning and fulfillment they gained from their work and reaffirms their desire to return to work at an appropriate point. Being at home full time can provide working mothers with the space to create a more fulfilling career in the future.[15]

If you decide that taking time off is part of your path, there are ways you can proactively approach this life stage to ensure you are better positioned to return to work when you are ready. Research suggests that 89% of working mothers who take time off want to return to work. Unfortunately, only 40% of these women will be able to secure the job they want in an industry they want.[12] With a little forethought and planning, working mothers can proactively manage their time off so they are well positioned to fulfill their reentry objectives.

If you think you want to return to your former profession, maintaining your professional skills is one way to stay connected and be prepared for reentry. Keeping up professional licensures or certificates is a relatively easy step a working mother can take to stay current with her prior profession. Lindsey, a social worker, stopped working six months after she returned from her first maternity leave. At the time, she found it difficult to manage work with a long commute, unstable childcare, and the demands of parenting. While at home, she had another child. As her children moved into middle and high school, she found herself longing to return to her work. As Lindsey had kept her professional license up to date by taking continuing education courses, it was much easier for her to return to her career as a therapist. Professional conferences and networking events provide working mothers with another mechanism for staying professionally current. While there may be costs associated with attending conferences or maintaining professional certifications, working mothers need to frame these costs as an investment in their career. Making this continued investment can help reduce future economic penalties associated with taking time off.

Maintaining relationships with former colleagues or mentors can also help a working mother stay professionally connected. Working mothers who choose to leave paid work sometimes cut themselves off from prior professional relationships, as they are uncomfortable with their work status and assume they have little in common with former colleagues. Working mothers need to move past these insecurities. Even women who are not currently working have a lot to gain and give in these relationships. Meeting for lunch, coffee, or even a playdate helps a working mother stay current and connected. When Natasha stopped working when her second child was born, she maintained what had been a close professional relationship with a former colleague. Years later, this relationship provided Natasha with her reentry opportunity. Natasha shared,

When Sari moved to another job, she reached out to me about a possible work opportunity. While I had not been thinking about going back to work yet, I jumped at the chance to work with Sari again as we had such a deep connection.

Work reentry cannot always be carefully planned. Staying connected with former colleagues can increase the likelihood that you will be aware of reentry opportunities when they arise.

For working mothers who do not want to return to their prior professions, time at home can become an extended opportunity to explore their next career move. Working mothers can take advantage of libraries and local continuing education programs to explore different career options and build new skills. These programs provide a low-cost method for building a résumé, developing social media and technical proficiencies, and strengthening interpersonal skills. Working mothers who have the financial resources may use their time at home to pursue a formal educational degree in a new area. With the proliferation of high-quality distance-learning programs and weekend and part-time programs, women may be able to earn a degree or professional certificate that will help with reentry.

Women will also want to use their personal and professional networks to explore different career options. This is a great time to repurpose those career exploration skills to learn what people in your network do or did in a former career. We have even heard of creative stories of mothers' groups offering speed-dating–style events in which stay-at-home and working mothers discuss their work experiences. Through these activities, working mothers can reflect on what they enjoy doing, what they are good at, and how this might translate to new career options.

Trisha, whom we mentioned in the previous section, benefitted greatly from her network as she began planning for return to work. Trisha left her job in operations planning to care for her children, who had significant learning needs. At first, Trisha thought she might want to return to work as a special education teacher, but after talking to other stay-at-home mothers who had been teachers, she decided this career option did not best suit her skillset. She realized that her skills in operations management made her particularly well equipped for handling the bureaucracy and logistics of educating children with special needs. She had had an easy time managing her own children's experiences and had informally advised many other families through that process. Propelled by this knowledge of her skills and how they did and did not fit possible career paths pertaining to special needs families, she eventually built a new consulting career in which she helped families navigate their children's special needs in the healthcare and education systems.

Volunteering and community board service presents another avenue for working mothers to continue to develop professional skills and explore new career options while they are at home. Volunteering can help working mothers adjust to the loss of their old professional identity and begin to develop a new identity.[15] Volunteering can also help working mothers be better positioned for work reentry. Carin had worked in college student services prior to taking time off when her son was born. When Carin's children started preschool, she became actively involved with the school. She chaired the parent board and began volunteering as a teacher after her children left the school. When a teacher left midyear, she was hired as a part-time teacher, which eventually evolved into a full-time position as an assistant director for the school.

Mothers are most effective in leveraging volunteer work toward reentry when they take the time to consider what volunteer work they want to engage in, what will be the best use of their skills, and how it might connect to reentry. The story at the start of the chapter provides a map of how one woman used volunteer opportunities to develop her leadership, communication, and computer skills, and to explore what she might find fulfilling when she was ready to return to work.

Beyond building new skills, volunteering can also help women who are not currently working build new relationships, which can support their work reentry. When Marissa's youngest son was diagnosed with a life-threatening illness, she left her career as a management consultant to stay home full time. As her son's health improved and he transitioned to elementary school, Marissa became involved in a series of strategic planning projects for local, community-based nonprofits. Through this unpaid work, she became known among her fellow board members for her strategic thinking and leadership skills. Another board member invited her to do a similar consulting project for his consumer goods company. This eventually turned into a full-time job. Choosing volunteer work that enables you to make a significant contribution can support your return to work either by raising your visibility or by providing you with impactful stories to share during a job interview.

Maintaining Optimism When Returning to Work

There is no right time or way to return to work. Some women are home for one or two years, others wait until their children enter elementary school, and still others wait to go back to work until their children leave home. Financial resources are frequently the driving factor behind women's decisions about when to return to work.[21,22] Many women return to work out of a desire to reestablish their income and to ease the financial pressures of looming college costs and retirement.[23] With the unpredictability of today's marketplace and shifting life circumstances, working mothers may return to work not out of choice but out of necessity. As Leticia explained,

> My husband is an entrepreneur and I needed to return to work because we needed the second income and, more importantly, we needed healthcare coverage. It would have been nice to take time to discover my true passion before I went back to work, but that wasn't an option for me. I needed to get back to work quickly, and the best way to do that was to go back to the industry I was in previously.

Working mothers also find themselves wanting to return to work because they miss the intellectual stimulation, the sense of accomplishment, and the recognition that comes from paid work. Working mothers are also often drawn back to work because they miss the work relationships that boost their confidence and self-esteem when working.[16]

Returning to work is not always easy. It can take much longer than you anticipate, and greater perseverence. To return to work, you will likely need to be creative, proactive, and patient as you pursue reentry. One strategy working mothers frequently mention using is accepting short-term project work with the long-term goal of finding a permanent position. This was Greta's path. She had been looking for a full-time position for close to a year with little success. As she continued to look, a friend offered her some project work. As Greta explained,

> I did some project work for a friend who ran a nonprofit. Through this, I learned about a temporary contract position at another non-profit to fill in for someone who was on maternity leave. Through these positions, I developed new marketing skills, particularly related to social media. This eventually led to my current full-time position in marketing and communications for an independent school.

Frustrated with her lack of initial reentry success, Greta made use of short-term opportunities, which became pivotal to her success in returning to work. Project-based work has the added benefit of demonstrating a working mother's commitment to returning to work, which lessens the risk some employers may see in hiring a mother who has been out of the paid workforce. Sometimes short-term work also turns into a more permanent position. When Shelagh decided she wanted to return to work, she reached out to her network and eventually was contacted by a former employee who was at a new company and was getting ready to go on maternity leave. While she was hesitant to take a three-month full-time position, as it would delay her search for more permanent work, she eventually agreed. The former employee ended up moving, and the temporary role became permanent.

In some industries, working mothers may want to seek out formal "returnship" programs to strengthen their résumé and build their confidence. These programs are typically structured over a three- to six-month period and provide working mothers with experiences similar to a college internship program. They help working mothers rebuild their skills and develop their confidence in returning to paid work. Formal returnship programs also provide women with a supportive cohort of individuals who are all in the same place and are facing similar struggles and opportunities. In STEM, accounting, professional services, and finance fields, returnships are increasingly popular, as they are a strategic human resource approach to reengaging working mothers. In most instances, organizations find returnship programs to be a cost-effective way to recruit talented employees, with the conversion rate from returnship participant to full-time employee being 50% to 90%.[24] On the home front, full-time returnships also enable working mothers to "try out" plans for managing home demands such as childcare arrangements, errands, and meals. With a returnship, a working mother can test out new routines at home, which further supports her work reentry.

In addition to focusing on finding opportunities to return to work, working mothers need to think about how to shift home responsibilities in order to minimize potential work/family challenges. Many working mothers who have been at home for a while have built active, busy lives. They may worry about being able to navigate home and family if they return to work. The ubiquitous exclamation "I don't know how she does it!" can lead working mothers at home to wonder if they, too, can "do it." Again, discussions with other working mothers can help alleviate fears and help women develop strategies for returning to work. Zara shared,

> When I began to think about returning to work, I first reached out to my friends who worked full time and had families. I wanted to find out how they managed their time and what advice they could give me. One thing everyone told me was the importance of paying for help at home and finding time for myself. When I did finally find a full-time position, this advice helped me make better choices about work and family.

Similarly, women will also want to have conversations with their partners and children about how life and responsibilities at home may need to shift given the changing demands as they return to work.

A PATH THROUGH ENTREPRENEURSHIP

According to the Small Business Association, women-owned businesses are on the rise in the United States. Recent data suggest that women-owned businesses—with a large percentage of those started by mothers—contribute nearly $3 trillion of the nation's GDP.[22] Entrepreneurship can be a meaningful career choice for working mothers who desire more creative, flexible, and fulfilling career options.[25] Many working mothers find entrepreneurship provides a greater opportunity for financial autonomy and wealth creation than working for someone else.[26]

When explaining why they were driven to start their own businesses, most women entrepreneurs with families mention autonomy over work/life management as a driving factor. Working mothers may pursue entrepreneurial career opportunities because they are frustrated with trying to fit into a workplace that is not supportive of family or that doesn't provide autonomy and flexibility. Hence, the desire to reduce work/family conflict often remains an important goal as working mothers develop their own ventures.[27] Running her own business can provide a working mother with greater autonomy and control. With this autonomy, working mothers are better able to manage workplace factors such as travel, commute, and schedule to create better alignment between work and family.[25] Furthermore, women entrepreneurs often find the accomplishments they experience with their own businesses are more exciting and uplifting than those experienced when working for someone else. The joy, satisfaction, and fulfillment women entrepreneurs experience at work positively affect how they approach home and family.[25]

With these opportunities also come potential challenges. Entrepreneurs' workloads are typically higher than those of white-collar or professional workers.[28] Entrepreneurs also experience more intense feelings of responsibility and commitment as they build their business ventures. For these reasons, entrepreneurs often continue to spend time and energy focused on their work even after the standard workday has ended, creating additional blurring of the boundaries between work and family life. This blurring is further heightened for women entrepreneurs, who typically experience greater work/family conflict than male entrepreneurs.[27] Women entrepreneurs may find there is little separation between work and home, as their businesses are integrated with all aspects of their lives.[29] While entrepreneurship may start as a strategy for creating work/family synergy, in reality it can create increased work/family demands for a woman entrepreneur. When women entrepreneurs are hampered by family responsibilities and work/family conflicts, they may find it harder to grow their ventures.[30]

All of this can have negative repercussions for their businesses. This challenge is even more pronounced for women who operate their businesses out of their homes.[31] Ina had started her own business as a way to continue to build her career while raising her two boys. Her husband's job required the family to move frequently, so being an entrepreneur provided the work flexibility Ina needed. Her business grew quite quickly, and she found herself presented with a unique offer to extend the business into new markets. Yet, with the expansion of the business, she found herself unable to care for her boys in the way that she desired. With pressure mounting on both sides, she ultimately decided to sell the business. She explained,

> I really wanted to see the business succeed but realized that I had taken on more than I could handle.

One way a woman entrepreneur can more efficiently manage work and family is by integrating her desires into her definition of success for her venture. Entrepreneurs typically measure success based on business growth, such as increased sales, market share, revenue, and profit. However, a woman entrepreneur who is also raising a family may be more interested in managing her venture's growth such that it fits with her family interests.[29] Just as we encourage working mothers to construct their own definitions of career success, women entrepreneurs may also find it valuable to develop a more comprehensive definition of success that includes both family and business. They can turn to these definitions as they make decisions about business and family that enable them to achieve the path they desire.

Beyond work/family management, another challenge women entrepreneurs may need to contend with are industry biases regarding the intersection between gender, motherhood, and entrepreneurship. Entrepreneurship is laden with masculine stereotypes, portraying the entrepreneur as a driven, ambitious, self-confident, assertive, and authoritarian male. These stereotypes can delegitimize the authority and power of women entrepreneurs.[32] As a result, women entrepreneurs may find all aspects of entrepreneurship more challenging, from securing funding to building a network of advisors and partners to being taken seriously by suppliers and customers.

This is especially true for women entrepreneurs who start businesses that are focused on women, children, or work/family issues. Felicity had launched a technology company focused on women's health after she had experienced a health crisis after the birth of her child. While she had received positive industry feedback, she found herself struggling to secure funding from technology-focused venture capital firms:

> When we started our second round of funding, we would be making pitches to these twenty-something guys whose careers were centered in high tech. Even though we were a tech-based business, they didn't get our business model. They would talk about the lack of growth potential of a "niche" business. I would ask how this can be a niche business if 50% of the world's population is female.

Felicity found she was more successful in securing funding when she targeted venture capital firms interested in women-led ventures.

Felicity's experience reiterates the importance of continuing to expand your network as a way to build your venture and manage your work/family path. Women entrepreneurs can find themselves so overwhelmed with growing their business and creating the family life they want that they do not have enough time to regularly network and build relationships that will support the business. Women entrepreneurs also find they are not as actively sought out as their male counterparts. As a result, they often have fewer developmental relationships than their male counterparts and than women in the corporate sector.[33] Cultivating these relationships can be particularly valuable in the early stages of a venture, where isolation and missteps can breed anxiety and doubt—particularly for women entrepreneurs.

As Claire, a working mother, began researching a new business opportunity, she reached out to a former business school professor who studies gender equity and women's entrepreneurship. Her professor provided Claire with guidance and advice and helped her connect with other women entrepreneurs. Claire shared,

> I needed the reality check from these other women to propel me to do this.

SEEKING SUPPORT FROM YOUR ORGANIZATION FOR YOUR HOLISTIC CAREER

It may seem funny to think about how your organization can support you when you are thinking about leaving the company in order to stay at home or start your own venture. Nonetheless, there are ways your organization can support you as you make these transitions, which can benefit both you and the company in the long run.

One way of seeking support is to help your organization be open to the possibility of diverse career paths and to help it recognize how prolonged engagement in other aspects of life could benefit your return to work. For instance, some organizations are becoming more open to the idea of extended leaves of absence. Eliora worked full time and had two children in college when she found herself struggling to meet the demands of her career and care for her aging parents, who lived in a different country. Before resigning from her position, she approached her employer about taking a one- to two-year unpaid leave to care for her parents. While her organization did not have a formal policy for this situation, they accommodated her request because they did not want to lose her. Working mothers who have unique expertise or a record of exceptional performance may find their organizations are more receptive to an extended leave. Another option working mothers can propose is to move to project or contract work for their current employer. This option enables a working mother to have more control over her work and adjust her schedule to manage her family responsibilities.

You might also encourage your organization, if it does not do so already, to maintain a database of working mothers who are currently at home but plan to return to work in the future. Organizations are becoming increasingly open to diverse employment arrangements, and former employees who are now at home present a skilled and knowledgeable labor pool. Often these women can be drawn upon to fill in when current employees are on maternity or family leave, or to provide additional support during busy seasons. Accounting firms frequently hire former employees who are now at home to fill in during audit season. As experienced workers who understand the organization, working mothers can fill a staffing shortage more quickly and effectively than simply hiring a random contract worker. Even if working mothers initially feel frustrated and dissatisfied when they leave their employer, over time these feelings often shift. Offering former employees the opportunity to come back on a short-term basis can help repair a relationship and pave the way for a potential rehire opportunity.[34]

Finally, if you are in a leadership position, you might think about how you can help your employees start to develop their own holistic models of their careers that include work/family synergy. When Charlotte went to work for a new company, she was surprised that her new manager wanted to talk about her personal and professional goals to define her objectives for the coming year:

While I knew the company talked about the importance of employees having rich, meaningful lives, I was still surprised when my manager asked me to think about my goals outside of work. I was hesitant to say anything, but he pushed me hard. I mentioned I wanted to have a vacation and not do any work. I just did that for the first time ever, and I am so thankful for his interest in me and my life.

Charlotte found she returned to work after her vacation more refreshed than she had been in the past and even more committed to the company and her job. When she transitioned into a management position later that year, she found herself taking a similar approach with her own employees. These conversations helped her build a team that was focused on work productivity and work/family synergy.

CHAPTER TAKEAWAYS

1. Careers are not necessarily hierarchical ladders, nor do they always involve either/or decisions. Embracing a more holistic definition of a career, which encompasses all the twists and turns one takes on the work/family path, is a sensible approach for most working mothers. No career choices are permanent; the work/life path is long and provides the space and opportunity for working mothers to make varied choices as they craft meaningful careers.

2. Taking time off from paid work can benefit working mothers both in their home and in their work life. Women need to carefully assess if taking time off is the right option for them, and then make sure they remain engaged during their time at home so they are well positioned when they want to return to work.

3. Entrepreneurship can be a fulfilling path for a working mother, but it is not without its challenges. Working mothers who start their own business ventures need to be attentive to the difficulties of managing an increasingly integrated home and work life, so that that they can grow their ventures while also creating the work/family synergy they desire.

REFERENCES

1. Shapiro, M., Ingols, C., & Blake-Beard, S. (2008). Confronting career double binds: Implications for women, organizations, and career practitioners. *Journal of Career Development, 34*(3), 309–333.

2. Ladge, J. J., & Greenberg, D. N. (2015). Becoming a working mother: Managing identity and efficacy uncertainties during resocialization. *Human Resource Management, 54*(6), 977–998.

3. Arthur, M. B., Hall, D. T., & Lawrence, B. S. (1989). *Handbook of career theory.* Cambridge, UK: Cambridge University Press.

4. Heslin, P. A. (2005). Conceptualizing and evaluating career success. *Journal of Organizational Behavior, 26*(2), 113–136.

5. Direnzo, M. S., & Greenhaus, J. H. (2011). Job search and voluntary turnover in a boundaryless world: A control theory perspective. *Academy of Management Review, 36*(3), 567.

6. Moen, P. (Ed.) (2003). *It's about time: Couples and careers* (p. xi). Ithaca, NY: Cornell University Press.

7. Hall, D. T. (2002). *Careers in and out of organizations.* Thousand Oaks, CA: Sage.

8. De Vos, A., & Van der Heijden, B. I. J. M. (2015). *Handbook of research on sustainable careers.* Cheltenham, UK: Edward Elgar Publishing.

9. Valcour, M., Bailyn, L., & Quijada, M. A. (2007). Customized careers. In H. Gunz & M. Peiperl (Eds.), *Handbook of career studies* (pp. 188–210). Thousand Oaks, CA: Sage.

10. Greenhaus, J. H., & Kossek, E. E. (2014). The contemporary career: A work–home perspective. *Annual Review of Organizational Psychology and Organizational Behavior, 1*(1), 361–388.

11. Meiksins, P., & Whalley, P. (2002). *Putting work in its place: A quiet revolution.* Ithaca, NY: Cornell University Press.

12. Hewlett, S. A., Sherbin, L., & Forster, D. (2010). Off-ramps and on-ramps revisited. *Harvard Business Review.* Retrieved from https://hbr.org/2010/06/off-ramps-and-on-ramps-revisited.

13. Allers, K. S. (March 5, 2018). Rethinking work-life balance for women of color. Retrieved from https://slate.com/human-interest/2018/03/for-women-of-color-work-life-balance-is-a-different-kind-of-problem.html.

14. Hewlett, S. A., & Luce, C. B. (2005). Off-ramps and on-ramps. *Harvard Business Review.* Retrieved from https://hbr.org/2005/03/off-ramps-and-on-ramps-keeping-talented-women-on-the-road-to-success.

15. Kanji, S., & Cahusac, E. (2015). Who am I? Mothers' shifting identities, loss and sensemaking after workplace exit. *Human Relations, 68*(9), 1415–1436.

16. Hewlett, S. A., & Luce, C. B. (2006). Extreme jobs: The dangerous allure of the 70-hour workweek. *Harvard Business Review, 84*(12), 49.

17. Maniero, L. A., & Sullivan, S. E. (2005). Kaleidoscope careers: An alternate explanation for the "opt-out" revolution. *Academy of Management Executive, 19*(1), 106–123.

18. Madowitz, M., Rowell, A., & Hamm, K. (2016, June 21). *Calculating the hidden cost of interrupting a career for child care.* Center for American Progress. Retrieved from https://www.americanprogress.org/issues/early-childhood/reports/2016/06/21/139731/calculating-the-hidden-cost-of-interrupting-a-career-for-child-care/.

19. Goldin, C., & Katz, L. F. (2008). Transitions: Career and family life cycles of the educational elite. *American Economic Review, 98*(2), 363–369.

20. Ruderman, M. N., Ohlott, P. J., Panzer, K., & King, S. N. (2002). Benefits of multiple roles for managerial women. *Academy of Management Journal, 45*(2), 369.

21. Zimmerman, L. M., & Clark, M. A. (2016). Opting-out and opting-in: A review and agenda for future research. *Career Development International, 21*(6), 603–633.

22. National Women's Business Council (2009, October, 27). *The Economic Impact of Women-Owned Businesses in the United States.* Retrieved from https://www.nwbc.gov/2009/10/27/the-economic-impact-of-women-owned-businesses-in-the-united-states/.

23. Elizabeth, F. C. (2007). Opting out and opting in: Understanding the complexities of women's career transitions. *Career Development International, 12*(3), 218–237.

24. Cohen, C. F. (2015). For professionals returning to work, there's power in the cohort. *Harvard Business Review.* Retrieved from https://hbr.org/2015/03/for-professionals-returning-to-work-theres-power-in-the-cohort.

25. McGowan, P., Redeker, C. L., Cooper, S. Y., & Greenan, K. (2012). Female entrepreneurship and the management of business and domestic roles: Motivations, expectations and realities. *Entrepreneurship & Regional Development, 24*(1-2), 53–72.

26. Elizabeth, A. W., & Beverley, J. W. (2007). Gender, age and self-employment: Some things change, some stay the same. *Women in Management Review, 22*(2), 122–135.

27. Jennings, J., & McDougald, M. (2007). Work-family interface experiences and coping strategies: Implications for entrepreneurship research and practice. *Academy of Management Review, 32*(3), 747–760.

28. Harris, J., Saltstone, R., & Fraboni, M. (1999). An evaluation of the job stress questionnaire with a sample of entrepreneurs. *Journal of Business and Psychology, 13*(3), 447–455.

29. Brush, C. (1992). Research on women business owners: Past trends, a new perspective and future directions. *Entrepreneurship Theory and Practice, 16*(4), 5–30.

30. Stoner, C., Hartman, R., & Arora, R. (1990). Work-home role conflict in female owners of small businesses: An exploratory study. *Journal of Small Business Management, 28*(1), 30.

31. Kirkwood, J., & Tootell, B. (2008). Is entrepreneurship the answer to achieving work–family balance? *Journal of Management & Organization, 14*(3), 285–302.

32. Jennings, J. E., & Brush, C. G. (2013). Research on women entrepreneurs: Challenges to (and from) the broader entrepreneurship literature? *Academy of Management Annals, 7*(1), 1–69.

33. Siri, T., & Sherry, E. W. (2011). The role of developmental relationships in the transition to entrepreneurship: A qualitative study and agenda for future research. *Career Development International, 16*(5), 482–506.

34. Fishman Cohen, C. (2016). Don't lose track of high performers who take a hiatus. *Harvard Business Review.* Retrieved from https://hbr.org/2016/01/dont-lose-track-of-high-performers-who-take-a-hiatus.

8

What to Expect from the Unexpected in Work and Family Life

I was miserable in my marriage and had developed a plan for when I was going to let my husband know I wanted a divorce. We had tried counseling for years, and it just was not working. I was worried about our daughter, but I knew if I was okay, she was going to be okay. I was at my wit's end with him, and I don't think our lack of communication and relationship was doing anyone any good. I would have asked for a divorce sooner, but then he lost his job, and while we were going to be okay financially for a little while, months had gone by and he still hadn't found a new job. There was one day when I came home from work and he was watching television with our daughter. She hadn't done her homework yet, dinner was not made, and there were piles of laundry. It was so frustrating, and I just knew I couldn't wait much longer. The day before I had prepared to finally tell him I wanted a divorce, I was diagnosed with breast cancer.

—KAYLIE, *a hospital administrator*

We wish we could have ended this book with the prior chapter focusing on the exciting and varied choices working mothers make as they forge their work/life path. However, work/life paths are not just about the choices we make: some choices are made for us. There is some truth in the saying "Life is what happens when we are busy making plans." Acute or chronic health issues, children's emotional or physical needs, or life-threatening illnesses, marital issues, or care needs of extended family members are just some examples of the disruptions working mothers may face. These disruptions vary in length and duration, but each comes with new and unique issues that need to be managed. Navigating these disruptions often requires a working mother to make adjustments along her work/life journey.

In this chapter, we explore some of the more common disruptions working mothers experience. We broadly categorize these based on whether they relate to the working mother herself, her nuclear family, or her extended family. You may think these disruptions won't be part of your path, and therefore you might be thinking about skipping this chapter. Unfortunately, from our research, we know most women will experience at least one of these disruptions as they contend with work and family. We hope that by discussing the unexpected and sometimes undiscussed aspects of navigating work and life, we can help working mothers become a bit more prepared for tackling these unexpected transitions.

HEALTH DISRUPTIONS IN A WORKING MOTHER'S LIFE

One of the most common complaints we hear from working mothers is that they do not have enough time to take care of themselves. They are so busy caring for those around them that they forget to take care of their own mental and physical health. It may then come as a surprise to learn that mothers who return to work full time after childbirth tend to have better physical health than women who work part time or not at all.[1] At age forty, full-time working mothers are typically mentally and physically healthier than women who stay at home or who work part time. The sense of purpose, self-efficacy, control, and autonomy working mothers experience as a result of work may offset the lack of attention women give to their own physical and mental well-being.[2]

However, while work in general may boost women's overall well-being, too much work remains a concern. The number-one killers of women are still heart disease and cardiovascular disease, both of which are strongly correlated to work stress.[3] Excessive work also can have a negative influence on working mothers' mental health. Long work hours, a high level of responsibility, lack of managerial support, and other job-related factors can all increase the stress working mothers experience. Mental health is also affected by home factors such as confidence in childcare arrangements and how involved your partner is in co-parenting.[4] When working mothers are worried about the care of their children, they often struggle to stay focused on work, which can lead to diminished work productivity. They may start to feel like they are failing at work and at home. Maintaining one's mental health can become an even more serious concern than physical well-being for working mothers.

Even when working mothers are paying attention to their own physical and mental well-being, unexpected health crises can occur. They may be prolonged, life threatening, and chronic, such as cancer or heart conditions, or they may be acute, such as a broken bone or surgery. Both authors have had to work through unexpected, acute health crises that affected how they managed work and family. For example, Jamie had a full rupture of her Achilles tendon in the middle of a semester. From the hospital, her first frantic calls were to her colleagues to find coverage for her classes, as there is no "substitute" system for college professors. She then called her friends to make sure someone could pick up her children after school. All of this was done before she had a diagnosis. Three days later she had surgery, which was followed by two weeks of heavy pain medication and four months of physical therapy. During this time, she had to find transportation to and from work, as she could not drive, and she had to meet two manuscript deadlines. She also had to create a new plan to get her three sons to two different schools, not to mention shop for groceries, cook, and do the laundry. She was fortunate that her workplace was supportive, and her colleagues covered the classes she missed. She had a good relationship with her ex-husband, so he provided help, and she hired additional childcare. Without financial security and a strong support system at work and at home, the work/life disruption caused by this acute health issue could have spiraled out of control.

Age, race, and other demographic factors all play a role in the kinds of health disruptions women face. As we discussed earlier in the book, older mothers may experience more challenges than younger mothers during pregnancy. After childbirth, older mothers may experience health advantages because they have more time and financial resources to devote to caregiving.[5,6] Marital status also impacts working mothers' physically and emotional well-being. Single mothers are more likely to experience depression and anxiety, particularly in the postpartum period.[7] Over the longer term, single working mothers face greater risks of heart disease, stroke, and chronic effects of sleep deprivation compared with their married peers.[8]

Race is a third element intersecting with gender, marriage, and age that affects working mothers' health prognoses. Working mothers of color are disproportionately affected by major health problems.[9] Black women are twice as likely as white women to be overweight, suffer heart attacks, or develop diabetes and autoimmune disorders. They are also at greater risk for other health conditions such as asthma, arthritis, and cancer.[10] During pregnancy and childbirth, women of color often don't have access to the same level of quality healthcare as Caucasian women do. Healthcare professionals also have been found to be less responsive to the physical and mental health concerns of women of color.[11] All of this further increases the health risks for working mothers of color. Serena Williams, the tennis superstar, is the unfortunate poster child for this discrimination. Days after giving birth, she was experiencing shortness of breath, which she mentioned to her healthcare providers. Even though they knew she had a history of developing blood clots in her lungs, they initially ignored her concerns. Serena continued to demand that her doctors be more responsive, which ultimately saved her life, though not without greatly increasing the time it took for her to physically recover from childbirth and delaying her return to tennis—her work.[11]

When health issues arise, working mothers will have to determine how best to manage the situation, be it for the short or long term. Working mothers may need to determine if they should negotiate a prolonged leave of absence or a flexible work arrangement in order to adjust their work and professional demands. As you consider what you may need to shift at work, you will want to investigate what policies or services are available to you that could be adapted to meet your specific situation. Formal workplace policies such as short-term disability, family and medical leave, and bereavement leave can be examined to see how they might be adapted. Working mothers will also want to rely on their internal network to learn how coworkers managed similar disruptions. Learning about others' experiences can help a mother determine the extent to which formal policies can be adapted to meet her needs.

Beyond the logistical challenges of health disruptions, these situations can also lead women to question their overall identity, where they want to spend their energy and time, and what legacy they want to leave behind. Working mothers may find themselves making shifts at work or at home as a result. For instance, Carmin was thrilled when she found out she was pregnant with triplets. She had been trying to get pregnant for a number of years, and her work colleagues celebrated her pregnancy. As she moved into her second and third trimester of pregnancy, the babies died one by one in utero. Overwhelmed by grief and depression, she found herself unable to return to her workplace and face her coworkers, many of whom she had previously considered family. Carmin took a leave of absence, as she needed time to evaluate her priorities and focus on her mental health. She realized that when she did return to work, she needed a fresh start in an organization where no one felt sorry for her and where nobody knew her family story. She eventually resigned and took a position in another firm.

Alternatively, some women find health disruptions may prompt them to reengage at work and become more focused on their professional lives. Amanda was diagnosed with cancer and shortly thereafter was laid off from work. She had a severance package, which included a few months of salary and healthcare. Her friends told her to take the time and focus on her health. However, she knew she needed to get back to work quickly for both financial and emotional reasons. She found a new job before her severance ran out. Amanda found that reestablishing her professional identity in a new organization kept her from letting the cancer define her. Reengaging in work helped Amanda emotionally work through her health crisis. How working mothers respond to health-related disruptions will vary greatly depending on the organizational context, their work/life stage, and their family circumstances.

FAMILY-CENTERED DISRUPTIONS

Despite the energy and care working mothers devote to their families, disruptions on the home front can still occur. Children, spouses, and marriages cannot be insulated from life's hardships. We refer to these events as *family-centered disruptions*, as they are disruptions related to one's nuclear family. Family-centered disruptions can be particularly problematic for working mothers, because they can trigger intense questioning about one's work/life choices.

Children-Centered Disruptions

The number of children who are likely to experience life challenges is on the rise. An estimated 30% of children under the age of eighteen will be affected by a chronic illness such as life-threatening allergies, diabetes, cancer, cerebral palsy, mental illness, or other physical disabilities.[12] Beyond illness, the number of children diagnosed with special needs (e.g., autism spectrum disorders, attention-deficit disorder or attention-deficit/hyperactivity disorder, dyslexia) is also increasing. According to the U.S. Census, more than 5% of school-age children (aged five to seventeen) have some disability that requires special education or services.[13] As mothers shoulder most of the caregiving responsibilities, the added demands of parenting children in these situations can lead to increased stress for working mothers.[14] Working mothers may also feel additional pressures at work, as they are experiencing greater financial pressures to meet the needs of their children. These additional pressures at work and at home can become overwhelming and may give rise to new fears about the future and the extent to which a working mother believes she will be able to nurture a healthy work and family life.[12]

While family leave policies are supposed to support the various caretaking needs of working mothers, few working mothers find these policies help them care for their children when they face an illness or have special needs. The care involved with children with disabilities or illness goes far beyond that of typical children. It requires constant interruptions, such as traveling to and from medical and professional appointments, staying with the child during hospital stays, and immediately responding when problems arise at school. These additional responsibilities can extend for months and even years. For instance, Patti, a single mother, had been temporarily living with her parents after she had been let go from her job. She had just accepted a new position and had plans to restart her more independent life when her daughter was diagnosed with a heart condition that required surgery and a prolonged stay in the hospital. Patti could not imagine how she could be fully dedicated to a new role in a new company and also take care of her daughter. After much heartache, she decided not to accept the new position. Six months later, as her daughter's health improved, she contacted the hiring manager again. The position had been filled, but the manager recommended she contact a different department that was now hiring. Patti secured a new position in the same company and started the next phase of her work/life journey.

Contrary to popular belief, the emotional burdens of family disruptions for single working mothers are not always that different than those experienced by partnered working mothers. Married or partnered women do not always feel supported by their spouses when caring for a child with special needs. Because they are shouldering the burden of care and not getting the support they need from their partners, married women may experience their own additional emotional burdens.[12]

Working mothers who are parenting children with special needs may be inclined to blame their work status for their children's challenges, or at least wonder if their working has made the situation worse. Charlotte, a public relations manager, and her wife adopted a two-year-old boy from Sierra Leone named Sekou. As Sekou got older, Charlotte and her partner learned Sekou had significant learning disabilities and psychological needs. While many of the learning disabilities could be addressed through school resources, Charlotte found it stressful to support Sekou's psychological needs. Charlotte knew that many of his challenges were the result of the trauma he had experienced as an infant, but she still blamed herself and wondered if Sekou's issues would have been eased if she had not continued to work full time. While she was thrilled to become a mom through adoption, her work was central to her identity and to her family's income. Her anxiety was further heightened because she was happy to go to work and leave Sekou with her partner; she found work to be a reprieve from the tension at home. On the day of Sekou's eighth-grade graduation, he was emotionally distant, as was typical for him. After the ceremony, he approached Charlotte, thanked her, and told her he loved her. Charlotte was emotionally overwhelmed to see Sekou connect in this way. Reflecting on that day, she shared that perhaps work may have helped her be a better parent to Sekou, because it provided her with the restorative distance she needed in order to be more supportive when she was with him. Charlotte's experience is not unusual. Work can be a source of social and emotional support and provide a respite from caregiving responsibilities for working mothers with special-needs and chronically ill children.[15]

When navigating child-related health issues, working mothers may feel even more isolated than their peers, as their unique circumstances set them apart from other mothers at work and in their community. Eva explained the struggles she experienced integrating work and caring for a son with autism:

I would like to work more than I do, but one of my sons is autistic and has some verbal issues, so I need extra time to tend to his needs. He needs me to pick him up, bring him home, and tend to his needs. If I were working full time, I would not be able to do all this. I worked full time for a couple of years, and it was very hectic. My son's needs were not being met and I was always rushing around. Working part time does help because it is easier and doesn't interfere with my family life, but obviously, it leads to new financial pressures.

Eva also felt more conflicted because she did not feel comfortable sharing her experiences with the other working mothers in her office. She didn't feel they could relate to the challenges she faced, when their biggest issues were things like forgetting to register a child for soccer. As Eva's story illustrates, working mothers who are caring for special needs children may isolate themselves from their colleagues. Beyond feeling that their colleagues do not relate to their situation, they may fear that they will be further stigmatized for their child's disability or illness.[16] While these concerns are not unwarranted, the demands of these caregiving situations, coupled with the stress of hiding one's experience and authentic self, may increase the emotional stress of not discussing one's life at work.

One way to combat this stress is to be more open and honest about the stress and pressure you are feeling as you care for your child. Over time, Eva began sharing her parenting story with her colleagues. She eventually learned of a number of other parents who also had children with significant special needs. Eva decided to form an affinity group in her organization for working parents of children with special needs:

> This is very close to my heart because of my son, and having a support group at work would be ideal. I am trying to organize parents and speakers together. My firm is supportive of this, and even though they are focused on children and community needs, this is not something we have for our employees.

Eva used her organization's policies around affinity groups to advocate for a new group that met her needs. Through the affinity group, she had access to organizational resources to fund special programs that would assist families with education, advice, and advocacy. By being creative and taking the risk of sharing her experience, Eva was able to get the support she needed from her organization.

Working Mothers Decoupled

Beyond children, the second most significant relationship for most working mothers is the one with their life partner. While working mothers continue to shoulder most of the caregiving and household responsibilities for a family, life partners provide emotional and social support that helps working mothers carve a positive path for themselves. However, not all life partners provide this support. As a result, the rate of divorce among working parents has risen exponentially in recent years.[17] Divorce is particularly straining for working mothers' emotional and physical health.[4] Compared to their married counterparts, divorced and widowed individuals have higher rates of acute and chronic conditions such as heart disease, cancer, depression, and other mental illnesses.[18] Divorced working mothers may also experience more work pressure, as they are now the sole breadwinners for their households. At the same time, working mothers may also feel greater demands at home as they parent and manage their households alone. These dual pressures can give rise to new tensions of integrating work and motherhood. Avery, whose former partner had moved to another state, explained the stress she felt:

> At work, it is hard because there is no one else in my same situation. They all have spouses. It is just easier for them. I don't always have a person that can help me. There is one person at work that is a single parent, but she has a long-time former partner who lives locally, so it is much easier for her to schedule things or have somebody pick up her children. Sometimes it's harder for me because I'm the only one that's home.

In the workplace, a change in marital status may also lead to changes in how coworkers and managers treat a working mother. Divorce can become one more identity beyond motherhood and gender that sets a woman apart. Divorced women may find themselves subject to awkward interactions with their coworkers as they tiptoe around their change in status. As a member of the executive team for a large nonprofit, Riya had to attend fundraisers, galas, and social events for work. She talked about how uncomfortable that aspect of her job became after her divorce:

> My boss actually said to me, "You are throwing off seating charts at the dinner parties."

She tried not to let these comments prevent her from staying engaged with this aspect of her work. Reflecting back on that time, Riya still felt positive about the choices she had made:

> Between my divorce and my long work hours, I had *über* parent guilt. Looking back, though, I know it wasn't an epic fail. My son turned out okay, and I had a lot to do with that.

In more family-supportive organizations, working mothers may find their managers will offer support before they even ask for it. Darlene was going through a highly contentious divorce and had a restraining order filed against her husband. Her manager offered to adjust her work schedule until she could find adequate after-school care for her daughter. He also worked with her to adjust her work responsibilities so she could manage the divorce process and establish new routines at home. Although there was no formal policy for Darlene's situation, her manager understood she needed time to settle her family concerns before she could reestablish a productive work/family routine.

Whenever possible, divorced mothers can benefit greatly by maintaining a positive co-parenting relationship with their former partners. The term *family incivility* refers to low-intensity negative behaviors that violate the norms of mutual respect in a family—even a divorced family.[19] Rudeness, insults, and other disrespectful behaviors can have lasting effects: when parents exhibit these behaviors, they are likely to be mimicked by their children.[20] Counseling can help a divorced couple reduce animosity and establish a new co-parenting model that leads to greater emotional and psychological well-being for both parents and children.[21] Clarity, civility, and advance planning around weekly schedules, vacations, and children's activities can also help a divorced working mother craft a more positive path. After her divorce, Barri established an agreement with her former husband in which they shared custody of their son. They also wrote into their separation agreement that her former husband would have their son the first two weeks in March, when she led a major industry conference. This arrangement eased her feelings of work/family conflict in the week before and then during the conference. She remarked that after the divorce, she found it easier to manage the conference; her husband took responsibility for their son in a way that he had not when they were married. If a civil, supportive co-parenting model with a former partner can be established, it will directly benefit a working mother and her children.

Working mothers often think they are alone as they manage a divorce, but some women may find there are ways their organization can help them that they might not have anticipated. Whether it is in the form of support networks, legal advice, or access to counseling, working mothers may find there are unexpected ways in which their organization and colleagues can support them as they work through the disruption of a divorce. Beyond the workplace, working mothers may also want to research community-based support. Within a community, there may be support groups, legal clinics, or other community programs that can help women work through a divorce and establish a "new normal."

CARING FOR AGING FAMILY MEMBERS

The *sandwich generation* is the term coined by sociologists to describe adults caring for both dependent children and aging or sick parents. Most individuals who are responsible for elder care are between the ages of forty-five and sixty-four, which often is when working adults are still caring for children.[22] Research suggests that 9% to 13% of dual-earner adult couples in the United States care for both children and frail or disabled parents for more than three hours per week.[23] Though about half of those individuals provide elder-care support for just under two years, 15.4% of people care for older relatives for more than a decade.[22] Elder care is expected to increase as baby boomers continue to age: between 5.7 million and 6.6 million caregivers will be needed by 2030 to support the elderly.[24]

While resources to help working mothers manage caregiving of children are growing, there is much less support available for elderly caretaking. The impact of elder care on women's careers can be dramatic, as this demand comes at a time when women's earning potential may be waning and when it is becoming increasingly difficult for women to reenter the workplace if they have taken time off.[24]

The stress of elder care occurs on multiple levels. Working mothers face new time demands and emotional stresses as they care for aging family members. Whether checking in on an elderly relative, cooking meals, driving him or her to and from appointments, managing finances, or providing direct care, elder care requires emotional energy, physical time, and cognitive space. Elder care itself can introduce new challenges for a working mother, as the care provided can become quite intimate and can result in role reversals between parents and children. The emotional toll of this role reversal creates new work/family stresses.[24] As one might expect, this burden is not necessarily shared equally by men and women. Women are more likely than men to be caring for their aging parents and relatives. Even when men and women are both providing this care, women spend more time on average than men.[25] Beyond the emotional stress of caretaking, there is also the potential financial burden of caring for aging relatives. The cost of elder care has soared, with expenses reaching as high as $14,000 per month.[26] Even if a working mother has the resources to pay for elder care, caregiving still requires a high level of emotional engagement and oversight that typically only a family member can provide.

Navigating elder care can also introduce new societal role pressures for a working mother. Having lived for years with the competing societal expectations of motherhood and professionalism, working mothers who are providing elder care may find themselves confronting a new societal pressure: "daughterhood." Janice Turner, a New York Times columnist, wrote about this issue when she discussed her experience caring for her aging mother who faced a health crisis. Having dealt with the crisis,

Janice returned to her work and her nuclear family in London. Upon her return, she received emails from readers judging her as "selfish and self-regarding" for returning to work. She wrote, "Just when you are free from being judged as a mother, you find yourself judged as a daughter."[27] Similar to motherhood and caring for children, "daughterhood" assumes that caring for aging parents, in-laws, and others is a daughter's responsibility, and that a working mother should prioritize this responsibility over work, but for many women, work is actually about being a good daughter, as it enables a woman to have the financial resources to take care of her parents.

Just as with a new baby, when caring for a sick or aging parent, a working mother needs to try to remember to make time to care for herself. Working mothers who are caring for elderly relatives may find themselves particularly vulnerable to anxiety and burnout.[28]

While childcare responsibilities lessen as children age, elder care responsibilities increase over time. There is always more to be done and concerns about what is to come next. It is easy to be self-critical and fearful of the future. If caretaking responsibilities become overwhelming, working mothers need to accept their limitations and reach out for help. Help can come in many forms. For emotional support, relying on friends or a mental health professional to develop strategies and ease the stress of navigating work and elder care may be beneficial.[28] Working mothers can research elder care resources in their community. Similar to childcare, there are different models of elder care ranging from care in one's home to adult care centers to continuing-care communities. These models vary in the amount of care provided and the cost. It is easy to focus solely on cost, but it is equally important to find a care arrangement that can ease the demands a working mother is experiencing so she can be more fully engaged at work and home. As with children, elder care should be seen as an investment rather than just a cost.

Working mothers may find their organizations and managers are not as attuned to the stresses of caring for elderly relatives. The 2015 SHRM Employee Benefits Report indicated that only 6% of employers provide an elder care referral service for their employees, with less than 1% of

employers providing additional elder care benefits such as geriatric counseling, onsite elder care facilities, access to backup elder care services, or
elder-care assisted living assessments. Similar to caring for children with
special needs, working mothers may need to become even stronger at
advocating for adjustments or for the support they desire. In requesting
a shift to a compressed work schedule to care for her parents, Hayley
commented on the challenges she faced in her organization:

> The struggle I had was most people in this situation seem to be
> young mothers who want to take time off to care for children. I am
> in my forties and my issues are different: I needed to find time to care
> for my mother when her health began to fail. My parents had always
> been there for me, and now it was my turn. That became my priority.

Hayley worked for a small business that did not have any family leave
policies. She spoke to her manager and the company owner to help them
understand elder care issues in general and her situation specifically.
She found that by educating her manager, he was more supportive when
she needed to accommodate her workday in order to help her mother.
Educating others was important to Hayley's ability to create her positive
path as she managed work and elder care.

Similar to how working mothers manage other life disruptions, work
can provide a valuable respite from the stresses associated with caring for
an elderly loved one. When Lucinda was returning to work after having her
first child, her mother was diagnosed with terminal cancer. She explained,

> I was crazy in the sense that things were very hectic for me. But
> coming back to work was the best thing for me. It kept me active
> rather than sitting around thinking about my mom and my daughter.
> So work was helpful in that sense. It also gave me just another reason
> to be more balanced in my life. Yes, I needed to spend more time
> with my daughter and mother, but I also still needed to keep my ca-
> reer going. That's the way I look at it. It was a hard time, but it was
> important to keep my career going. I wanted to still be out there

progressing in my job, in my organization. I needed that in order to have the income and energy to care for these people who were depending on me.

LOSS, GRIEF, AND WORK

Being part of a family and being connected emotionally also means that at some point one is likely to be confronted with loss. The death of a loved one is a traumatic experience, leaving survivors with feelings of helplessness, fear, and often an immediate sense of catastrophe.[29] An individual may experience a range of physical and mental reactions to trauma, including numbness, sleep disturbances, difficulty concentrating, and trouble making decisions. Traumatic loss can trigger feelings of extreme guilt, which interrupt a person's ability to perform his or her regular daily activities.[30] Depending on the nature of the death and the individual, it can take anywhere from months to years to move forward with life.[31] Grieving and adjusting to the death of a loved one is likely to disrupt women's lives at home and at work and, in some instances, lead to new choices on their work/life path.

There has been quite a bit of research focused on how individuals recover from the death of a loved one. The grieving process does not follow a linear path; rather, an individual typically oscillates between feelings of loss, in which one is focused on the lost relationship with the deceased, and feelings of restoration, in which one is focused on moving forward.[32] This oscillation between loss and restoration is part of the healing process, as it helps an individual acknowledge the loss while also beginning to create a new future.[32]

What is absent from most discussions of bereavement is how individuals adjust to a life trauma in the context of their work and professional life. How one connects with colleagues, reengages at work, and makes sense of the trauma at work all have implications for how a working mother crafts her work/life path. As Sheryl Sandberg, COO of Facebook, stated about her return to work following the sudden death of her husband:

For me, starting the transition back to work has been a savior, a chance to feel useful and connected. But I quickly discovered that even those connections had changed. Many of my coworkers had a look of fear in their eyes as I approached. I knew why—they wanted to help but weren't sure how. Should I mention it? Should I not mention it? If I mention it, what the hell do I say? I realized that to restore that closeness with my colleagues that has always been so important to me, I needed to let them in. And that meant being more open and vulnerable than I ever wanted to be.

As this quote illustrates, returning to work following the death of an immediate family member requires a working mother to manage shifting relationships with colleagues and shifting boundaries between life and work. For some individuals returning to work, reestablishing work routines, connections, and identity can help with the healing process.[33] Work roles can even help women craft a new identity for themselves that honors their loss. Gabriela, a family psychologist, had a private practice focused on families and adolescents when her teenage son died in an accident. Over time, she shifted her practice to focus on bereavement and families recovering from the loss of a child. Gabby's identity as a mother whose child died became intertwined with her professional identity. For other working mothers, death may spark a desire to transition away from work and their professional life, at least for the time being. Some working mothers find they need time off to focus solely on their family as a way to move forward from their grief. Whatever path a mother chooses, we know that how her colleagues and organization respond to her affects her ability to move forward and craft the next phase of her work/life path.[33]

Similar to Gabby's experience, working mothers may also find it helpful to channel their grief as part of the healing process. Sheryl Sandberg did this when she wrote about her experience in *Option B* and established a foundation to help women recover from the death of a partner. Starting or becoming engaged in a nonprofit, or establishing a scholarship in a loved one's memory, can also be a helpful way for a working mother to heal. When it comes to grief, there is no clear path for moving forward.

Working mothers need to rely on the strength of their families and their professional lives to carve the path that best suits them.

CONSIDERING A LEAVE OF ABSENCE

As most of the stories in this chapter illustrate, when working mothers experience a life disruption, they may consider taking a leave of absence. Because of the nature of most of these disruptions, it can be hard to know what a working mother needs, what types of work adjustments might be helpful, or how long she might need to be out of work. As women consider a leave of absence, they should be mindful of the possible adverse career effects we have discussed in earlier chapters. Taking a leave of absence—regardless of the reason—can have negative career implications for both men and women, resulting in lower salary increases and fewer promotions.[34] Despite these potential career implications, the emotional benefits of taking time off can outweigh any negative impact.

To manage possible negative repercussions of a leave of absence, a working mother will want to revisit the discussion regarding navigating maternity leave in Chapter 3. Here, we only mention a few high-level points. First, while organizations may have a bereavement policy, it likely only covers a few days or a few weeks away from work. Women who experience life disruptions can investigate what other human resource policies they can leverage as they advocate for the leave they desire. As with maternity leave, working mothers can set clear expectations with their managers about how much time off they desire and what their role will be when they return. Similar to maternity leave, time off does not need to be an all-or-nothing prospect. Given the benefits work can provide for navigating life disruptions, working mothers may find it useful to stay engaged in some capacity, both for their emotional well-being and for their professional identity. Staying in communication with work helps women stay informed about work and organizational changes and involved in key discussions. Keeping colleagues informed of the situation may also ease the tension and reduce the need for awkward or imposing conversations about one's family life when one returns.

GARNERING SUPPORT TO NAVIGATE UNEXPECTED TRANSITIONS

Garnering support at work to navigate unexpected life transitions can be particularly difficult, since working mothers' experiences and needs are likely to vary tremendously. It would be virtually impossible for an organization to create a portfolio of benefits and policies that could support working mothers across all potential disruptions.

For this reason, working mothers will frequently need to rely on their managers to gain the support they need from the organization. This can be difficult, as not all managers are open to or knowledgeable about the additional stresses and responsibilities working mothers shoulder as they cope with these disruptions. In most instances, though not all, working mothers will benefit from being open with their managers about their situation and advocating for what they need. Earlier in the chapter, we shared Hayley's story of how she used an educational approach with her manager to help him understand the added burden of caring for elderly relatives. Educating her manager made it easy for her to then negotiate the accommodations she needed. If there are benefits that might ease your burden, such as counseling or referral services, you might want to gather data to help your organization find financially feasible options and to explain why these benefits are important to all employees, not just you.

We also encourage working mothers to reach out to their managers sooner rather than later. Working mothers often try to carve a path through a disruption on their own because they are afraid of disclosing the situation to their manager or simply because they are so used to solving problems on their own. Managers can be an important advocate and a source of support to help a mother handle the unexpected. For instance, a number of years back one of the authors (Danna) had a sudden health crisis that was potentially life threatening. She found herself in the hospital awaiting surgery two days later. One of her first calls was to her department chair. It was the day before surgery, and it was unclear when or if she would be able to return to work. Her department chair was likely worried, as classes started in a few days and he needed to find coverage, but on the phone he was kind and reassuring and told her to focus on her health. When surgery was over, she learned the original diagnosis had been wrong and she was going to make a full recovery. Still, she had undergone major surgery, and she was grateful that her department chair had found a colleague to cover her classes for a few weeks so she could recover. If she had not reached out to her department chair, she likely would have stepped back into the classroom a week after major surgery.

Finally, working mothers can garner support from their organization by being more supportive themselves when colleagues face these unexpected disruptions. Sending flowers, cards, personalized gifts, or a meal service reminds an employee that the organization cares about him or her as a person. Attending a wake, shiva, or funeral service or making a hospital visit are all ways to support colleagues as they work through difficult life situations. In so doing, working mothers can help build an organizational or departmental culture in which unexpected disruptions are acknowledged and where employees support each other through good and bad circumstances. There is no doubt you will benefit from such a culture, if and when you need the help.

CHAPTER TAKEAWAYS

1. As much as you plan for and forge your work/life path, you are likely to experience some unexpected life disruptions—whether a personal health crisis, a child-centered health issue, divorce, an elderly relative's care needs, or the death of a loved one—that will challenge your status quo.
2. Sometimes a working mother's first response to a life disruption is to take time off from work. While this may be helpful for some

women, others find that their work can provide an important reprieve when facing a difficult life circumstance.

3. Because these life disruptions vary so much from individual to individual, it is not likely that organizations will have clear policies that provide a working mother with the support she needs. Working mothers will need to advocate for what they want in both the short and long term as they sort through these unexpected turns in their work/life path.

REFERENCES

1. Damaske, S., & Frech, A. (2016). Women's work pathways across the life course. *Demography*, *53*(2), 365–391.
2. Frech, A., & Damaske, S. (2012). The relationships between mothers' work pathways and physical and mental health. *Journal of Health and Social Behavior*, *53*(4), 396–412.
3. Cohen, I. (2011, July 26). Heart @ work. *Working Mother*. Retrieved from https://www.workingmother.com/health-safety/heart-health-and-work.
4. Ross, C. E., Mirowsky, J., & Goldsteen, K. (1990). The impact of the family on health: The decade in review. *Journal of Marriage and the Family*, *52*(4), 1059–1078.
5. Davis-Kean, P. E. (2005). The influence of parent education and family income on child achievement: The indirect role of parental expectations and the home environment. *Journal of Family Psychology*, *19*(2), 294.
6. Harding, J. F., Morris, P. A., & Hughes, D. (2015). The relationship between maternal education and children's academic outcomes: A theoretical framework. *Journal of Marriage and Family*, *77*(1), 60–76.
7. Scharte, M., Bolte, G., & GME Study Group. (2012). Increased health risks of children with single mothers: The impact of socio-economic and environmental factors. *European Journal of Public Health*, *23*(3), 469–475.
8. Almendrala, A. (2016, January 6). Almost half of single moms struggle with this health problem. *Huffington Post*. Retrieved from https://www.huffpost.com/entry/single-parents-sleep-study_n_568c09eae4b014efe0dbe060.
9. Omara-Alwala, A. (2012, September 7). Black women face health discrimination in America. *Forbes*. Retrieved from https://www.forbes.com/sites/womensenews/2012/09/07/black-women-face-health-discrimination-in-america/#741ff0b877d5.
10. Barnes, Z. (2017, March 30). 8 Health conditions that disproportionately affect black women. *Self Magazine*. Retrieved from https://www.self.com/story/black-women-health-conditions.
11. Villarosa, L. (2018, April 11). Why America's Black mothers and babies are in a life-or-death crisis. *New York Times Magazine*. Retrieved from https://www.nytimes.com/2018/04/11/magazine/black-mothers-babies-death-maternal-mortality.html.

12. Vickers, M., Parris, M., & Bailey, J. (2004). Working mothers of children with chronic illness: Narratives of working and caring. *Australian Journal of Early Childhood, 29*(1), 39–44.

13. Brault, M. W. (2011, November). *School-aged children with disabilities in U.S. metropolitan statistical areas: 2010.* U.S. Census Bureau, American Community Survey Briefs, Report Number ACSBR/10-12. Retrieved from https://www.census.gov/library/publications/2011/acs/acsbr10-12.html.

14. Anastopoulos, T. D., Guevremont, D. C., Shelton, T. L., & DuPaul, G. J. (1992). Parenting stress among families of children with attention deficit hyperactivity disorder. *Journal of Abnormal Child Psychology, 20*, 503–520.

15. Li, A., Shaffer, J., & Bagger, J. (2015). The psychological well-being of disability caregivers: Examining the roles of family strain, family-to-work conflict, and perceived supervisor support. *Journal of Occupational Health Psychology, 20*(1), 40–49.

16. Rosenzweig, J. M., Malsch, A. M., Brennan, E. M., Huffstutter, K. J., Stewart, L. M., & Lieberman, L. A. (2011). Managing communication at the work-life boundary: Parents of children and youth with mental health disorders and human resource professionals. *Best Practices in Mental Health: An International Journal, 7*, 67–93.

17. Bianchi, S. M., Robinson, J. P., & Milke, M. A. (2006). *The changing rhythms of American family life.* New York, NY: Russell Sage Foundation.

18. Smith, J. C., Mercy, J. A., & Conn, J. M. (1988). Marital status and the risk of suicide. *American Journal of Public Health, 78*(1), 78–80.

19. Lim, S., & Tai, K. (2014). Family incivility and job performance: A moderated mediation model of psychological distress and core self-evaluation. *Journal of Applied Psychology, 99*(2), 351–359.

20. Maccoby, E. E. (1992). The role of parents in the socialization of children: An historical overview. *Developmental Psychology, 28*(6), 1006–1017.

21. Kruk, E. (2012). *Family therapy and parenting coordination to reduce conflict.* New York, NY: Sussex Publishers.

22. U.S. Department of Labor, Bureau of Labor Statistics. (2015). *American time use survey, eldercare.* Retrieved from https://www.bls.gov/tus/charts/eldercare.htm/.

23. Neal, M. B., & Hammer, L. B. (2007). *Working couples caring for children and aging parents: Effects on work and well-being.* Mahwah, NJ: Lawrence Erlbaum Associates Publishers.

24. O'Donnell, L. (2016, February 9). The crisis facing America's working daughters. *The Atlantic.* Retrieved from https://www.theatlantic.com/business/archive/2016/02/working-daughters-eldercare/459249/.

25. Butler, R. N. (2007). Who will care for you? *AARP Bulletin.*

26. Tribune Wire Reports. (2015, July 20). Families face tough decisions as cost of elder care soars. *Chicago Tribune.* Retrieved from https://www.chicagotribune.com/lifestyles/health/ct-elder-care-costs-20150720-story.html.

27. Turner, J. (2017, May 18). The good daughter. *New Statesman.* Retrieved from https://www.newstatesman.com/politics/health/2017/05/good-daughter.

28. Mayo Clinic Staff. (2018). *Tips for taking care of yourself.* Mayo Foundation for Medical Education and Research. Retrieved from https://www.mayoclinic.org/healthy-lifestyle/stress-management/in-depth/caregiver-stress/art-20044784.

29. Herman, J. L. (1997). *Trauma and recovery* (Rev. ed.). New York, NY: Basic Books.

30. Hazen, M. A. (2003). Societal and workplace responses to perinatal loss: Disenfranchised grief or healing connection. *Human Relations, 65*(2), 147–166.

31. Maciejewski, P. K., Zhang, B., Block, S. D., & Prigerson, H. G. (2007). An empirical examination of the stage theory of grief. *Journal of the American Medical Association, 297*(7), 716–723.

32. Stroebe, M., & Schut, H. (2010). The dual process model of coping with bereavement: A decade on. *OMEGA: Journal of Death and Dying, 61*(4), 273–289.

33. Hazen, M. A. (2008). Grief and the workplace. *Academy of Management Perspectives, 22*(3), 78–86.

34. Judiesch, M. K., & Lyness, K. S. (1999). Left behind? The impact of leaves of absence on managers' career success. *Academy of Management Journal, 42*(6), 641–651.

9

Allies, Not Enemies

Garnering Support from the Men in Our Lives

I was promoted less than a year after our second child was born, and I think my husband was even more excited than I was about it. For him, it wasn't about money, although that was certainly a plus; it was more about the recognition of all my hard work and that I would be the youngest person to be promoted to this particular leadership role. He told me right away that he would do what he could to make it work alongside his full-time job. We added more childcare, and when I began to travel and attend more dinners and other events, he was very understanding and supportive. He wants me to succeed just as much as I want him to succeed. Perhaps this is a function of how we started when we were dating. I made it clear to him that I was career oriented and I did not expect to be a stay-at-home mom. He was clear with me that he wanted to be involved in his kids' lives, so knowing that upfront helped, and I think it is probably what attracted us to one another.

—LYNDSEY, *technology manager*

Playing off the phrase "behind every great man is a great woman," Anne-Marie Slaughter argued just the opposite—that is, "behind every great woman is a great man"—when advocating for the importance of men supporting their wives' careers and addressing the gender pay gap.[1] Working mothers cannot tackle all of the inequities they face alone. Societal and gender role expectations are powerful and shape organizational expectations and the way we all think about appropriate roles men and women should play. We have the potential to alter those assumptions when men and women work together to shift gendered norms around work and caregiving.

In this chapter, we explore how men can play a significant role in supporting women as they create positive paths through work and motherhood. We begin by discussing the benefits for mothers, children, and fathers of men who are caregiving partners. We then address the challenges and opportunities many fathers face as they take on more caretaking and household responsibilities. Like women, men are beginning to approach their careers differently, with greater interest in making space for life outside of work but may face different challenges when they integrate fatherhood and work. Finally, we turn our attention to the workplace and how men can act as allies and support working mothers at work. To get this support from men, women need to give support—a topic we discuss throughout this chapter.

BALANCING ACTS OF WORKING FATHERS IN THE TWENTY-FIRST CENTURY

In discussions of work and family, we often forget that many working fathers are managing similar complexities to working mothers. Scott Behson, author of *The Working Dad's Survival Guide*, argues that fathers need the same support as mothers, and we need to bring these issues to the forefront of organizational practice. Our research echoes this point. We have found that fathers are challenged by gender role expectations about caregiving and work that mirror the societal norms working mothers face.

Undoubtedly, the role of fathers has shifted dramatically in the past decade. Nonetheless, twenty-first-century working fathers are still pushing against traditional models of fatherhood. Just as society has historically placed mothers as caregivers, fathers have been assumed to be the family breadwinners. It was assumed that a father's primary contribution to a family was as the provider. Therefore, fathers were expected to be removed from their children, other family members, and household responsibilities, because their work takes them outside the home.[2] Fathers also often receive a "fatherhood premium" in their compensation at work. They are still frequently given higher salaries and more frequent promotions because, as the presumed family breadwinners, the assumption is that they need additional career benefits to support their families.[3]

Today, generational changes and shifting family structures are altering these desires and expectations of working fathers. Increasingly, fathers need and want to be more involved in caretaking.[2] Fathers, particularly Millennial ones, express a strong desire to be involved parents and to define their role as an integration of breadwinner and caregiver.[4] For instance, Jack explains how he has structured his work/family path to provide time for work and caretaking:

I drop my daughter at daycare every morning by 8 a.m. My wife also works full time, so we are doing five-days-a-week daycare. In addition to working full time, my wife also teaches three nights a week. With my wife's schedule, I need to leave work on time and go pick up my daughter. If I need to work after my daughter is asleep, I have my laptop, so I can access everything I need. Generally, I do a lot after she goes to bed. So, family does "interfere" with my schedule to some extent, but I really enjoy the time with my daughter.

Like mothers, fathers also want to integrate meaningful careers with being active parents.[5] Jack went on to explain that if he were to solely focus on being a breadwinner, as is expected of most men, he would have to shift his work/family arrangement:

If I want more money, I've got to put in more hours. I think it comes down to that. And the hours spent with my daughter are not something I want to sacrifice.

The clash between societal expectations of fatherhood and modern fathers' desires has led to conflicting ideals of what it means to be a working father.

Gendered norms around work and caregiving also mean fathers feel judged at home when they are active caregivers. We frequently hear fathers complain about being out with their children and being asked if they are "babysitting" or being praised for "helping their wives" when in fact all they are doing is being fathers. Fathers who are active caregivers are seen as special, simply because they are men. When a mother engages in the same behaviors, no one notices, because it is "normal."[6] Fathers also get tired of being portrayed as less capable caregivers, a norm perpetuated by the media and pop culture.[7]

David shared his frustration with how teachers and other parents responded when he regularly brought his daughter to daycare in mismatched clothing:

> If I were a mom, I would be praised for letting my daughter dress herself and make her own choices. People would applaud me for helping her begin to develop her autonomy and to buck the trend of controlling, helicopter parenting. As a dad, everyone just assumes I can't match clothes and my wife isn't there to help me.

Even at a daycare center, where most families have two working parents, gendered expectations of fathers abound.

Negative assumptions of fathers can be even more pronounced depending on one's racial or cultural identity. For example, Matt Prestbury started a successful Facebook group called "Black Fathers" to combat the negative image that black fathers are disengaged parents who leave their children to be raised by single mothers. Prestbury is using this group to highlight images of loving and engaged fathers, to help black fathers connect with and support one another, and to change the narrative of what it means to be a black father.[8]

At work, fathers also face biases when they try to combine work with caregiving. This message is most often conveyed in how an organization approaches paternity leave and men's desires for flexible work arrangements. Only 12% of private-sector workers have access to paid parental leave policies.[9] When paternity leave is offered, it is usually short and unpaid. This may partially explain why 96% of American fathers go back to work within two weeks of a baby's birth. Taking paternity leave has been shown to lead to decreased earnings for the first five years of a child's life.[10] Fathers' awareness of these consequences may explain why only 40% of men choose to use paternity leave, even when they have access to it.[11] In fact, professionally employed fathers who had access to paid parental leave cite workplace pressures as the primary reason why they chose not to use these policies.[12] Men appear to be just as worried as women about being stigmatized and penalized for being an engaged parent. This may be why some research suggests fathers experience even greater work/family conflict than mothers.[13]

Tom Stocky, VP of product development at Facebook, explained how these expectations and biases affected his choice to use his four-month paternity leave benefit. He famously blogged,

> When I tell people I'm on a four-month leave, it's typically followed by surprise that I'm actually taking it. Parents wonder why would I want to subject myself to that torture, and non-parents wonder why I would want to sit around and do nothing for four months. Everyone wonders why I would want to do what is surely a career-limiting move. This last one was especially interesting to experience, because in some ways people said to me what they didn't feel permitted to say to women. Would my project still be there when I got back? Wouldn't my ambitious coworkers use this as an opportunity (maliciously or not) to advance themselves at my expense? Wouldn't I be viewed as being less committed to my work, thus stunting my own advancement for the foreseeable future? I did not know the answers to these questions, but I viewed this as an important enough experiment to find out.[14]

Coworkers see paternity leave as a choice, whereas maternity leave is not. In making this choice, men are violating gendered expectations associated with masculinity, leading them to face even greater questioning of work commitment than women who take maternity leave. When fathers are able to work past these biases, they experience many benefits of work/family integration. A father's satisfaction and engagement in work is more positive when he is actively involved at home with his children.[15]

One of the unique issues working fathers face in managing work and family is that they have fewer role models to draw upon than working mothers. Without positive role models, they may be less likely to share their feelings for fear that others at work might see them as less of an ideal worker or less of a man. Gary, a software developer, shares the struggles he feels because he does not have models to follow as he navigates work and fatherhood. He explains his struggle with wanting to continue to pursue a demanding career while also wanting to be available to his daughter:

> I want to be super-successful and have this long title and lots of letters after my name . . . But I don't want to do that at the expense of being a good father. I don't know what that balance is regarding the percentage of each.

WORKING MOTHERS BENEFIT FROM INVOLVED FATHERS

Helping fathers become active caregivers benefits working mothers' well-being and engagement at work and home. Encouraging fathers to take paternity leave, as was discussed previously, is important because it moves a couple toward a more equitable distribution of home responsibilities. When men are active caregivers, they develop a "parental caregiving neural network" and, like women, they become more attuned to an infant's state and more emotionally connected to their child.[16] This may help explain why fathers who take paternity leave experience increased child–parent engagement and are more involved in children's daily care nine months after birth.[17] This pattern has been found even when fathers take just two weeks of paternity leave. Children also behave differently when both parents are active caregivers. Children shift more easily between parents providing caregiving, with the added benefit of having two different, but equally engaged, parents.[18] This, in turn, benefits mothers, who feel less stress and guilt as their children are not solely dependent on them for their needs, and consequently leads to a positive impact on women both in their careers and at home.

In short, fathers' involvement in caregiving has a positive influence on the health, well-being, and career progression of working mothers.[19] Furthermore, couples who share caregiving equitably have more sex and are less likely to divorce.[20]

The benefits of co-parenting for fathers, mothers, and children are well defined. What is less straightforward is how a couple can create and main-tain a model of shared caregiving. Even with shifts toward this model, fathers still lag behind working mothers in the time they devote to house-hold and childcare responsibilities. While two-thirds of fathers say they want to share caregiving equally, only about one-third actually do.[12] On average, married fathers who work full time spend about 1 hour and 17 minutes per day on caregiving responsibilities. By comparison, married mothers who work full time spend about 2 hours and 4 minutes daily on childcare.[21] Furthermore, many working fathers still see themselves purely as the helpers or backup providers, with working mothers remaining the primary caregivers.[4]

One of the biggest challenges for working mothers is the mental and emotional load they carry.[22] The popular press has noted how in families where both parents work, mothers overwhelmingly carry the mental burden of remembering home- and child-related responsibilities like doctor's appointments, school paperwork, filling out forms, signing up for camps and extracurricular programs, and so forth. It's usually up to mothers, whether they are working or not, to remember all of that. To share this mental load, having a discussion with one's partner is definitely an important step to take. However, often the response from dads is, "I am happy to help, absolutely! Just tell me what to do, and I'll take care of it!" This helps with the offloading of doing the actual tasks, but NOT with the offloading of remembering all the tasks to be done—hence the term "mental" load.

The challenge for heterosexual couples is to debunk gendered expectations around breadwinning and caregiving. It is not surprising that same-sex couples tend to share childcare and household responsibilities more equitably and tend to be more equally involved in their roles as parents.[23] These couples do not start from heteronormative assumptions about caregiving and breadwinning, so they make work and caregiving decisions based on what each partner wants and enjoys doing at work and home.[24] This is does not imply that all same-sex couples are immune to the challenges of one partner being overburdened by the mental load of household and child-related responsibilities. All couples should start these conversations by focusing on what each partner enjoys and feels confident at, rather than what is expected of each partner, as they determine their co-parenting strategy. A more detailed discussion of co-parenting can be found back in Chapter 3.

We do want to remind working mothers that they will likely need to actively and continually support their male partners to help them stay committed to a co-parenting model. As work shifts or as children age, shared caregiving can easily revert back to more traditional roles. For example, as a father's work role or employer changes, he may find himself responding to new organizational pressures that make it harder to integrate work and family. On the other hand, as children age, some fathers find themselves wanting to become more involved in their activities and academic lives. As with all aspects of your path through work and motherhood, shared care arrangements are not static. We encourage couples to discuss how childcare and household arrangements may shift whenever there are changes to a home or work schedule. For instance, when Juliette accepted a new job, she and her husband sat down to discuss how they might need to shift daycare pickup and drop-off arrangements for their son. Initially her husband assumed she would now be doing all pickup and drop-off duties because her new job was just 10 minutes from their house, but Juliette had hoped to use the extra time to exercise and take some time for herself. They ended up coming up with an entirely new pickup and drop-off plan that enabled them both to create some extra time in their days to exercise more regularly. Beyond responding to scheduling shifts, regular conversations about shared caregiving and household responsibilities are just as important to a couple's health as are regular conversations about finances or schedules. It may take some extra time and energy to sustain shared caregiving and breadwinning, but sharing these responsibilities is critical to building a life that enables both working parents to thrive at work, at home, and as a family.

VARIED WORK CHOICES FOR WORKING FATHERS

> I sold my business, staying on part time as a consultant. I thought about going into other careers, but then my children needed me. I had three kids in three different schools. I adapted by working from home, working out of Starbucks, and at one point I even rented office space near one of my boy's schools because it was 40 minutes from our home. I would have stayed on as a consultant, but then I missed a game when my son got his first home run because I was on a conference call, and that changed everything for me. Now I have created a portfolio career—a mix of jobs I like to do—and I can also be full time with my kids. I can drive anywhere and I don't miss things.
>
> —DENNIS

We do not hear much about fathers who alter their career trajectories to better accommodate work and family integration, but it is becoming more common as fathers, like mothers, want time to care for their families and children. Working fathers want to be successful in their careers, but they also want to be committed to their families. More frequently, they are making career choices that are based on their desires to be active caregivers.[25]

Some fathers are making this shift by adjusting the trajectory of their career. In a study conducted by Massachusetts-based Bright Horizons, about half of new parents (including men) said they have opted for a lower-paying job with more flexibility and better family-friendly benefits. More than two-thirds of working parents (again, men included) said they considered not returning to their same employers after having their first child, and about 60% stated that they would switch employers for a job with greater flexibility.[26] In the same survey, 69% of working fathers reported they had considered changing jobs because of family responsibilities. This is particularly evident in the professional services industry, where firms have trouble retaining women and men in their early thirties because of work/family conflicts created by long hours and extensive travel.[27] Even at the upper echelons of organizations, male senior executives who are in line for top leadership positions say they have little desire to become CEO if it interferes with their family lives.[28]

More frequently, fathers are also making use of flexible work arrangements to better integrate work and family. Boston College Center for Work and Family conducted research on 1,000 professionally employed fathers and found that 75% of them reported using flextime, 57% worked from home at least some of the time, and 27% used compressed workweeks. However, working fathers do not have equal access to workplace flexibility. Men in low-status jobs are significantly less likely to ask for and take advantage of flexibility for non–work-related tasks such as caregiving.[29] Rather than negotiate a formal flexible arrangement, men are more likely to informally shift when they work or how they work. This was particularly true for men who held senior-level positions. Malcolm, a partner in a law firm, stated he rarely felt guilty when he left early or rescheduled meetings to fulfill home responsibilities. He told his firm that when his daughter was born, he was going to be very involved in her life while still remaining committed to the company. Interestingly, he was not asking permission, nor was he formally negotiating a flexible work arrangement; he was simply informing his partners of his plans.

Flexibility has similar work/family benefits for fathers as it does for mothers. Fathers who have access to and use flexible work schedules have greater job satisfaction, report increased morale and commitment to their organizations, enjoy improved relationships with their coworkers, and are more productive.[30] Unfortunately, most flexible work programs are targeted toward mothers, which reinforces the belief that it is more acceptable for women than men to adapt their careers to accommodate family demands.[2] Consequently, fathers often face a harsher flexibility stigma than women when they shift their work schedules for family reasons.[31] This may partially explain why many working fathers often "fake" their work hours to pass as being an ideal, committed worker.[32] However, such faking can lead fathers to feel less authentic at work, which likely has adverse effects on their engagement and work productivity. Men and women need to work together to make flexible work arrangements more acceptable.

A more dramatic shift some working fathers are making to manage work and family is to take time off from work to be a full-time parent. In 2012, there were more than 2 million fathers who were deemed "stay-at-home dads." While that only represents about 7% of fathers with children, that figure has risen from 4% in 1989.[33] Fathers' reasons for staying at home have also changed. While some are at home due to illness, disability, or joblessness, 21% of fathers said they were specifically staying home to care for their children and households.[33] Typically, the decision for a father to stay home is driven by the same considerations as a mother. Financial circumstances, earning power, and values around childrearing influence men's choices.[34] For many couples, the determination of who will stay home is simply a question of who is earning more and has more earning potential.

While media and advertisements are drawing attention to the "involved dad," the stigma of full-time fatherhood remains strong. Full-time fathers face additional challenges of finding friends, being accepted by full-time mothers, and maintaining their self-esteem when they are not breadwinners. When Julian and his wife decided he would take time off to care for their three children, they were surprised by the reactions they received from their "gender-enlightened" family and friends: jokes about who "wears the pants" and "weekly allowances" abounded. A mother may also struggle as she relinquishes the majority of caregiving to a stay-at-home dad. Women may find it difficult to be confident that they are good mothers if their partner is doing the majority of childcare.[35] Even when both members of a couple are fully committed to a father staying home, it can be difficult to defy family, work, and societal pressures.

In sum, when we support working fathers, mothers, fathers, and families all gain. Women are more likely to break through the "maternal wall" when they have a spouse who is involved in childcare and household responsibilities. While fathers face gender biases that are similar to mothers' experiences, actively supporting fathers at home and work may help to lessen this stigma over time for all. Encouraging equality in the home as it relates to childcare and household responsibilities not only paves the way for further sharing of responsibilities but also models for other parents how couples (unmarried, married, and divorced) can make this work. It also provides children with a positive model of co-parenting, which hopefully encourages them to do the same when they become parents. In this way, the next generation becomes indoctrinated in new norms around work and childcare.

MALE ALLIES AT WORK

Just as working mothers can more easily change gendered expectations around caregiving by engaging their male partners, working mothers can more easily shift gendered assumptions about work by garnering support from male coworker allies. Some experts argue that gender equality, which is essential for changing the dialogue around work and family, is only attainable if women actively engage male colleagues, bosses, and mentors.[36] Given that the majority of senior business leaders are still men, they often have the power and influence to shift this dialogue.[37]

Male allies include men—both fathers and non-fathers—who engage with, support, and advocate for working women and minorities in the workplace. Effective male allies provide support by listening, empathizing, and publicly advocating for gender equality, work/family integration, and more broad-based diversity issues. Male allies understand that the pursuit of gender equality is not just for women—it benefits men as well.[36] Male allies see that they too are constrained by traditional gender norms and look for ways to challenge the status quo. By working together, men and women can create new norms that put men and women on a level playing field at work and at home.

To become allies, men must begin by understanding the power and privilege they experience in the workplace. They need to start to understand how the dominant culture in most organizations favors white men. Homogeneity in organizations, especially in senior leadership roles, tends to breed a culture of sexism and racism that can undermine women and minorities.[38] Recognizing this for white men is not easy. Bill Proudman, cofounder of White Men As Full Diversity Partners, uses the analogy of a fish in a fishbowl to explain this challenge.[39] Men know how to operate in organizations because the culture mirrors the values and norms in which they have been raised. It is hard for them to see the culture around them, just like a fish cannot see the water. Men often have to be challenged and pushed out of their comfort zone to "see the water" and recognize how that culture impacts access, engagement, and career opportunities in the workplace.[39] Helping men to see this culture can be difficult, since they may fear that their male colleagues will criticize their support of women or that their female colleagues may blame or judge them.[39]

Men are often able to move beyond these fears and become allies when they have first-hand experiences with women who work. While being married to a working mother or being raised by a working mother provides men with some insights into the challenges women experience, nothing provides a stronger impetus for becoming an ally than having a daughter. In explaining why he was a feminist, former President Barack Obama said,

I was raised by a single mom who spent much of her career working to empower women in developing countries. I watched as my grandmother, who helped raise me, worked her way up at a bank only to hit a glass ceiling. I've seen how Michelle has balanced the demands of a busy career and raising a family. Like many working mothers, she worried about the expectations and judgments of how she should handle the tradeoffs, knowing that few people would question my choices . . . but I also have to admit that when you're the father of two daughters, you become even more aware of how gender stereotypes pervade our society. You see the subtle and not-so-subtle social cues transmitted through culture.[40]

Having daughters has a significant impact on the hiring and promotion decisions men make. In the finance industry, senior partners with daughters have been shown to be more likely to hire and support female investing partners.[41] Having a daughter helps fathers "see the water" and ignites their desire to change organizational dynamics for the better.

On the other hand, men who maintain traditional gender roles at home may need more help in becoming allies. Heterosexual men in traditional marriages may just not be as aware of the issues working mothers face. As such, they may have more implicit biases against women at work. They are more apt to view the presence of women in the workplace negatively and deem organizations with women leaders as less effective.[42] Because men in traditional marriage structures have arranged work and home in a way that parallels societal norms, they may be less enlightened about the challenges working mothers face. Without an understanding of gender and work/family issues, these men are less aware of how traditional work environments make it difficult for both men and women to integrate work and family. These men may need more assistance to "see the water" before they can step into an ally role.

Once they begin to identify as male allies, there are no shortage of ways that men can encourage and promote working mothers. The simplest step male allies can take is to actively seek out connections with working mothers to learn about their experiences. Asking questions and listening to a working mother can help men begin to understand how women experience the intersection between work and family as well as other workplace inequalities. Male allies can support women further by actively engaging other men in discussions about gender and work/family issues even when women are not in the room. Sometimes it can be easier to confront one's biases when the issue is raised by someone in one's own identity group. In other words, men may be more likely to listen to the challenges working mothers face when they hear about them from other men.[43] Similarly, men can help advocate for organizational changes related to work/family policies. Organizations may be more responsive to men when they are advocating for formal policies or cultural changes that enable employees to create a positive path through work and parenthood.

Perhaps the most powerful action male allies can take is to proactively mentor and support working mothers in their career development. Implicit biases often shape who mentors whom, such that men are more likely to build informal mentoring relationships with men.[44] This dynamic limits mentorship opportunities for those from diverse backgrounds—particularly women and women of color. It also hurts an organization's ability to cultivate a diverse workforce. Male allies can counteract these tendencies by actively seeking out women to mentor or by offering to participate in formal mentoring programs for women. Being open, suspending judgment, and acknowledging differences are all critical to making these relationships work. Male allies can then provide the emotional and instrumental support working mothers need as they navigate work and family and pursue new career opportunities.[44]

Just as fathers need support from working mothers to become engaged co-parents, men at work also require support and encouragement from working mothers to step into the role of allies. Working mothers may find they need to invite male colleagues into conversations on gender equality or navigating work and family. Rather than simply speaking to other working mothers about work/family issues, working mothers can also reach out to male colleagues as they discuss these issues. These conversations can naturally open up the opportunity to discuss gender issues in the organization. Working mothers can invite men to join affinity groups or attend discussions related to gender or work/family concerns. As they become more engaged, men will begin to understand gender and work/family issues in their organizations and become part of the solution, rather than the problem.

WHAT MALE ALLIES NEED FROM THEIR ORGANIZATIONS

Organizations, like working mothers, also need to more actively engage men in changing the current gendered discourse that is hindering women in their careers and in creating new patterns around work and family. Organizations can do this in two ways. First, they can consider how to support working fathers directly so that work/family is no longer framed as a women's issue. Second, as organizations focus on building leadership programs that support women, they can also think about how to build programs that support male allies who are committed to changing the gendered discourse in organizations.

A relatively simply way to support fathers is to provide men access to parental leave, preferably a paid parental leave. While birth mothers may need additional leave to accommodate physical recovery from childbirth, mothers and fathers benefit when they both have access to the same parental leave policies. Updating policies and language to counteract outdated norms and assumptions about who is the main caregiver of a family is a major step to gaining parity. Organizations can also offer fathers similar benefits and resources that are provided to working mothers. For example, Deloitte provides working mothers and working fathers with equal access to individual and group coaching as they navigate work and family after the birth of a child.

Senior leaders, particularly fathers, will want to make sure they are building an organizational culture that is supportive of fathers being active caregivers. The negative experiences in the workplace that can come from being an engaged father can be substantially reduced when fathers feel their managers and organizations are supporting their efforts to integrate work and family.[15] One way that senior male leaders can signal their support is by using these policies themselves. When Norway changed its parental leave policy to motivate working parents to split the eight months of paid leave, fathers' use of parental leave rose from 3% in 1993 to 70% in 2006. A driving force behind this change was the influence of peers. Fathers who had a coworker or sibling who took paternity leave were significantly more likely to take leave. The influence of peers accounted for

21% of the increase in fathers' participation in the parental leave program. This influence was even more pronounced when that peer was a manager.[45] Tom Stocky, the VP of Facebook who took a four-month parental leave and was quoted earlier in this chapter, found that his leave had a significant impact on shifting the Facebook culture to better support fathers' engagement at work and at home. Prospective fathers would reach out to him to inquire about his leave and the impact it had on his career and family. As one Facebook employee shared,

> I had just become a new manager . . . but he made it clear this is something that Facebook will accommodate. It just made me feel so much less nervous.[46]

Senior male leaders who take parental leaves reduce the stigma of paternity leave and model for prospective fathers and colleagues that men can be both engaged parents and successful professionals.

To increase the involvement of men, organizations may want to think about how to use cohort models in the same way that they do for women leaders. For instance, AB Volvo has created a male-only program that cultivates male ally cohorts. This program enables men to have male-only dialogues to discuss gender and work/family issues without fear of being blamed or judged by other male or female colleagues. The program showcases senior male allies and provides participants with reverse mentoring, in which female colleagues share experiences they have had related to gender, leadership, and work/family management. Through assignments and measured deliverables, men begin to adopt the role of ally. As an ally cohort, these men can then also rely on one another to confront gender biases in the organization.[47]

Finally, organizations can support the development of male allies by altering the assumption that conversations about work/family and women in leadership positions are solely for women. Historically, these topics have been "women's" initiatives that have been run and attended by women only. Women-only initiatives create silos that exclude men from the conversation and simply reinforce traditional notions of gender roles.

Sometimes women-only conversations are appropriate, but if the discussion is about gender equality and how to better support working parents, men can and should be at the table. Encouraging men to become involved in these initiatives can further strengthen working mothers' legitimacy and shift the conversation to one that is inclusive of all.[43]

CHAPTER TAKEAWAYS

1. Societal and gendered norms are slowly but surely changing. More and more working fathers are seeking tangible ways to become more involved caretakers—and are confronting similar biases and challenges to those faced by working mothers.

2. Expanding support opportunities for working fathers—such as parental leave policies, role models, and flexible work arrangements—can benefit both men *and* women in an organization.

3. Cultivating male allies in the workplace can be a significant way to shift gendered expectations, raise awareness of the struggles faced by working mothers and minorities, and influence organizational policies and practices.

REFERENCES

1. Slaughter, A.-M. (2014). Behind every great woman is a great man. *Huffington Post*. Retrieved from https://www.huffingtonpost.com/annemarie-slaughter/gender-gap-2013_b_4636850.html.

2. Burnett, S. B., Gatrell, C. J., Cooper, C. L., & Sparrow, P. (2013). Fathers at work: A ghost in the organizational machine. *Gender, Work & Organization, 20*(6), 632–646.

3. Budig, M. J. (2014, September 2). The fatherhood bonus and the motherhood penalty: Parenthood and the gender gap in pay. Retrieved from https://www.thirdway.org/report/the-fatherhood-bonus-and-the-motherhood-penalty-parenthood-and-the-gender-gap-in-pay.

4. Harrington, B., & Fraone, J. S. (2016). *The new Millennial dad: Understanding the paradox of today's fathers*. Boston, MA: Boston College Center for Work & Family, Carroll School of Management.

5. Humberd, B., Ladge, J. J., & Harrington, B. (2015). The new dad: Navigating fathering identity within organizational contexts. *Journal of Business and Psychology, 30*(2), 249–266.

6. Coe, A. (2013, January 23). Dads caring for their kids: It's parenting, not babysitting. *The Atlantic.* Retrieved from https://www.theatlantic.com/sexes/archive/2013/01/dads-caring-for-their-kids-its-parenting-not-babysitting/267443/.

7. Levs, J. (2015). *All in: How our work-first culture fails dads, families, and businesses—and how we can fix it together.* New York, NY: HarperCollins.

8. Prestbury, M. (2014, August 5). Fathers, we can be here for each other. *Huffington Post.* Retrieved from https://www.huffingtonpost.com/matt-prestbury/fathers-we-can-be-here-fo_b_5651665.html.

9. U.S. Department of Labor. (2015). *Factsheet: Paid family and medical leave.* Retrieved from https://www.dol.gov/wb/resources/paid_leave_fact_sheet.pdf.

10. Rege, M., & Solli, I. F. (2013). The impact of paternity leave on fathers' future earnings. *Demography, 50*(6), 2255–2277.

11. Williams, M. (2013, January 6). 40% of fathers do not take paternity leave. *The Guardian.* Retrieved from https://www.theguardian.com/careers/fathers-choose-not-to-take-paternity-leave.

12. Harrington, B., Van Deusen, F., Fraone, J. S., Eddy, S., & Haas, L. (2014). *The new dad: Take your leave.* Boston, MA: Boston College Center for Work & Family, Carroll School of Management.

13. Matos, K., & Galinsky, E. (2014). *National Study of Employers.* New York, NY: Work and Families Institute.

14. Stocky, T. (2013, July 7). Facebook Post. Retrieved from https://www.facebook.com/tstocky/posts/996111776858.

15. Ladge, J. J., Humberd, B. K., Watkins, M. B., & Harrington, B. (2015). Updating the organization man: An examination of involved fathering in the workplace. *Academy of Management Perspectives, 29*(1), 152.

16. Abraham, E., Hendler, T., Shapira-Lichter, I., Kanat-Maymon, Y., Zagoory-Sharon, O., & Feldman, R. (2014). Fathers' brain is sensitive to childcare experiences. *Proceedings of the National Academy of Sciences of the United States of America, 111*(27), 9792–9797.

17. Tanaka, S., & Waldfogel, J. (2007). Effects of parental leave and work hours on fathers' involvement with their babies: Evidence from the millennium cohort study. *Community, Work & Family, 10*(4), 409–426.

18. Deutsch, F. (1999). *Halving it all: How equally shared parenting works.* Cambridge, MA: Harvard University Press.

19. Mundy, L. (2013). *The richer sex: How the new majority of female breadwinners is transforming our culture.* New York, NY: Simon and Schuster.

20. Boushey, H., & O'Leary, A. (2009). *The Shriver report: A woman's nation changes everything.* Washington, DC: Center for American Progress.

21. U.S. Department of Labor, Bureau of Labor Statistics. (2015). *American time use survey: Charts by topic: Care of household children.* Retrieved from https://www.bls.gov/tus/charts/childcare.htm.

22. Hartley, G. (2018). *Fed Up: Emotional Labor, Women and the Way Forward*. New York, NY: HarperCollins.

23. Bryner, J. (2010, February 9). *Children raised by lesbians do just fine, studies show*. Live Science. Retrieved from https://www.livescience.com/6073-children-raised-lesbians-fine-studies-show.html.

24. Slaughter, A.-M. (2024). Why women still can't have it all. *The Atlantic*. Retrieved from https://www.theatlantic.com/magazine/archive/2012/07/why-women-still-cant-have-it-all/309020/.

25. Johnston, K. (2017, February 9). Would you give up pay for family time. *Boston Globe*. Retrieved from https://www.bostonglobe.com/business/2017/02/08/parents-sacrificing-pay-for-family-friendly-benefits/1ZAAzrI5CSSkfXMzU05yUM/story.html.

26. Bright Horizons. (2016). *Modern family index 2016: Labor pains: What employees expect when they're expecting*. Retrieved from https://solutionsatwork.brighthorizons.com/~/media/44bd67c4a27b47cd8a6c0d871a998853.

27. Behson, S. (2015). *The working dad's survival guide: How to succeed at work and at home*. Melbourne, FL: Motivational Press.

28. Hurst, N. (2005, November 20). Fewer interested in occupying corner office. *Boston Globe*, G2, 98.

29. Brescoll, V., Glass, J., & Sedlovskaya, A. (2013). Ask and ye shall receive? The dynamics of employer-provided flexible work options and the need for public policy. *Journal of Social Issues*, 69(2), 367–388.

30. Bowers, K. (2014, March 19). A mother's work: Special report. *Working Mother*. https://www.workingmother.com/special-report/mothers-work-special-report.

31. Williams, J. C., Berdahl, J. L., & Vandello, J. A. (2016). Beyond work-life integration. *Annual Review of Psychology*, 67, 515–539.

32. Reid, E. (2015, April 28). Why some men pretend to work 80-hour weeks. *Harvard Business Review*. Retrieved from https://hbr.org/2015/04/why-some-men-pretend-to-work-80-hour-weeks.

33. Parker, K., & Livingston, G. (2018, June 13). *Facts about American fathers*. Pew Research Center. Retrieved from http://www.pewresearch.org/fact-tank/2018/06/13/fathers-day-facts/.

34. Harrington, B., Van Deusen, F., & Iyar, M. (2012). *The new dad: Right at home*. Boston, MA: Boston College Center for Work and Family.

35. Dowd, N. E. (2000). *Redefining fatherhood*. New York, NY: New York University Press.

36. Center for Women and Business at Bentley University. (2017). *Men as allies: Engaging men to advance women in the workplace*. Retrieved from https://www.bentley.edu/files/2017/05/02/CWB%20Men%20as%20Allies%20Research%20Report%20Spring%202017.pdf.

37. McKinsey and LeanIn. (2015). *Women in the workplace Report*. Retrieved from https://www.mckinsey.com/business-functions/organization/our-insights/women-in-the-workplace.

38. DeTurk, S. (2011). Allies in action: The communicative experiences of people who challenge social injustice on behalf of others. *Communication Quarterly, 59*(5), 569–590.

39. Proudman, B. (2015). *Why the fish must see the water: Helping men see their own culture.* White Men As Full Diversity Partners. Retrieved from https://wmfdp.com/wp-content/uploads/2015/05/why-fish-must-see-the-water.pdf.

40. Obama, B. (2017, August 4). Exclusive: President Barack Obama says, "This is what a feminist looks like. *Glamour Magazine.* https://www.glamour.com/story/glamour-exclusive-president-barack-obama-says-this-is-what-a-feminist-looks-like.

41. Gompers, P., & Wang, S. Q. (2017). *And the children shall lead: Gender diversity and performance in venture capital.* National Bureau of Economic Research Working Paper No. 23454. Retrieved from https://www.nber.org/papers/w23454.pdf.

42. Desai, S. D., Chugh, D., & Brief, S. P. (2014). The implications of marriage structure for men's workplace attitudes, beliefs, and behaviors toward women. *Administrative Science Quarterly, 59*(2), 330–365.

43. Ashcraft, C., DuBow, W., Eger, E., Blithe, S., & Sevier, B. (2013). *Male advocates and allies: promoting gender diversity in technology workplaces.* National Center for Women in IT, Boulder, CO. Retrieved from https://www.ncwit.org/resources/male-advocates-and-allies-promoting-gender-diversity-technology-workplaces.

44. Murphy, W., & Kram, K. (2014). *Strategic relationships at work: Creating your circle of mentors, sponsors, and peers for success in business and life.* New York, NY: McGraw Hill Professional.

45. Dahl, G. B., Løken, K. V., Mogstad, M., & Salvanes, K. V. (2016). What is the case for paid maternity leave? *Review of Economics and Statistics, 98*(4), 655–670.

46. Douglas, D. (2016, February 8). How to get dads to take parental leave? Seeing other dads do it. *National Public Radio.* Retrieved from http://www.npr.org/2016/02/08/465726445/how-to-get-dads-to-take-parental-leave-seeing-other-dads-do-it.

47. Prime, J., Moss-Racusin, C. A., & Foust-Cummings, H. (2009). *Engaging men in gender initiatives: Stacking the deck for success.* Catalyst: Workplaces That Work for Women. Retrieved from https://www.catalyst.org/knowledge/engaging-men-gender-initiatives-stacking-deck-success.

Epilogue

*Where Do We Go from Here: Achieving
and Sustaining Maternal Optimism*

While women have made great strides in the workplace over the last several decades, it is far too early to declare victory. Women still hold a disproportionately small number of executive level positions and high-growth entrepreneurial ventures. Although many factors contribute to this lag, the key issue that we have focused on in this book is the persistent expectation that working mothers must choose between being "ideal" mothers and "ideal" workers. Consequently, women have become consumed with how to best manage the intersection of work and family while trying not to succumb to the outdated gendered norms and expectations or neglect their families. Regardless of the type of work, parenting stage, or family situation, working mothers are often troubled about not being able to put 100% into either role. We have described many moments that lead women to begin to question who they are, what is important to them, and whether they want to or how they will blend work and family. In contrast with many other books, we do not believe that work and family should be an either/or proposition. "Having it all" is unattainable only when we allow societal or organizational influences to dictate what "having it all" means. What is required is a fundamental shift away from letting others prescribe how to blend work and family to allowing individuals to construct their own definitions of being "good" working mothers. When guided by their own values and needs rather than by gendered assumptions, individual working mothers can craft a work/life path that is fulfilling to them and is filled with optimism and hope, rather than guilt and regret.

The goal of this book is to guide you through various work/family transitions and raise awareness of the key challenges and opportunities you will face over time. Secondarily, we hope that by providing some direction, you may be able to communicate with your manager, peers, and human resources professionals about how they may be able to better support you and other working mothers in your organization. As we have stated many times throughout this book, we do not believe there is a "one size fits all" definition or approach to being a working mother or to any of the small or large decisions working mothers must make. Similarly, there is no "one size fits all" strategy for organizations to approach work/family practices in support of parents who work in their firms. However, there is a collective action working mothers, and their organizations, can take to break the vicious cycle of outdated norms and gender stereotypes that make navigating work and family so challenging. The data and stories that are the foundation of this book only serve as a starting point to empower working mothers and their organizations to change these deep-rooted assumptions and societal expectations.

We believe that collective action begins where the last chapter ended, with women and men sharing responsibility for caregiving and sharing the burden of gender bias until it fades away. Women and men need to be equal partners in ensuring that work and family integration occurs in mutually reinforcing ways. An equal partnership requires moving past conversations about how men can support working mothers to how we can better support one another. Men cannot simply be involved in caregiving; they also need to take on equal ownership and advocacy for changing societal and organizational expectations for how we integrate work and family. They too will have tenuous moments, but the goal is not to unload the work/family conflict onto men. Rather, it is to find ways to alleviate the conflict and increase the opportunities for work and family to enrich one another for both mothers and fathers. To change the gendered nature of the work/family conversation requires confronting and shifting expectations so that work and family are roles that are not viewed as being at odds with one another.

Where, then, does this leave the role of caregiving? If we continue to treat caregiving as a devalued role, will fewer individuals decide to have children? We are already beginning to see evidence that Millennials are delaying marriage and family or deciding not to have children at all. In 2013, Wharton Professor Stew Friedman studied the partner relationship and childbearing intentions of young men and women. He was surprised to find that a large percentage of undergraduates had low intentions of having children. These choices seemed to result from seeing their parents and those of prior generations struggle to have a successful career and simultaneously manage a family. Women in particular viewed having children as being at odds with having a successful career, which they saw as a priority.[1] While it is highly likely that these women's views will shift over time, the sad reality is they still believe they have to choose between the two roles. If we are going to transform the conversation such that women do not have to feel bad if they want to have a career, we need to elevate the status of caregiving. While the aspiration for this elevation might be that eventually caregiving is valued equally with work, for now, minor shifts in how caregiving is valued could create major changes in alleviating the pressure and stigmatization individuals experience as they navigate work and family.

One step toward shifting this judgment and elevating the status of caregiving is for individuals, primarily women, to finally bring a truce to the "mommy wars." For example, "mom-shaming" (that is, criticizing mothers as to how they parent) is on the rise.[2] Interestingly, most women are mom-shamed by other mothers, including their own mothers and mothers-in-law! How, then, can working mothers ever come out ahead when experiencing mom-shaming at home and maternal bias at work? Taken together, all of these behaviors, while often subtle, only serve to devalue caregiving further. For those on the receiving end, it is very difficult to shut out these judgments, which limit any chance for achieving and/ or sustaining maternal optimism. However, following the basic premise of this book and embracing your own choices around work and family while valuing and learning from the choices other women are making will foster a greater degree of maternal optimism and hopefully create a contagious effect. Mothers can create a stronger, more inclusive culture around caregiving by connecting with other mothers who have made different choices and exploring how to be supportive, rather than judgmental, of these differences. Mothers who are involved in community leadership can advocate for school and community programming that enables all parents to participate actively, rather than just those who are home full time. Mothers who are working need to openly value and support women who are staying at home, both while they are home and if/when they choose to transition back to work. Working together, rather than against one another, is critical to creating a culture that is more embracing of all work/family choices.

Elevating the status of caregiving also requires shifts within our workplaces. In organizations, you and your allies can begin making these shifts by becoming more public about the time you are spending caregiving and the joy, and challenges, you experience in this aspect of your life. If you are in a managerial role, you can help colleagues who have less power by creating coalitions and advocating on behalf of your organizations to provide opportunities for all workers to be engaged and active caregivers. Organizations need to go beyond offering internal policies that support caretaking by acting as advocates to encourage other organizations and the government to challenge the status quo. Well-respected organizations often create industry shifts as other firms emulate their actions or by lobbying industry groups to put out statements around organizational support for caregiving. Similar lobbying of the government can be done by powerful CEOs of large, successful organizations with generous support for caregiving. In this way, we no longer are asking individuals to shoulder this burden alone. You can be the agent for this type of change in your organization.

In the United States, caregiving is primarily the responsibility of the individual family, with few resources provided by organizations or the government. Thus, parents are often left to their own devices to manage tough and expensive choices. Why should an organization or the government provide paid leave or support flexible work arrangements? Why should taxpayers or a company bear the cost of a decision an individual or a couple has chosen to make about having children? One important reason is that children are the economic future of a nation and a thriving economy. Thus, organizations are dependent upon children receiving adequate caregiving, family support, and the education they need to be successful adults. Because of this dependency, we need to think about shifting some of the responsibility for caregiving away from solely the individual. This change needs to happen at societal, governmental, and organizational levels. We need to reframe government initiatives around maternity leave and childcare not just as policies that support working mothers, but also as practices that support the development of the next generation and the overall economy.

Achieving and, more importantly, sustaining maternal optimism does not come easy. However, if you can begin to learn how to embrace your own work/life path, you can become more confident in your own decisions and more open to the choices of others. In doing so, you can become the change agent that leads the collective action we need from the men in our lives, the organizations they lead, and the broader society at large.

REFERENCES

1. Friedman, S. (2013). *Baby bust: New choices for men and women in work and family.* Philadelphia, PA: Wharton Digital Press.
2. Jones, A. R. (2017, April 26). The rise of the mean moms. *Marie Claire.* Retrieved from https://www.marieclaire.com/culture/a26300/bully-moms/.